D1570890

THE BUKE OF THE HOWLAT

SCOTTISH
TEXT
SOCIETY

The Scottish Text Society
Fifth Series
no. 12

RICHARD HOLLAND

THE BUKE OF THE HOWLAT

Edited by
Ralph Hanna

The Scottish Text Society
2014

First published 2014 by The Scottish Text Society

ISBN 978-1-89797-639-5

A Scottish Text Society publication
Published by The Boydell Press
an imprint of Boydell & Brewer Ltd
PO Box 9, Woodbridge, Suffolk IP12 3DF, UK
and of Boydell & Brewer Inc.
668 Mt Hope Avenue, Rochester, NY 14620–2731, USA
website: www.boydellandbrewer.com

The publisher has no responsibility for
the continued existence or accuracy of URLs for external or
third-party internet websites referred to in this book, and
does not guarantee that any content on such websites
is, or will remain, accurate or appropriate.

A CIP catalogue record for this book is available
from the British Library

This publication is printed on acid-free paper

Printed and bound in Great Britain by
TJ International Ltd, Padstow, Cornwall

MIX
Paper from
responsible sources
FSC
www.fsc.org
FSC® C013056

For Sally Mapstone

Contents

Preface

An editor's first indebtedness is always to those libraries that have facilitated his work. Here, like all researchers into matters Scots, I have been particularly blessed by the welcoming generosity of the Manuscripts Department of the National Library of Scotland. I am especially indebted to Kenneth Dunn, Manager of the Department, for arranging my two protracted sessions with John Asloan's manuscript, the basis of my edition.

I am also grateful that this edition has received elaborate patronage. Nearly all its final draft was composed in spring 2012, during my tenure as Fellow of the Radcliffe Institute for Advanced Study, Harvard University. As all past Fellows will know, the Institute provides an environment intensely helpful and munificent (if not downright sybaritic) in which to pursue one's studies. I am especially grateful to Liz Cohen and Judith Vichniac, not simply for their support but also for not inquiring too closely about what I was about during my Fellowship, since I pursued the interests of the Scottish Text Society while allegedly engaged in another project. I also remember with great fondness stimulating conversations, frequently tinged by various Scottish products, with my fellow Fellows, Tayari Jones and John Plotz.

Perhaps my greatest debt is to the Scottish Text Society (and its publishers, Boydell & Brewer). Between them, Nicola Royan, Rhiannon Purdie, and Caroline Palmer have efficiently transformed some rather dodgy computer files into an elegant book. But this volume could not have achieved whatever finish it now possesses without the most constructive reading anything I have produced has ever received. I am particularly grateful to Priscilla Bawcutt, Sally Mapstone, and Jeremy J. Smith for a wealth of criticisms and suggestions, many of which have saved me from acute public embarrassment. Sticklers that all three are, they will not be satisfied with what has emerged; readers should assume that they are responsible for all the persuasive bits and ascribe the rest to a pigheaded editor, immune to expert advice.

For anyone who has engaged in Scottish studies in the last twenty-five years, the dedication of this volume will require no explanation. Sally Mapstone's contributions to this field have been immense, and she has inspired a new generation of engaged scholars, many of them products of the thriving programme she has singlehandedly built up in Oxford. Dogged, organised, precise, and inspirational, she has managed to convince this confirmed (Piers) plowman that his avocation for Scots was not simply personal idiosyncracy. My gratitude – and it should be Oxford's as well – for Sally's conversation and companionship over many years is here inadequately expressed.

References and Abbreviations

AA   *The Awntyrs off Arthure at the Terne Wathelyn*, ed. Ralph Hanna (Manchester, 1974)

Bruce   *Barbour's Bruce*, ed. Matthew P. McDiarmid and James A. C. Stevenson, 3 vols, STS 4th ser. 12, 13, 15 [vols 2, 3, 1, respectively] (Edinburgh, 1980–85)

Bower   Walter Bower, *Scotichronicon*, gen. ed. D. E. R. Watt, 9 vols (Aberdeen, 1987–98)

Cln   *Cleanness*, ed. J. J. Anderson (Manchester, 1977)

DL   'Death and Liffe', ed. John W. Hales and Frederick J. Furnivall, *Bishop Percy's Folio Manuscript: Ballads and Romances*, 3 vols in 4 (London, 1867–68), 3:49–75

DOST   *The Dictionary of the Older Scottish Tongue*, 'www.dsl. ac.uk'

Dunbar   William Dunbar, *The Poems*, ed. Priscilla Bawcutt, 2 vols, Association for Scottish Literary Studies 27–28 (Glasgow, 1998) [*TMW* 'The Tretis of the tua mariit wemen and the wedo' = poem 3, 1:41–55; *Flyting* 'The Flyting of Dumbar and Kennedie' = poem 65, 1:200–18]

EETS   Early English Text Society

EETS os 98   *Minor Poems of the Vernon Manuscript*, ed. C. Horstmann (London, 1892)

Flytyng   see Dunbar

GG   *The Knightly Tale of Golagros and Gawane*, ed. Ralph Hanna, STS 5th ser. 7 (Woodbridge, 2008)

GGK   *Sir Gawain and the Green Knight*, ed. J. R. R. Tolkien and E. V. Gordon, rev. Norman Davis, 2nd edn (Oxford, 1968)

Henryson   Robert Henryson, *The Poems*, ed. Denton Fox (Oxford, 1981)

Latham   R. E. Latham et al., *Dictionary of Medieval Latin from British Sources*, currently 15 fascicles (London, 1975–)

MA   *Morte Arthure*, ed. Mary Hamel (New York, 1984)

ME   Middle English

MED   *The Middle English Dictionary*, 'quod.lib.umich.edu/m/ med'

O&N   *The Owl and the Nightingale: Text and Translation*, ed. Neil Cartlidge (Exeter, 2001)

OE	Old English (usually forms of 'Old Anglian/Old Northumbrian')
OED	*The Oxford English Dictionary*, accessed through OXLIP
OF	Old French
ON	Old Norse (usually forms of Old Icelandic)
Pearl	*Pearl*, ed. E. V. Gordon (Oxford, 1953)
PF	Geoffrey Chaucer, *The Parliament of Fowls*, *The Riverside Chaucer*, 3rd edn, ed. Larry D. Benson et al. (Boston, 1987), 383–94
PPB	William Langland, *Piers Plowman: The B Version*, ed. George Kane and E. Talbot Donaldson (London, 1975)
PTA	'The Parlement of the thre ages', ed. Turville-Petre 1989, 67–100
Quat	*The Quatrefoil of Love*, ed. Israel Gollancz and Magdalen M. Weale, EETS 195 (London, 1935)
Rauf	'The Taill of Rauf Coilyear', ed. Bawcutt and Riddy 1987, 94–133
SJ	*The Siege of Jerusalem*, ed. Ralph Hanna and David Lawton, EETS 320 (Oxford, 2003)
SJB	'St John the Baptist', *Three Alliterative Saints' Hymns*, ed. Ruth Kennedy, EETS 321 (Oxford, 2003), 19–23
SJE	'St John the Evangelist', *Three Alliterative* (as the prec.), 10–18
SS	'Somer Soneday', ed. Turville-Petre 1989, 140–47
STS	Scottish Text Society
Susan	'A Pistel of Susan', ed. Turville-Petre 1989, 120–39
TDK	'The Three dead kings', ed. Turville-Petre 1989, 148–57
TMW	see Dunbar
WA	*The Wars of Alexander*, ed. Hoyt N. Duggan and Thorlac Turville-Petre, EETS ss 10 (Oxford, 1989)
Wallace	*Hary's Wallace*, ed. Matthew P. McDiarmid, 2 vols, STS 4th ser. 4–5 (Edinburgh, 1968–69)
Whiting	Bartlett J. Whiting, *Proverbs, Sentences, and Proverbial Phrases from English Writings Mainly Before 1500* (Cambridge MA, 1968)

The 'Black' Douglases

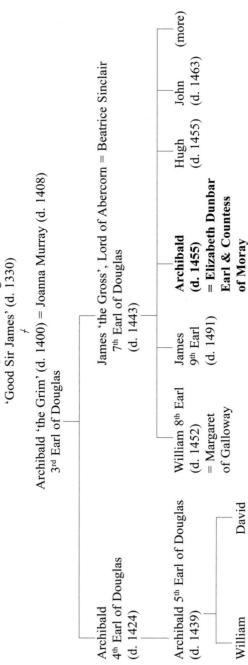

James, Lord of Douglas
'Good Sir James' (d. 1330)

Archibald 'the Grim' (d. 1400) = Joanna Murray (d. 1408)
3rd Earl of Douglas
†

Archibald
4th Earl of Douglas
(d. 1424)

Archibald 5th Earl of Douglas
(d. 1439)

William
6th Earl of Douglas
(d. 1440)

David
(d. 1440)

James 'the Gross', Lord of Abercorn = Beatrice Sinclair
7th Earl of Douglas
(d. 1443)

William 8th Earl
(d. 1452)
= Margaret
of Galloway

James
9th Earl
(d. 1491)

**Archibald
(d. 1455)
= Elizabeth Dunbar
Earl & Countess
of Moray**

Hugh
(d. 1455)

John
(d. 1463)

(more)

† : illegitimate

Derived from Tables 4 and 5 in Brown 1998 (pp. 98, 228).

xiv

Introduction

The Sources of the Text

This edition of Richard Holland's *Buke of the Howlat* joins, and is dependent upon, the earlier presentations by F. J. Amours (1892–97, 47–81, 287–317) and Felicity Riddy (Bawcutt and Riddy 1987, 43–84, 323–40), in addition to the transcription offered by William A. Craigie (1923–25, 2:95–126).[1] As its predecessors, it derives the majority of its readings from the three early witnesses to the text, in chronological order:

Cambridge University Library, Sel.1.19: a single printed leaf, with lines 537–99, from its fonts and format probably the remains of one of Walter Chepman and Andro Myllar's spring 1508 pamphlets, the first examples of Scottish printing (hereafter **C**);[2]

Edinburgh, National Library of Scotland, MS 16500 (formerly Acc. 4233; 'The Asloan Manuscript'), fols 213[r]–28[v], the poem copied on a paperstock datable 1509 x 1524 (hereafter **A**);

Edinburgh, National Library of Scotland, MS Advocates' 1.1.6 ('The Bannatyne Manuscript'), fols 302[r]–10[v], copied by George Bannatyne 'in tyme of pest ... | Frome our redimaris birth To knaw it heir | Ane thowsand Is Fyve hundreth Threscoir awcht [1568] (fol. 375) (hereafter **B**).

C The Chepman-Myllar print

David Laing discovered and removed most of this leaf from a Dundee municipal protocol book covering actions during portions of 1529 and 1530 (Laing 1867, 15–16). Some thirty years ago, a small strip, missing from the foot of the leaf in Cambridge, was identified in the binding of another Dundee municipal book, retained in Dundee City Archives, the protocol book for 19 November 1526–12 July 1528.[3] This strip supplies

---

[1] For Riddy's editorial responsibility for the text, see vii. Earlier presentations of the poem occur in Pinkerton 1792, 3:146–88; Laing 1823, and Diebler 1893.

[2] For general discussions of Chepman and Myllar, see Mapstone 2001, 4–11, and Hanna 2008, xi–xxiv.

[3] For the original scholarly treatment of the leaf, see Beattie 1938–45 and, for the strip preserved in Dundee, Donaldson 1980–83, with full images, joining both fragments, and transcription.

the feet and descenders of several letters that one could previously iden-
tify only hypothetically.

The Howlat appears here in the same format as that used for the
same printers' edition of *Golagros and Gawane* (the colophon there
dated 8 April 1508). There are exactly five stanzas to the leaf, and thirty
printed lines to the side (following manuscript practice with works in
this stanza, the short thirteenth line is printed opposite the eleventh).[4]
In *Golagros*, while stanzas regularly run over the boundaries between
rectos and versos, they never run over the boundaries between leaves,
and each verso ends with a multiple of 65 text-lines. However, the
surviving leaf from *The Howlat* has not been so carefully produced
and awkwardly splits stanzas across all page boundaries. The extant
leaf includes stanza 42/line 2 to stanza 47/line 1 (lines 537–99 of this
edition). The compositors probably went 'off sequence' as the result
of omitting lines, one might suppose by either dropping or failing to
account for lines 370–71 (an omission repeated in **A**).[5]

Given that only a single leaf from this Chepman and Myllar produc-
tion survives, inferences about the volume from which it came must
remain speculative. But the similarities in format to *Golagros*, as well
as the general consistency of practice in the spring 1508 prints, allow
some educated guesses. Like Chepman and Myllar's other productions,
The Howlat will likely have appeared as a sequence of quarto quires,
each containing six leaves;[6] three such units would have been sufficient
to present the poem. One might also assume that, like Chepman and
Myllar's other 1508 prints, sig. A i[r] would have been reserved for a
title-page, with blank verso, and the text would have begun at the top
of sig. A ii[r]. Given these formatting practices, *The Howlat* should have
ended about three-quarters of the way down sig. C iv[v]. In other products
of the press, sig. C vi[v] was reserved for Myllar's device, and this would

---

4   The format is actually 32 (or in the case of the verso of the leaf bearing the
    The Howlat, 33) lines to the page, since in both books, a line is left blank
    between stanzas.

5   See the note to line 370. Although the Chepman-Myllar print of *Golagros*
    omits three lines, these are isolated single instances (291, 333, 553), and the
    compositors easily adjusted their count so as to regularly conclude stanzas
    at the foot of each verso. Indeed, the last of these three omissions was not
    inherited, as the others may have been, but occurred during the print produc-
    tion, when a compositor overlooked the final line that he should have set on
    p. 23.

6   For the exact mechanisms involved in this form of production, see Hanna
    2008, xi, xxi–ii, and xlii–iii n.47.

have allowed, again as in other productions from the press, room for a small 'filler' text, running from the foot of sig. C iv^v to sig. C vi^r. In such a reconstruction, the surviving leaf probably represents sig. B v of the whole.

The discovery of both fragments associated with Dundee materials re-enforces provenance evidence associated with the remainder of Chepman and Myllar's work of spring 1508. Signatures scattered through the collected products of the press in the National Library of Scotland include individuals associated with Fife, on the opposite side of the Tay from Dundee. The surviving single leaf of *The Howlat* confirms that our knowledge of Chepman and Myllar's output remains incomplete and that what survives for us may depend upon the activities and tastes of a single collector or small group of them, perhaps specifically locally prominent administrative figures, in eastern Scotland.[7]

A 'The Asloan Manuscript'

This is the largest early Scots miscellany, probably less than half surviving, but still extensive: 304 single paper leaves, now inlaid in paper mounts.[8] The scribe John Asloan produced a contents table for the entire book (fols iii^r-iv^r, printed Craigie 1923–25, 1:xiii–xv), numbered to seventy-one items, in modern conceptions about sixty separate texts. Of these, thirty-four are lost entirely, and seven further items lack materials, usually at either the head or the end. *The Howlat* is the fiftieth text of the volume in Asloan's count.

Cunningham demonstrates (128–29) that, as it survives, the manuscript represents fourteen separate 'booklets' or fascicles. Asloan copied small groups of texts into discrete runs of quires and formed the full manuscript by joining these in what he deemed an appropriate order.[9] *The Howlat* fills the tenth of these originally separate units, the

---

7 On the provenance of the National Library copies, see Hanna 2008, xii, xxi, with further references.

8 For a fine description, on which much of the following depends, see Cunningham 1994 (I supply further references on specific points parenthetically in the text). For extensive discussion of the texts included, see van Buuren 1996.

9 Although the original binding already contained glitches. The four central folia of the last surviving quire (the 21st) had become dissociated from the remainder (Lydgate's 'Complaint of the black knight'/'The Maying of Chaucer'). Asloan failed to notice this, arranged the leaves to appear as an independent text at fols 243–46, and assigned them item 54 in his table of contents ('Ane ballat of luf'; see Cunningham 1994, 114, 116, 117–18).

sixteen-leaf (the normal form in Asloan's folio folding) quire 16 of the surviving materials (Cunningham 126). The poem appears on one of the two paperstocks (of six evidenced here) appearing most frequently in the surviving book, the stock Cunningham designates *f*. The water-mark is a blazon with three fleurs-de-lis, a crown above and letter 't' below, identifiable as Briquet no. 1748, its other uses datable 1509 x 1524 (Cunningham 119, 120).[10] This stock appears in quires 13–18, fols 167–262, leaves bearing the surviving texts Asloan identified in his table of contents as nos 21, 50–53, 55–56 of the whole. One might infer that this segment, along with missing portions of the book – the large lacuna between fols 212 and 213 (where *The Howlat* begins), bearing the intervening texts 22–49 – formed a core to Asloan's book, all on this single stock.

Although a large number of preceding quires have been lost, the table reveals that, just as in the Bannatyne manuscript, *The Howlat* originally sat among a sequence of comparable 'fables'. Asloan's items 39–52, of which only the last three (*The Howlat* is no. 50) survive, were: 'Colkebie sow', the now unknown 'Buke of þe otter and þe ele', 'The flyting of Dunbar and Kennedie', six of Robert Henryson's *Moral Fables*, and two lyrics (probably 'filler' at the end of the booklet preceding this text).[11] Following *The Howlat*, and still extant, are the 'Talis of þe fyve bestis' and Henryson's second 'moral fable' ('The Two Mice').[12] As Cunningham suggests (129), these relevant lost materials preceding *The Howlat* may have occupied three separate booklets ('The Flyting' in one of these, perhaps rather incongruously intruded here).

As at eight other points in the book, the colophon to *The Howlat* includes a scribal signature, 'Per manum Iohannis Asloan' (Cunningham 130), and Asloan wrote the entire book, excepting a single quire.[13] As

---

[10] For further discussion, including beta-radiograph images of the watermarks, see van Buuren 1982, 5–20.

[11] At least arguably, the second of these, 'A ballat of treuth', may have been the Chaucerian lyric ('Fle fro the presse ...'); there is another Scots copy in Cambridge University Library, MS Kk.i.5.

[12] On the text order, also relevant to the Bannatyne manuscript, and for commentary, see Fox's introduction to Henryson, lxxvi (xxxv–ix describes the same two sources as here). The end of Asloan's 11th booklet contains 'þe crying of a play', and materials on paperstock *f* conclude, in a further booklet, with Henryson's *Orpheus* and 'Þe Thre prestis of Peblis'.

[13] One G. Myll is responsible for fols 137–50 ('Þe Spectakle of lufe'). In addition to those images provided by van Buuren, mentioned in the next sentence, and the frontispiece above, reproductions of Asloan's hand appear

4

van Buuren demonstrates (1966; cf. 1982, 26–30, both with images), the Edinburgh scribe and notary John Asloan is also responsible for copying in at least the following manuscripts: Oxford, Bodleian Library, MS Douce 148, and Edinburgh, National Library of Scotland, MS Advocates' 19.2.3.

In the Bodleian manuscript, Asloan wrote fols 1^r–44^v, 139^{rv}, 257^{rv} (in smaller script to match the format of a second scribe, as also the first leaf of the next portion), 300^r–36^v. The manuscript, in the main, presents Lydgate's *Troy Book*. But this appears to have been copied from a fragmentary exemplar, and the text has been filled out, partly by Asloan, with fragments from *The Scottish Troy Book* sometimes ascribed to John Barbour. The text here is headed 'Ihesus maria' above Asloan's red-ink heading, 'Heir begynnes þe troy buke Translatit by monke of Bery ...'; fol. 336^v has the colophon, 'Heir endis þe sege of Troye writtin and mendit at þe Instance of ane honorable chaplaine schir Thomas ewyn in Edinburgh'.

The colophon indicates the patron for whom Asloan helped produce the volume. Thomas Ewen was a longtime chaplain of St Giles. As the description above indicates, this copy was indeed 'mendit'. At least initially, Asloan and the main scribe began by sharing out the copying, apparently each responsible for a large section. But they seem to have discovered that, following fol. 290, they had only a single quire from the end of Lydgate's text (the current fols 301–11). This they supplemented with the indigenous version of Trojan history.

Asloan appears as a 'mender' of texts in a second volume identified by van Buuren, Edinburgh, National Library of Scotland, MS Advocates' 19.2.3, fols 1^r, 10^r–11^v, 137^{rv}, 199^{rv}, 247^{rv} (in significantly smaller script), 414^{rv} (probably), 423^{rv}, 426^{rv}, and 447^r–48^v. The manuscript contains a slightly damaged copy of Andrew Wyntoun's *Original Chronicle*, and Asloan's activity is limited to supplying leaves replacing those earlier lost. As van Buuren points out, in addition to the differences in hand from that responsible for the majority of the text, Asloan's stints here are distinguished from surrounding materials by being written on a different paperstock from the remainder.[14] One might note that this manuscript

at Craigie 1923–25, 2:facing xii (fol. 109) and facing 141 (fol. 236); examples of brief segments van Buuren 1966 and 1982, frontispiece (fol. 169) and 14 (fol. 179v); and (a composite image from three separate folios) at Thomson 1819, facing 1.

[14] Fol. 415^{rv} *may* be in Asloan's hand, but a good deal of the book, from fol. 380 onwards, resembles Asloan's script in a generic sort of way. In addition

is in a contemporary binding, and clasps from the lower board to the upper, like a continental, rather than an insular book.

Further identifications of Asloan's work depend on aligning specific script features appearing in these three stints, a substantial volume of materials, with those attested in other books. I would identify the following distinctive features, illustrated on the frontispiece reproduced here, the first side of *The Howlat*, **A** fol. 213ʳ.[15]

In general, Asloan's hand is relatively large and rather rounded and erect. Most typically, it lacks two features frequently associated with contemporary secretary scripts. It displays minimal forward lean, and Asloan does not indulge in the exaggerated shading traditional on the long strokes of *s* and *f*. A number of features are potentially distinctive.

Asloan very frequently shows decorative strokes on the graphs *e* and *r*, when they appear in word-final position (see further the discussion at pp. 56–57). Traditionally, final -*e* in British scripts is written with two or three strokes, two forming the left-hand bow of the letter and the third, which joins the right end of the first stroke, its 'tongue'. In Asloan's script, this last stroke of the graph, in final position, is regularly extended, either horizontally or obliquely.

However, in Asloan's script, this 'tongued' form alternates with two other, more exaggerated ways of completing the letter in final position. Most strikingly, Asloan often writes -*e* with an extended leftwards loop, frequently over the top of several preceding graphs, for example in line 2 *grene*. Alternatively, he adorns the graph with a tail-like stroke, extending to the right, as in line 22 *sure* or 26 *bure*. Final -*r* is subject to the same embellishment; the looped form appears in 12 *Reveir* (as also in the words with which it rhymes in lines 10–11), while the same word is written with the trailing stroke in line 14 *Rever*.

Like most secretary scripts after 1440 or so, Asloan regularly writes *w* as a reduced version of the form inherited from anglicana scripts. This usually has an exaggerated initial stroke derived from representations of *v* in initial position. However, Asloan also utilises a form comprised of two rather loopy minim-like strokes with a circular stroke on the right end of the graph. One may illustrate the two forms in line 18, where inherited secretary reduced *w* appears in *was* and *with*, but the round *w* in *lowne*. As these examples indicate, the latter form represents a

---

to this book-copying, van Buuren 1982, 22 mentions two notarial instruments, both with Asloan's sign, for which, see her 1982, 8.

[15] For further comments on the script, see the account of the transcription at pp. 53–57 below.

positional variant, for use in medial positions; it is one of the more prominent features that gives Asloan's hand its relatively rounded and curvy aspect.

The graph *s* is among those forms most anciently associated with specific forms for word-final position, and Asloan's handling displays potentially idiosyncratic behaviours. The form traditionally associated with secretary scripts, 'beanshaped' *-s* , appears thoroughly absent from Asloan's repertory. The uniquely Scots ß-form occurs frequently; for it see line 20 *Becauß* or 25 *Alß* (these are rendered in the edition *Becaus*, *Als*). But, as this plate will indicate, Asloan more frequently in final position uses a sigmoid *-s* with a high trailing loop. Examples appear in line 16 *branchis* or 17 *blossomes*.

There is a variety of gracenotes potentially of aid in distinguishing Asloan's hand. The graph *h* provides another example of a medial variant. Within the word, and especially in common sequences such as *quh-* and *-ich-*, Asloan renders the graph as a nearly vertical pair of left-to-right loops (rather resembling the form of traditional modern German cursive). For examples, see line 14 *riche* and 16 *branchis*. One might note here in passing that line 14 *riche* also displays Asloan's customary rendition of 'round *e*', the letter reduced to a backward-leaning minim and dissociated tailed dot; for further examples, see line 15 *ane*, or the two instances of *þe* in line 16.

Other features of the hand are potentially of use for identifying heretofore unrecognised bits of Asloan's scribal oeuvre. The lower, usually open loop of secretary *g* frequently, particularly in initial position, loops back up to join the head of the letter, as in line 8 *greable gift* and *godhed* (but for an example not in initial position, see line 14 *resting*).[16] The graph *y* is written as a *v*-shape on the line with lower loop extending from the right end of the *v*. Asloan has a pronounced tendency to render the final minim in a series (sometimes even in isolated instances of *-i/-n*) as a descender, for example in line 7 *sessoun*. Finally, there is a limited number of clearly otiose strokes, on the whole conventional. In final position, *-n* regularly has a terminal loop, as in line 7 *sessoun*; and when medial *h* has the usual bow plus foot form, it is frequently crossed, as in the rhymewords of lines 23–25. Both these strokes occur together in line 11 *Withoutin*.

---

[16] Note also the exaggerated form of line 17 *on*, with a concluding loop taken back to head of the word, reminiscent of the handling of *g*; the same encircling loop also occurs in Asloan's rare use (he prefers the full *and*) of the Tironian nota for 'et'.

On the basis of my sense of Asloan's duct and of his persistence in these features, I would reject one of van Buuren's possible identifications of the hand, in London, British Library, MS Harley 4700 ('auld laws' of Scotland). This is certainly the kind of book one might have expected the notary (and thus legal scribe) John Asloan to have copied. However, much of this book is composed in Latin, which might be seen as constructing a different scribal practice from the vernacular materials. Certainly, I see nothing that distinctively reminds me of Asloan in these portions. Yet the volume also includes a considerable amount of material in Scots. Again, I see nothing here directly reminiscent of the hand in the three poetic manuscripts, and any resemblance is largely generic, features widespread in early sixteenth-century Scots secretary hands.

However, van Buuren's association (1982, 27) of Asloan with another book deserves considerably more attention. This is Wemyss Castle (Fife), a manuscript of Wyntoun's *Original Chronicle*. Van Buuren, who was able to examine the manuscript – now unfortunately unavailable to scholars – does not simply identify the script as Asloan's, but also associates the paperstocks in the volume with ones that appear in other books he certainly copied. On the basis of the sample leaf Amours provides (1903–14, vol. 2 [STS 50], frontispiece), although some distinctive Asloan features are not illustrated in this one-page selection (e.g. the high loop as extended tongue of -e), the script of this volume should be described as 'impressively like', or 'very likely Asloan'.[17]

I have seen further unpublished images of the manuscript, photographs made by the late Jeremy J. Griffiths on a visit to Wemyss Castle in the early 1990s. From these, I would say that this ascription might well be plausible. The script is far from identical in detail with other writings convincingly ascribed to Asloan; most particularly, majuscules are frequently not of the forms testified in Asloan's other books, and the nearly vertical double-looped *h* is absent, even in sequences such as *quh*- and -*ich*-, where it is elsewhere especially pronounced. But enough Asloan crochets, e.g. the long final minim of a series and round medial *w*, remain for one to feel sanguine about the identification. One may face here the difficulty of assessing a script varying over what may have been protracted periods, but, by the same token, the anthology now in the National Library was certainly copied over a extended period and remains largely consistent in its script practices.

---

[17] Incidentally, the frontispiece to Amours 1903–14, vol. 5 (STS 56), appears to have found one of Asloan's leaves in Advocates' 19.2.3.

B 'The Bannatyne Manuscript'

This important and extensive miscellany is available (and meticulously described) in the full facsimile, Fox and Ringler 1980. Just as **A**, this book was built up from a number of smaller independently produced fascicles or booklets, although these have been subjected (as **A** apparently was not) to explicit organisational procedures. Here *The Buke of the Howlat* appears near the end, in what is formally introduced (fol. 298ʳ) as 'the fyift pairt of this buik, contenyng the Fabillis of Esop, with diuers vþir fabillis and poeticall workis, maid and compyld be diuers lernit men 1568'; this heading is followed on fol. 298ᵛ by a poem introducing this section of the whole. In Fox and Ringler's account (xii), predicated (like Cunningham's description of **A**) on watermark sequences, this portion includes fols 299–375 (the end of the volume) and represents two originally separate bookets; the division between them follows quire 31 and fol. 356. Fox and Ringler collate the relevant segment of the volume as quires 27^{14} 28^{10} 29^{12} 30^{12} 31^{10}. *The Howlat* is completely contained in the first quire of this sequence (fols 299–312).

As his title for this portion of the arranged volume implies, Bannatyne responds to the poem within the same generic framework, the fable, as is implicit in Asloan's contents ordering. However, Bannatyne's conception of fable is considerably more expansive than Asloan's, even leaving aside the promise of additional 'poeticall workis', a locution that probably refers to Dunbar's 'The Thrissill and the rois' (fol. 342ᵛ) and 'The Goldyn targe' (345ʳ), together with other items at the end of this section.[18] Central to the presentation is extensive reproduction of Henryson's *Moral Fables*, the prologue and ten items from the collection in total. But these are interspersed with other materials; *The Howlat*, for example, appears between Henryson's 'Preaching of the Swallow' and 'The Fox and the Cock', perhaps a deliberated sequence of 'bird-poems'. The presentation of *The Fables* is interrupted by two other Henryson poems, 'Orpheus and Eurydice' (fol. 317ᵛ) and 'The Bludy serk' (fol. 325ʳ); Bannatyne might have construed these as generically similar to 'fables' in that each includes a separate 'moralitas'. The second fascicle comprising this 'pairt of this buik' includes further materials generically comparable to this portion, for example, the beast-story 'Colkelbie sow'

---

[18] For a full list of the contents here, see Fox and Ringler 1980, xxxviii–xl. These materials are now extensively supplemented in Bawcutt 2008; for recent studies of the book, see her 126 n.2.

(fol. 357[r]) and Henryson's dialogue with concluding moral, 'Robin and Makin' (fol. 365[r]).

Author and Date

As has long been recognised (cf. Amours 1892–97, xxiii–vi), there is considerably more evidence for assigning *The Buke of the Howlat* an exact provenance than exists for most medieval poems. This material occurs in the poem's concluding stanza, where the poet 'Holland' wittily insures the transmission of his name by including it in rhyming position. In addition, this panegyric stanza associates the poet with the household of Archibald Douglas, earl of Moray, and his wife, Elizabeth Dunbar.[19]

Following Marion Stewart's impressive assembly of information (1972), we have considerable biographical information about Archibald Douglas's clerical servant, Richard Holland.[20] Since this Holland was well launched on a clerical career early in the 1440s (and appears to have died in English exile in early 1480s), he was probably born around 1410. As Amours first points out, several poetic details would suggest that Holland originally had come from Orkney,[21] and Stewart offers ample evidence suggestive of an Orkney background (3, 10–11). In 1457, Holland was identified as priest and canon of Kirkwall (and he may have held the position for as much as a decade previously, whether or not he was resident). Both 'Holland' and the surname 'Ratter', which may be used once to refer to him (13), are Orkney names; while the second may communicate the name of his family, the first is a toponym, a field-name several times instanced in Orkney. When Holland first appears in the records, in 1441, he is said to be of Caithness diocese (that is, he was ordained there) and engaged with the earl of Ross (at this point, the Lord of the Isles, Alexander MacDonald; see pp. 43–45) in Inverness.

Like a great many other late medieval men in orders, Holland appears to have seen clerical service as a career move, not an engagement with

[19] For Elizabeth Dunbar, see further 989n.
[20] On patronised clerks and their service to the Douglases, see Brown 1998, 193–94.
[21] Most notably, the offhand reference to the local locution *þe lang reid* 698, and the use of the placename *Burone* 896 as an term to express geographical distance.

the *cura animarum*. He appears most prominently in the historical record as seeking preferment to well endowed postings in collegiate institutions, positions which will have involved him most directly in administrative tasks, rather than spiritual ones. In such a context, being 'serviceable' to great men, utilising his literate and administrative talents in support of a lordly household, would have been a desideratum. In return, Holland would have expected to receive lordly influence in ecclesiastical appointments (which might have obviated having to pay him a salary for his contributions to an efficiently run household).[22]

The search for preferment seems to have rendered Holland's career a particularly contentious one. (This is a reason why records of his activities survive; legal spats always leave extensive 'parchment trails'.) Holland became engaged in a sequence of acrimonious disputes over various benefices and offices. In 1444, he was already an imperial notary and prebendary of Kirkmichael in Ross diocese, and the first reference clearly associating him with the Douglases (22 February 1449/50) identifies him as notary public, secretary to Archibald Douglas, earl of Moray, and rector of Halkirk, 'a simple prebendary of Dornoch cathedral' (Stewart 1972, 5). Laing provides (1867) two facsimiles of Holland's hand and his notarial sign, attached to documents (dated 1455 and 1457) he copied and attested for the Douglases; there the cross that conventionally forms such a 'sign' is flanked by four Douglas hearts.[23]

Given Holland's ongoing legal wrangles over a possible appointment as archdeacon of Caithness through the mid-1440s, he is unlikely to have been a Douglas adherent at that time. He may have abandoned a similar battle over the precentorship of Moray cathedral, still alive in the early 1450s, following the failure of the Douglases' rebellion against King James II in 1455.[24] This rising, his employers' response to the king's murder of William, the 8th earl Douglas, and his subsequent attacks on the family, effectively shattered whatever hopes Holland may have harboured for ecclesiastical advancement.

Holland appears to have been an active participant in the failed revolt, and for most of the remainder of his life, his exact whereabouts remain

---

[22] Cf. the comments on literate education and its social usefulness, Hanna 2011, 187–90.

[23] See Durkan 1985, xix, who first identified the significance of this feature and found parallels in the work of other Douglas notaries.

[24] See Stewart 1972, 6–9, for a discussion of a precentor's duties and their possible influence on the musical knowledge displayed in the poem.

unknown. Laing summarises (1867) a document in which his vicarage at Ronaldshey in Orkney was transferred to a new incumbent in 1467. The latest references to his activities include his exclusion from a Scots general pardon of 1482 and a safe conduct issued by Richard III in 1483. The last, as other records, point to his continuing service to 'his' family, likely attendance on and service to Archibald's brother, James, nominally 9th earl Douglas, during his lengthy exile in England. Holland may have had some role as messenger or negotiator as James pursued his aims against James II and III, with some support from Edward IV's Yorkist court. There Douglas hopes were intermittently perceived as useful in reasserting the English overlordship sought earlier by Edward I. But exile may have introduced a considerably more cosmopolitan view, and Holland could well have been in places such as Carrickfergus in Ulster (part of the Lordship of the Isles, allies to the earl of Ross) or in France on military service.

However, all these events long postdate the composition of *The Buke of the Howlat*, which is, as I have already noted, more narrowly datable, on internal grounds, than most medieval poems. As the concluding stanza indicates, Holland's composition must postdate Archibald Douglas's marriage to 'the dove of Dunbar', Elizabeth Dunbar, countess of Moray; his gaining the Moray inheritance (and title); and his taking up residence at Darnaway Castle (Morayshire). These events occurred in 1442, 1445, and 1447, respectively, and the last provides a *terminus a quo* for the work. Equally (and obviously), there is a fixed *terminus ad quem*, Archibald's death at the battle of Arkinholme – and the destruction of the Black Douglases as a political force – in 1455. However, one can probably narrow the possible period of composition still further and place the poem before James II's murder of William Douglas in December 1452. After that date, the poem's effusive statements of Douglas loyalty to the Scottish crown would seem distinctly implausible.[25]

However, the concluding stanza of the *Howlat* is far from the only place where the poem offers detail capable of being aligned with historical record. As a result – and reflective of a persistent effort to read Holland's poem through the lens of contemporary Scottish politics – a distinguished series of studies has sought a narrower chronological

[25] For this historical background, see Brown 1998, 267–72, 276, 293, 307, etc.; McGladdery 2005, 181–82.

placement.[26] This specification, as all who deal with the problem recognise, depends upon Holland's extensive (and precisely detailed) descriptions of the heraldic devices borne by his humanised birds.

Here perhaps the most telling evidence is provided by the description of the papal arms (lines 339–51), which are those associable with the antipope Felix V. Since Felix, the secular lord Amadeus of Savoy, surrendered his claim to the papacy in 1449, the poem cannot have pretended to the historical accuracy Holland appears to have sought after that date. In general, recent accounts, following Riddy, have situated composition during summer 1448. This chronological placement answers Holland's apparent reticence (lines 599–603) on the perquisites of Hugh Douglas, earl of Ormond. As Riddy argues (1986, 9–10), one would hardly expect Holland to have ignored Hugh's victory over the English in the battle of Sark (not the Channel Island but the river forming part of the western border with England), 23 October 1448. Such a dating would place the poem slightly earlier than any surviving historical record of Holland's association with Archibald Douglas, a point to which I will return below.

This historical detail all speaks to the poem as Douglas panegyric, at least initially offered as material entertaining a household or retinue. However, *The Buke of the Howlat*, even in the face of James II's destruction of the Douglases, seems to have achieved reasonably immediate circulation. As early as *c.* 1461, a reference to *The Howlat* may appear in the *Liber Pluscardensis*: 'Jacobus vero de Douglas ibidem [in the Holy Land] diem clausit extremum. Qui amplius de hac materia scire desiderat, ad legendam dicti excellentissimi principis in nostro wlgari compositam transeat, ubi ad longum reperiet'.[27] Moreover, *The Howlat* remained an influential resource for later authors (and Holland a person to be referred to with admiration) for well over a century, as Amours indicates (1892–97, xxxiii–iv).

---

[26] See particularly McDiarmid 1969, Riddy 1986, and Mapstone forthcoming 1, all with a wealth of further historical detail, summarised Royan 2006, 59–60 and especially 60 n.23. For more extensive discussion, see pp. 31–34, deeply indebted to these earlier scholars.

[27] 'But James Douglas died in the same place [in the Holy Land]. Whoever wants to know more about this matter should go to the account of that most excellent prince written in our own Scots, where he will find it at length.' Amours makes this suggestion (1892–97, 300); I cite Skene 1877–80, 1:263–64. But for an alternative interpretation of this record, see p. 40.

13

Certainly, the strongest commendation of Holland's work is offered by his inclusion in catalogues of the great dead poets of Scotland. He appears prominently – in the first example joined with Barbour – in both Dunbar's 'Timor mortis'/'Lament for the makaris' (Bawcutt's poem 21, 61) and Lyndsay's 'The Testament and complaynt of our soverane lordis papyngo' (19). Both poets follow (and in Dunbar's case, participate in) a sequence of direct appropriations of *The Howlat*, beginning in the 1470s.

Probably the earliest, and a particularly canny, example appears in Hary's *Wallace* (11.130–49). When Wallace insists on leading the vanguard in battle, Lord Stewart recounts for him the fable of the owl, as part of an angry presentation of Hary's hero as overreacher. Stewart's citation, which insists that 'Dcym Natur tuk off ilk byrd but blame | A fayr fethyr', can refer only to Holland's account. Moreover, Stewart's closing riposte, that Wallace's desire for precedence relies upon investing himself with resources proper only to others – 'This makis it thow art cled with our men. | Had we our awn, thin war bot few to ken' – directly answers the specific, if often elided, terms of Holland's moral (see further below, pp. 33–34). Of course, Wallace is no owl, and Hary implicitly argues here, in his revisionist account of the War of Independence, that his hero is not just comparable to, but better than, James Douglas, Holland's foil to the owl – and better than Douglas's beloved king as well.

A second late fifteenth-century appropriation of the poem occurs in the copy of Chaucer's 'Parliament of fowls' that appears in Bodleian Library, MS Arch. Selden. B.24. This version of the text, in a book produced for the Sinclairs of Ravenscraig (Fife), transmits the Chaucerian original only to line 602. Thereafter, it provides a unique conclusion (fols 151r–52r), in which Nature responds to the lower birds' demand 'for to ben delyvered' (*PF* 491), ignores Chaucer's central eagles, and promptly pairs off all the birds. The action concludes:

> The foulis flawe aweye as they were wilde,
> By two and two and noght by one allone.
> Sum flaw to forest, and als sum flawe to feild,
> And in a thrawe there was noght levit one
> Of grete and smale, bot all were forth gone –
> Sauf anerly an oule þat hie gan ȝout
> Was leuit behind than of all that rout. (fol. 152r)

Chaucer's redactor here recalls not only Holland's complaining isolated owl, but the mixed landscape, 'forest … and feild', that Holland describes at the poem's opening. '3out' echoes a verb Holland uses to describe his antihero's outcry (cf. line 102, where it is joined with the more usual '3oule'); and although 'hie' here means 'loudly', it equally reminds one of the lofty behaviour that precedes the bird's downfall (e.g. line 905).[28]

Not just the anonymous compiler whose work underlies the Selden version of Chaucer's 'Parliament', but the finest Middle Scots poets engaged with *The Howlat*. Although a great deal more elaborately conceived, Robert Henryson may draw on Holland's initial evocation of natural order when he describes his narrator's walking out at the opening of 'The Preaching of the Swallow' (*Moral Fables* 1622–1712). Bannatyne's juxtaposition of the two poems certainly highlights this connection, as it also does both narratives' reliance upon clerical bird-councils that achieve minimal effect. William Dunbar's borrowings are most recognisable in places where both he and Holland choose to follow well-established traditions (and thus, may represent coincident choices of received materials). But they often involve verbally exact detail that implies that Dunbar's mentioning Holland in 'The lament' represents but one part of a more pervasive reminiscence of his predecessor. And Bellenden's translation of Boece's chronicle certainly draws on Holland's account of James Douglas's 'crusade', down to a direct reference to 'þe Haly Graiff' (cf. lines 444, 471).[29]

Holland's influence remained vital well into the reign of James VI. In his 'Anser to ane heland manis invectiue', one of the latest poems written in the thirteen-line stanza Holland probably introduced into Scots, Alexander Montgomerie cites one or two lines from the Irish bard's Gaelic (certainly Holland's line 802, perhaps also 798). And Lekpreuik's 1571 edition of Barbour's *Bruce* inserts a dozen-line passage elaborating on James Douglas's fatal heroism with material the printer derived from *The Howlat*.[30]

---

[28] Mapstone first identified and discussed this echo; see 1996, 15; and 1999b. In addition, line 648 in the Selden conclusion, 'Sum piked him, sum proyned, sum song songis', may echo *Howlat* 22; see the text note there.

[29] See, for example, the notes to 138 ('The Thrissil and the rois', Bawcutt's poem 52), 718ff. ('Ane Ballat of our lady', Bawcutt's poem 16), and 795 ('The Seven deadly sins' and 'The Flyting', Bawcutt's poems 47 and 65, respectively). For Bellenden, see Batho and Husbands 2:297–98 (*Chronicles* 15.2).

[30] See *Bruce*, the collations at 20.429 and 1:109, 430n. For a small citation, see 491–94n.

Holland's Language

Given that *The Buke of the Howlat* has a named and identifiable Scots author, investigating its language would not appear an especially pressing pursuit. This investigation should throw up evidence only of well-known features of late medieval Scots. However, all is not exactly what one might expect. The following analysis begins by offering evidence of Holland's handling of the eighteen points listed and discussed in the earlier edition of *Golagros and Gawane* (Hanna 2008, xxv–xxx, with full references to historical grammars). In most instances, I restrict myself to offering the first three examples of relevant features.

Point 1: OE long a /ɑ:/ is retained as a low vowel, but probably fronted to /a:/ (not general ME long open o /ɔ:/). This feature, common to all northern English dialects, as well as Scots, is best illustrated by examples of OE long a in rhyme with the long a that developed in ME from other sources, mainly OF long a and OE short a in contexts lengthened in ME:

> *pape* (OE *pāpa*) 80:*cape* (OE *cæppe* or OF *cape*) 82:*schap* (cf. OE *gescap*) 84:*grap* (OE *grāpian*) 86

> *behald* (OE -*háldan*) 87:*cald* (ON *kalla*) 91[31]

> *haife* (cf. OE *hafast*) 118:*saif* (OF *salver, sauver*) 120:*laif* (OE *lāf*) 122:*conclaif* (OF *conclave*) 124

However, during a sustained block of the poem, Holland relies exclusively on 'southern English' rhymes that require OE long a to represent long open o. These occur in situations where OE long a rhymes with words having either long close or long open o:

> *fold* (OE *fólde*) 321:*behold* (OE -*háldan*) 325

> *oist* (OF *[h]ost*) 326:*most* (OE *māst*) 328:*cost* (OF *coste*) 330:*boist* (OF **boster* v.?) 332

> *gold* (OE *góld*) 340:*behold* 342:*inrold* 344 (OF *reillier;* see the text note):*fold* 346

> *gold* 360:*bold* (OE *báld*) 364

Rhymes of this type recur at 526 and perhaps 530, the first a particularly interesting example: *befor* (OE -*foran*) 522:*sore* (OE *sār*) 524:*þore* (cf. OE *þār*, ON **þár*) 526:*more* (OE *mār*) 528. The form *thore* is mapped

---

[31] This traditional collocation (widely dispersed in northern ME from before 1300) actually represents a half-rhyme, of short a with long a, but would be unavailable in Southumbrian ME; cf. modern hold/called, reflective of those developments.

at McIntosh et al., dot map 322 (1986, 1:385); it is primarily recorded in about a dozen Linguistic Profiles representing scribes located in fringe areas of western and southwestern Yorkshire. This is an area where copyists with secure Midland backgrounds, and thus o-forms, might well be aware of conservative unrounded northern /a/. The spelling represents an analogical back-formation from this northern form, and Holland displays expected Scots *thar* in rhyme at 184.[32] For further discussion of the Holland's marginal yet persistent 'Anglicisms', see below pp. 18, 20, 23.

Point 2: Just as retention of OE long a marks northerly English dialects, so also does the retention of the sequence OE āw/āg/āh as a diphthong au/aw, as opposed to more southerly ou/ow. Examples of this feature, shown by rhyme with words having historical short a (the usual source of ME au/aw diphthongs), occur at:

rawis (ME *rawe,* origin obscure, but implicitly with vowel ā) 244:*caus* (OF *cause*) 245:*sawis* (OE *sagu*) 246

awne 938 (OE *āgen*):*knawin* (OE *cnāwen*) 940:*drawin* (OE *dragen*) 942:*schawin* (*shāwen* < OE *sc(e)āwode*) 944

Point 3: In northern English and Scots, OE long o was raised to a high rounded vowel, probably fronted /y:/, but rhyming with words in earlier u:

ruf (OE *rōw*) 14:*abuf* (OE *abufan*) 16:*luf* (OE *lufu*) 18:*huf* (OE *hōfian*) 20

lufis 750:*behufis* (OE *behōfian*) 753

hone (ME *hōne,* of obscure origin) 886:*done* (OE *dōn*) 888:*sone* (OE *sōna*) 890:*abone* (*abūn* < OE *abufan*) 892[33]

Points 4–7: Rhyme confirms a variety of verbal inflections typical of northern English and Scots. Both the present third singular and the present plural of verbs share the same ending *-es* (points 4 and 5); the feature is adequately demonstrated in the two cross-rhymes 146–50, 706–10. However, when a pronominal subject occurs immediately adjacent to the verb, it shows no inflection (point 6, 'the Northern pronoun rule'); this feature occurs uniquely at 613 (most of the poem is written

---

32 Cf. the similar variation with the word 'lord' (OE hlāford), the Northern/ Scots form ('laird') in /a/ at 193, in contrast to the 'general English' usage in /o/ at 530. For the persistence of this particularly 'southern' vocalism in early Scots verse, see Aitken 1983, 26–31 (although few of his cited examples show the local persistence of Holland's use here).

33 For fuller discussion, see Jordan 1934, 77 (¶54) and 46 (¶26); Aitken 2002, 39 (¶7.1). Cf. further point 10 below.

in the past tense, and there is thus little opportunity to exhibit this item). Rhyme also confirms that the present participle has the termination common in northern English and Scots, *-and* (point 7):

> *cunnand* 204:*-sand* 208
> *-lestand* 997:*Holland* 1001

Point 8: The northern and Scots form for SHALL (OE *sceoldan*) is *sal* with initial /s/, and Asloan's universal spelling is *sall* (*sal* in the sequence *sal be* 123, 441). Holland's knowledge of the form is probably confirmed by the initial rhyme at 123: 'Thai sal be **sembl**it full **sone** – þat þow **se sall**'; and 577: 'Fra **son**nis of þe **Sax**onis. Now gif I **sall** schewe'. But neither line offers unproblematic evidence: the first is hyperalliterated, and the word is not absoutely necessary for rhyme; while the second might be interpreted as an example of an aa/bb rhyming pattern (and thus 'southern English' *schall*). Matters are not clarified by Holland's willingness to crossrhyme /s/ with clusters conventionally separate in alliterative practice, such as /š/ and /sk/ (see below, p. 48 and n.81).[34]

Evidence for the past tense SHOULD, in northern ME and Scots *suld*, is similarly murky. Again, Asloan routinely provides Scots spellings, excepting two provocative examples of *shold*, at 415 and 676. On both occasions, although these occur in the short lines of the 'wheel', where alliteration appears optional, both examples could rhyme initially /s/. But both examples also provide the end rhyme, here with words like *gold* (OE *góld*), and Asloan's spellings may be his recognition that in both cases the form represents 'southern English' *s(c)holde* (OE *sceolde*).

Point 9: In some parts of northern England, and routinely in Scots, OE eh/ēh develops as long close e. Such rhymes occur very frequently:

> *e* (OE *ēaga*) 67:*be* (OE *bēon*) 69:*de* (*degh* < ON *deyja*) 71:*me* (OE *mē*) 73
> *ʒe* (OE *gē*) 114:*me* 115:*de* 116
> *fle* (OE *flēon*) 140:*entre* (OF *entrée*) 141:*hie* (OE *hēah*) 142

Point 10: Unlike *Golagros and Gawane*, where examples occur frequently, *The Howlat* offers minimal evidence for northern ME and Scots lengthening of short /i/ in open syllables. The only plausible example is *bewschyris* 148(:*materis* 144:*efferis* 146:*steris* 150). This form may reflect earlier *-schiris* (with short /i/), but more probably represents the vowel of OF *sieur* rendered as /e/, an example of

---

[34] For example, '**Sall** I never **sene** be into **Scot**land' 485.

Holland's relatively frequent reliance upon nonce- or artificial forms (see pp. 21–22, 49–50).

Point 11: In restricted parts of northern England but widely in Scots, the verbs *make* and *take* display contracted forms, the infinitives *ma* and *ta*, third singulars *mase* and *tase*, and past participle *tan*. *The Howlat* displays only a restricted range of these forms, the infinitive *ta* 880(:*ga* 884, OE *gān*) and participle *tane* 145(:(-)*ane* 147 and 151, OE *ān*:*gane* 149, ON *gegna*). Analogous examples of the latter occur at 209 and 885(:*schane* 891, OE *scān*).

Point 12: The northern ME and Scots development of OE ōg/ōh to a diphthong *iu*, is widely attested:

> *drewe* (OE *drōh, drōg-*) 170:*knewe* (OE *cnēow*) 172:*trewe* (OE *trēow*) 174:*ynewe* (OE *genōg*) 176
>
> *ynewe* 282:*trewe* 286
>
> *hewe* (OE *hiwe*) 431:*reskewe* (OF *rescouer*) 433:*knewe* 435:*ynewe* 437

Point 13: In Scots, the historically distinct long vowel /a:/ and the diphthong /ai/ coalesce at an earlier date and more regularly than occurs in northern English. Rhymes between earlier /a:/ and /ai/ are abundant:

> *fair* (OE *fæger*) 15:*bair* (OE/ON *bār-*) 17:*levar* (-*ar* < OE -*ere*) 19[35]:*pair* (OF *paire, peire*) 21
>
> *chancillar* (-*ar* < OF *c[h]ancel-er*) 204:*fair* 205:*mistar* (-*ar* < AN *mester*) 206
>
> *tane* (*tāne* < OE *tacen*) 209:*plain* (OF *plain, plein*) 211:*ane* (OE *ān*) 213:*ran* (Gaelic *rán*?) 215

Point 14: In later Middle Scots, as is well-attested in *Golagros*, the vowel formed by this earlier coalescence of earlier /a/ and /ai/ may also rhyme with words having earlier long open e. Given its fixed date of composition, *The Howlat* provides important evidence for dating this development; on the basis of the poem, where conjunction of /a/, /ai/, and /ɛ:/ is *not* attested, this change occurred subsequent to Holland's poetic career, as Aitken notes.[36] Cf. 200 and the textual note there for an example of Asloan's obscure back-spelling in this phonetic context.

Point 15: In Scots, but no variety of English, earlier French -*ng*- (the -*gn*- of Modern French *digne*, not the sound of OE *ring*) rhymes with words with native -*ng*- (rather than usual ME -*n*-), including the verbal noun in -*ing* (OE -*ung*). Examples include:

---

[35] For the vowel here, see the discussion at pp. 21–22.
[36] See Aitken 2002, 131–50 (¶ 22) and the discussion at Hanna 2008, xxix.

mornyng (*morgning, morwening* < OE *morgen* + *-ung*) 157: *appering* (cf. OE *-ung*) 159:*lyng* (OF *ligne*) 161:*takynnyng* (OE *tācnung*) 163

thing (OE *þing*) 166:*leving* (OE *-ung*) 167:*digne* (OF *digne*) 168

king (OE *cyning*) 470:*thing* 472:*ryng* (AN *rengner*) 474:*hyng* (cf. OE *hēng*) 476

However, the 'English' form may also occur:

lyne (as if showing compensatory lengthening to /i:/ after loss of /g/?) 841:*syne* (*sīn* < OE *siþþan*) 845

Holland also displays the unusual analogical past tense *rang* 'reigned' 937:*fang* 939 (cf. OE *fangen* pp.), etc.[37] At 48–52, the rhyme *gowlyne* (again cf. OE *-ung*):*holyne* (OE *hollin*) implies, at least in this customarily unstressed context, the simplification of the OE sequence *-ng(-)* [ŋŋ] to simple [n], a feature occurring sporadically across the full range of English dialects. Compare further *syngis* (OE *singan*) 712:*begynnis* (OE *beginnan*) 714. Both examples can be paralleled in earlier Scots (and the rhyme of 841–45 may not be 'English' but an example of these developments). These then are susceptible to one of two explanations. Either they represent 'historical' rhymes, a licence still alive for Shakespeare, in which any nasal may freely rhyme with any other; or they indicate the prevalence of the simplification of [ŋŋ] to [n].[38]

Point 16: In Scots, /v/ and /w/ coalesce, probably exemplified once in alliteration: 'The said purse**want** (cf. OF *-suivant*) bure quhar he **away wend**' 629.[39]

Point 17: Holland probably offers no evidence of the Scots rhyme

---

[37] A past tense formed by analogy; in this development, where the French verb has become a homonym with OE *ringan* 'to ring, resound', Holland construes it as sharing all that verb's grammatical forms.

[38] See, for example, the rhymes at *Bruce* 3:241–42 (*fechtyn:syne*), 4:243–44 (*syne:fechtyn*), 4:512–13 (*syne:outyne/huntyn(e)*), 5:405–6 (*wyne:mellyne*); Kennedy, *Flyting* 494 (*myten:flyting*); the more extended examples at *Legends of Saints* Theodera 135–36 (*hand:wrang*), Eugenia 805–6 (*endynge:fynde*); and see further 276n. The rhyme *wyne:keching* at Theodera 429–30 is exact for consonance, but *keching* represents a back-spelling, commonplace all through the *Legends*; that form depends upon /ng/ and /n/ having become indistinguishable, so that the spelling of one historically distinct sound might be used to represent the other as well.

[39] Although, yet once again, the verse form is ambiguous, and the line might be construed as an example of aa/bb with alliteration in the first halfline on **said** and **-se-**.

between earlier long o and long u. The sequence of rhymes at 365–71 juxtaposes words all with earlier forms in long o.

Point 18: However, Holland provides ample evidence of earlier Scots long o rhyming with French loans in /y:/:

> *sure* 22 (OF *sure, seure*):*bure* (*bōre* pt. < OE *boren* pp.) 26
>
> *fure* (OE *fōr*) 79:*pure* (OF *pure*) 81:*mure* (cf. AN *meur*) 83:*sure* 85
>
> *luke* (OE *lōcian*) 295:*duke* (OF *duke*) 299

A further linguistic issue concerns Holland's perhaps cavalier attitude to the vowels of (usually) unstressed syllables in rhyme.[40] Rhyme provides ample evidence for the customary collapse of final inflectional syllables, e.g. *reird* 13 or *restord* 531.[41] Yet equally, these are often restored, as necessary, most typically in forms rhyming /i/, e.g. *planit*(:*layne it*) 850/852 or *recordis*(:*restord is*) 656/658.

However, in a variety of further instances, Holland places unstressed suffix syllables in rhyme with syllables normally stressed – and thus with relatively fixed vocalism. Here he relies upon the variety of potential renditions of unstressed vowels in Scots. In contrast to English, and down to present-day Scots, there is a good deal of variation here, and the artificiality involved in granting stress to a syllable where it is customarily absent allows the actualisation of such variation.

Nearly universally in Holland's handling, whatever their etymological sources, customarily unstressed suffixes forced into stressed rhyming service are reproduced as /a(:)/. Examples would include the rhymes of the *-er* of the comparative (OE *-ra*) at 19 and 173; the suffix of actant nouns (OE *-ere*) at 189, 374, and 771 (*-er* < OF at *mistar* 207; but contrast *-er* at 231; and cf. the spellings at 743 and 747). For *-el* rhyming on /a/, see 729/731 (OE *engel*, OF *angele*; and OF *boel, buel*, respectively) and more distantly 930, where *possible* rhymes as if *-able*. For the superlative suffix *-est* (OE *-ost*) rhyming on /a/, see 453 and 967/969. Finally, the suffix OE *-nes* rhymes on /a/ at 75, 110, 239, and 309 (contrast 395), and its handling is apparently extended to comparable treatment of OF *-esse* in *mastres* 32 and *richas* 674. On at least

---

[40] In contrast, one might note the bravura technique of a number of functionally monorhymed stanzas, e.g. 612–24 or 885–97. In these examples, a single consonant rhyme runs through the entire stanza, and only the vowels of the alternate lines are differentiated; such a form is universal in *TDK*.

[41] This is the only feature of unstressed vowels taken up in Aitken 2002; see 69–73. In what follows, I am particularly indebted to Jeremy J. Smith's wise counsel.

one occasion, routine /a/ in such examples points to a probable textual corruption (see *nuris* 275 and the textual note).

These formations are of various sources, adventitiously gathered. Nearly all might be paralleled in the rhyming uses of early Scots poetry, where they occur as occasional variants, not the universal forms that Holland makes them. Certainly most widespread, probably representing normal Scots usage, would be the rendition of *-nes* as *-nas*. Asloan spells the form as such at 75 and 309, and not simply the spelling, but the rhyme, is widely attested in early poetry. In other examples, although instances elsewhere may be isolated, Holland's practice may be paralleled in texts such as *Legends of Saints*, *Bruce*, *Wallace*, Hay, and Henryson.[42]

This listing scarcely exhausts the adjustments in expected forms dictated by rhyme. A variety of examples, like those in unstressed syllables, provides nonce-uses with non-etymological vowels. For example, OF *sir(e)* appears to rhyme on long e in 148 (see above, pp. 18–19) and OF *parfit* with long i in both its rhyming uses (182, 992).[43] With the last example, compare *dovle* 59 with long u, rather than the short vowel of the etymon, OE *dull*.

In addition to offering evidence phonologically useful, Holland's rhymes also confirm a variety of specifically Scots forms, often representing common items, e.g. *firth* 23, *feid* 61 and 165, *speik* ('speech') 242, *oft-syis* 274, (?) ȝald 289, *hart* 388/477/502, *hyng* 476, *amang* 494, *clas* 'clothes' 673, *sa* 'so' 793, *wald* 785, *smidy* 'smithy' 825, *sang* n. 943. As already noted, rhyme routinely shows apocope of the inflectional syllables *-is* and *-id/-it* (see 245 and 442, 344, respectively),

---

42 Unambiguous examples of *-nas* in rhyme (*Bruce* has frequent was:-nes, e.g. 4.35–36, which might rhyme either on /e/ or /a/) include *Wallace* 7.147–48, 381–82, 917–18; Hay, *Alexander* 4654–55; Henryson, *Moral Fables* 705–7, 720–23, 1104–6. Hay, *Alexander* 4902–3 rhymes *place* and *riches* (= richesse). For *-er* rhyming /a/, see *Wallace* 6.165–66, 271–72; Hay, *Alexander* 5021–22, 5495–96; Henryson, *Moral Fables* 1272–74; Dunbar, 'Seven deadly sins' (Bawcutt's poem 47) 34–35. Rhymes in *-el* sounded /a/ probably represent assimilation to the common suffix OF *-aile*, but cf. Hay, *Alexander* 5695–96 (yewall 'jewel':all) For *-est* rhyming /a/, see *Wallace* 6.379–80.

43 This rhyme, attending to vowel quality /i/, not quantity /iː ~ i/, is widely attested, e.g. *Bruce* 6:357–58 (wice 'vice':is). For further examples, see *Bruce* 3:241–42, 4:243–44, 5:405–6; *Legends of Saints* Theodera 429–30; Eugenia 445–46, 805–6; Hay, *Alexander* 5139–40, 5707–8.

yet entirely typically, in a poem devoted to expansive variation, some rhymes require full rendition of these syllables (see 852).

This linguistic exercise proves fruitful precisely because of Holland's commitment to extensive variation. A great many features imply the poet's interest in drawing unpredictably upon a range of forms, far from all of them items one might associate with Scots at all. Here one might recall the discovery of prominent 'anglicised' features associated with points 1, 8, and 15 above. Moreover, such features are not limited to information derived from rhyme, but also matters of lexicon and of local readings. Mackay (1981, 201–2) notices a number of peculiarities in Holland's choice of vocabulary; she specifically identifies some of this selectivity as 'Lydgatian', but a more general characterisation as 'English' might be appropriate. Similarly, a number of lines remain metrically suspect, at least within a Scots context. But for example, line 243 would probably alliterate unproblematically, were Scots *gaf* to read as distinctly southern ME *yaf*, and on two occasions, where the transmitted Scots forms do not rhyme, their English synonyms would (see the notes to lines 230, 782). Holland's language is exuberant in its variousness and pursuit of parallel forms scarcely widespread in Scots. Perhaps the main point to derive from this linguistic analysis is the deliberated wittiness, extending to very small choices among a range of options, associated with this fine poet's production.[44]

Literary Sources and Holland's Poem

As Bannatyne (and implicitly, Asloan) saw, Holland's *Buke of the Howlat* is a 'fable'. However, such an account requires immediate qualification; a fable of the type 'De bubone et aliis volatilibus' provides only a frame for the poem, the actual narrative business of lines 1–130, 846–1001 alone. There the account is accompanied by, or set within, as Bawcutt and Riddy say (1987, 43), a *chanson d'aventure*; this provides, as I will suggest, an important accompaniment to the specific fable-moral Holland draws. It is further significant that this particular fabular confirmation only frames the poem, for as I will also argue, Holland engages in a standard example of a specific type of *amplificatio* (one considerably less restrained than the precise Henryson).

---

[44] On variation in early Scots (here mainly a discussion of the spelling system), see Aitken 1971.

Ultimately, Holland's source, just as Henryson's in his *Moral Fables*, is a commonplace fable for schoolboys (and a type of text regularly imported into adult contexts as a preacher's *exemplum*). Its most widely disseminated form is of the type the great historian of the genre, Léopold Hervieux (1893–99), identifies as 'The proud jay and the peacock' ('De graculo et pavonibus', as the late medieval standard, Walter of England, has it). In one form or another, this anecdote goes back to the fable-collection ascribed to 'Phaedrus', probably composed in the reign of Claudius (A.D. 41–54), and it appears widely, its antihero one of a range of various proud, if unsightly, birds. (A 'graculus', after all, in medieval Latin, might represent a jackdaw, crow, or rook.) Among other versions available in the British late Middle Ages, one might notice those of Vincent of Beauvais, Alexander Nequam, Walter, and Odo of Cheriton.[45]

It is this last version that McDiarmid, in an important intervention (1969, 282–84 et passim) conclusively identifies as Holland's immediate source. McDiarmid is certainly, given Holland's meticulous rendition of Odo's moral at lines 970–84, correct. This text runs:

> Contra illos qui iactant se habere quod non habent
> Cornix, semel uidens se turpem et nigram, conquesta est aquile. Aquila dixit ei quod mutuo reciperet plumas de diuersis auibus. Fecit sic. Accepit de cauda pauonis, de alis columbe, et sicut sibi placuit, de ceteris auibus. Cornix, uidens se ornatum, cepit deridere et inclamare contra alias aues. Venerunt igitur aues et conquerebantur aquile de superbia cornicis. Respondit aquila, 'Accipiat quelibet auis suam pennam, et sic humiliabitur'. Quo facto, cornix relicta est turpis et nuda.
>
> Sic miser homo de ornatu suo superbit. Set accipiat ouis lanam suam, terra li[m]um, boues et capri corium suum, cirogrilli et agni suas pelles, et remanebit miser homo nudus et turpis, et ita fiet saltim in die mortis, quando nihil secum afferet de omnibus bonis suis.

---

45 For discussion and texts, see Hervieux 1893–99, 2:7, 140–41 (Phedrus proper), 167, 210 ('Romulus'), 239 (Vincent's Romulus-derivative), 254, 269, 307, 332 (Walter), 399 (Nequam), 467, 489–90, 603, 760. Cf. McDiarmid 1969, 290 n.29; Holland's revision to make the owl his antihero draws on conventional lore about this bird, discussed in the note to line 48. On further contemporary use of Odo's fables, by Walter Bower, see Mapstone 1999c, 44–45.

Item hoc exemplum ualet contra diuites qui pro multitudine diuitiarum gloriantur, sed Deus quandoque omnia aufert, et sic humiliantur.[46]

While the general outline of Odo's account – and particularly its moral – will be familiar to readers of the poem, Holland's rendition certainly involves recourse to literary works more august than the fable tradition. In Odo's account, both the owl and the other aggrieved birds approach the eagle, as king of birds, to seek redress. This regal figure appears prominently enough in *The Buke of the Howlat* (see, for example, lines 313–18), but no longer in the same unqualifiedly executive role as in the fable. Instead, Holland presents the owl appealing to a mixed council of ecclesiastical (headed by the peacock) and secular officials, a testimony to a prominent form of contemporary political decision-making, the church council (cf. McDiarmid 1969, 278–79, 285–86). Moreover, the actual ingrafting of the owl's newly acquired feathers is not a free avian gift, as it were, but requires the intervention of a supernatural power, 'Dame Natur, þat noble mastres' (32).[47]

These features should immediately recall Chaucer's 'Parliament of fowls'. That poem, of course, presents birds within a governmental metaphor comparable to that in *The Howlat*, and in it, while eagles

[46] For the text, see Hervieux, fable 3, 4:180–81:

Against those who boast that they have what they do not

Once the crow, perceiving that he was black and ugly, complained to the eagle. The eagle told him that he should receive in turn feathers from the various birds, and the crow did so. Thus, he took feathers from the tail of the peacock, from the wings of the dove, and, just as it pleased him, others from various birds. Then the crow, perceiving himself decorated in this way, began to mock and lay charges against the other birds. Therefore the birds went and complained to the eagle about the crow's pride. The eagle answered, 'Let each bird take its own feather, and he will be humbled'. Once they had done this, the crow was left ugly and bare.

In the same way, wretched mankind prides himself about his ornament. But should the sheep take back its wool, the earth its slimy bits, bulls and goats their hides, squirrels and lambs their pelts, wretched mankind will be left naked and ugly. And he will be made so immediately on his death-day, when he can carry nothing away with him from among all his goods.

This example also has force against rich men. Some of them feel ennobled on account of their many riches, but God sometimes takes away all their things, and thus they are humbled.

[47] One should note that the common noun 'nature' appears routinely in versions of this fable, either incidentally in the anecdote proper, or as part of the moral, a warning about deserting one's proper state (*natura*).

25

are certainly prominent, they are subjects (and engaged in pursuits amatory, rather than regal). Moreover, the executive role in Chaucer's account is reserved for Nature, 'the vicaire of the almyghty Lord' (*PF* 379). Holland certainly knew the poem, as a few selected verbal details indicate. For example, 'All se-fowle and seid-fowle' (238) evokes two of Chaucer's four parliamentary 'estates', and the peculiar usage 'þe walentyne' (918) probably alludes to the Chaucerian linkage between saint's day and the mating of *volatilia* (see *PF* 309–10, 504, 512). Further details confirm Holland's knowledge of the English poet. The jay's tricks at lines 772–75, 790–93 echo the lightshow arranged by the 'subtile tregetour[e]' (*Canterbury Tales* F 1141) of Orleans in 'The Franklin's Tale',[48] and the allusion to 'þe frute of þe erd and Godis fusoun' (979) may echo 'The Miller's Prologue' (A 3165) – although both poets may here draw independently upon a common proverbial utterance.

However, Holland's independent recourse to Chaucer's marked source, 'Aleyn in *The Pleynt of Kynde*' (*PF* 316), Alain of Lille's *De planctu naturae*, is far more pervasive than are allusions to the greatest medieval English poet.[49] Indeed, it might be argued that Holland's entire poem has been generated from a particularly academic *jeu d'esprit* predicated upon Alain's poem. The Latin author writes a work in which Nature complains (the title as subjective genitive). Holland inverts the grammatical relations, a technique he might well have learned from Alain, notorious for his grammatical metaphors. He thereby produces a work in which the 'unnatural' owl complains *against* Nature (objective genitive). As McDiarmid points out, even this conception (and the substitution of a sordid owl for the traditional 'graculus' or 'cornix' of the fable) might be predicated upon Holland's reading of *De planctu*:

> Illic bubo, prophetia miserie, psalmodias funeree lamentationis precinebat. Illic noctua tante deformitatis sterquilinio sordescebat,

---

48 Thus, ships appearing in the hall at *Canterbury Tales* F 1143–45, an image of great 'hertes' and a deer hunt at 1189–94, knights jousting on a plain and 'his lady on a daunce' at 1198–1201. Further examples of Holland's frequent echoes of *PF* (or at least coalscence in detail between the two poems) are mentioned in the textual notes; see particularly 212, 226, 229, 239, 256, 318, 651, 771, more distantly 761 and 762 ('The House of fame'), and 896 ('The General Prologue').

49 Once again, see McDiarmid's seminal account, 1969, 281, 290 n.34; the subsequent citations are from Häring's edition (1978).

ut in eius formatione Naturam fuisse crederes sompnolentam. Illic cornix ... (2/167–69, p. 818).[50]

Large swatches of *The Howlat* might readily be ascribed to the influence of *De planctu naturae*. For example, the poet's opening ramble into nature, where he sees birds and blossoms in juxtaposition (1–32), might well answer 7/29–36 (p. 832), a description in which the air filled with birds and the grove and the land with leaves and flowers re-enforce one another as a sign of Nature's orderedly various and recreative power.[51] Or, in contradistinction to Chaucer's presentation, where Nature is simply present, as if the literarily ordinary accompaniment to landscape, in *De planctu*, as in *The Howlat*, the goddess must descend from heaven to address (in *De planctu*, to lament) an emergency situation.[52] Holland's recall of the Latin prosimetrum occasionally extends to very precise detail, for example in his nonce-usage *sytharist* (757 'zither or harp'), recalling 'alauda quasi nobilis citharista ... citharam presentabat in ore' (2/189–91, p. 816).

Of course, like Chaucer (cf. *PF* 323–64), Holland most vividly recalls – and most of my citations above come from this portion of the poem – the description of Nature's mantle (2/138–95, pp. 813–16). This

---

50 'There the horned owl, prophet of misery, was singing the psalms of funeral lamentation. There, the night-owl grew vile in a dung-pit of so great deformity that you would believe that Nature had been drowsy when making it. There the crow ...' Häring's note ascribes the distinction between the two species of owl to Isidore, *Etymologiae* 12.7.40; while Holland has been inspired by the language in which Alain describes his second type of owl, Chaucer echoes only language associated with the first: 'The oule ek, that of deth the bode bryngeth' (*PF* 343).

51 Cf. Chaucer's evocation of the same passage – excepting the branches, reasonably conventional in medieval natural descriptions: 'And in a launde, upon an hil of flouers, | Was set this noble goddesse Nature, | Of braunches were here halles and here boures ...' (*PF* 302–4).

52 Cf. 4/8–9 (p. 821): 'Virgo ... a celestis regie emergens confinio, in mundi passibilis tugurium curro uitreo ferebatur' ('The girl ... emerging from the confines of the heavenly palace, was carried in a glass chariot into the hovel of this world, susceptible to suffering'); or 8/2–5 (p. 832): 'An ignoras que terreni orbis exorbitatio, que mundani ordinis inordinatio, *que mundialis curie incuria, que iuris iniuria*, ab internis penetralibus celestis archani in uulgaria terrenorum lupunaria me declinare coegit?' ('Do you not know what "exorbitant" deviation from the earth's orbital course, what disorder of the world's order, *what carelessness by the world's carers/courtiers, what injustice to justice*, has compelled me to descend from the innermost recesses of heaven's secrets to the common whorehouses of the earth?') (my emphasis).

passage, like much else in *De planctu naturae*, forms an elaborate poetic catalogue, a listing of all the birds Alain could think of, in short compass – a technique, as I will argue, inspiring Holland's primary imaginative work of *The Howlat*. Chaucer's birds, in his catalogue, form a rowdy list that testifies to Nature's plenitude (which is also inherent in Holland's appropriation of Alain), and are mainly depicted in their proverbial/ textualised existence. Holland's interests are other, an emphasis on birds native to Scotland – if not actually, as the poem, in its complimentary mode, occasionally implies (cf. lines 157–58), fluttering about the Douglas seat at Darnaway – and a witty effort at finding equivalences between *observed* bird detail (not necessarily of great sophistication) and social states:

> The dow, Noyis messinger,
> Rownand aye with his feir,
> Was a corate to heir
> Confessionis hale. (231–34)

Here the cooing pairedness of doves is presented as an emblem of the confessional (cf. Chaucer's 'The wedded turtil, with hire herte trewe', *PF* 355). Proverbially, (turtle)doves are 'true' and paired, and thus both sincere – giving a 'hale' [complete] confession, in accord with one catechetical requirement – and discreet – the auditor preserving the secrets told him by the other. The biblical allusion (echoed at 809–17, 989–90) evokes the bird's worldly sanctity and may further remind one of its connection with the Holy Spirit, vehicle for that grace necessary to absolution. Holland cleverly actuates functions that might be appropriate to humans out of something that resembles observed bird-lore.[53]

But the influence of Alain's cataloguing on *The Buke of the Howlat* is more pervasive still. Here one might consider a stanza in most respects thoroughly superfluous, lines 755–67. This provides an elaborate indication of what might not have needed expression, the musical instruments in use at the birds' banquet (which, of course, do not quite exist, since melody comes from song-filled bird-throats, cf. Alain's 'citharam

---

[53] Cf. Amours 1892–97, xxxiii: 'the quaint and mildly satirical aptness with which each bird plays its part in the drama stamps the poem with an originality all its own'. For an extensive discussion of the turtledove here, see Scheibe 1997.

presentabat in ore'). Again, the list has probably also been inspired by Alain, here *De planctu*, section 17 (pp. 872–73).[54]

This poetic technique, of including a list not altogether necessary, dovetails with a venerable alliterative genre, the poetic *þula* or catalogue. Traditionally this offers a way for expressing, within a literary tradition given over to purposeful variation, the poet's capacity, the expansive range of materials at his disposal. Such is quite clearly the case in the earliest English example, portions of which were once imagined as having been composed in the early sixth century. The Exeter Book 'Widsith' is mainly comprised of a listlike series of references to the heroic accounts the poet/speaker claims he is prepared to recite.

þula should, however, be contrasted with the normal métier of alliterative poetry, variation. The latter reflects a fundamentally metonymic impulse, the proliferation of general synonyms for the same person or object ('warrior', 'sword', 'horse', etc.). While catalogues may include such multiplications of the same, they differ fundamentally in conception. In them, the poet imagines a broad class category (in *The Howlat*, 'all birds', as aligned with 'all ecclesiastical and noble offices') and breaks it into constituent parts for rhetorical display. Rather than multiples of the same thing/topic, one is provided a range of multiple possibilities, in certain respects outside the expected scope of alliterative metonymic rhetoric. After all, of Holland's birds, only those of prey fill the social niches that provide traditional alliterative subjects.

Most particularly, catalogue allows the display, not only of comprehensive learnedness (the best catalogue is that most detailed), but also of carefully chosen (and often, wittily precise) multiple register. Both metonymy and catalogue fuse in one of Holland's great delights in the poem, display of a specifically 'clergial' or 'dictaminal' rhetoric. This gathering of all usefully honorific forms of address – essential to Holland's professional career in the formulation of documents, both papal and magnatial – is presumably what line 253 describes as 'termes in test'.

This unifying rhetorical technique demonstrates the strength and thematic focus that McDiarmid (1969, 277–78) evokes to expose the weakness of earlier accounts. These he characterises as complaints against 'a succession of spirited but purposeless scenes' or 'a merely occasional poem, slightly conceived and carelessly shaped'. I would

---

[54] Amours, followed by Riddy, provides a fine note with later parallels (1892–97, 309), and cf. McDiarmid 1969, 290 n.42.

concur with McDiarmid's powerful, if somewhat idealising, view of the poem as upholding 'natural order', but I would find that order in Holland's rhetorical plenitude or variousness. This would include that *copia verborum* that catalogues demand, as well as the moral harmonies McDiarmid wishes to applaud. Further, in this interest in verbal expansiveness, the poem looks ahead to a rich set of forms later prominent in Scots. One need only point to the obverse of Holland's usually panegyric efforts, the poetic flyting, with its victor being the person most profusely stocked with apposite insult, or Dunbar's *Tretis of the tua mariit wemen and the wedo*, a differently satiric kind of contest, which strives for an extensive listing of the most vilifying terms for men.

In the poem, cataloguing is expressed through a complicated combination of features, to only two of which I draw attention here. One striking emphasis, appropriate enough in a narrative centred about an owl achieving – and losing – a strikingly particoloured 'featherhame', would concern blazon and colour. On the one hand, 'colour' is a word deeply embedded within rhetorical tradition (and self-presentation), the *colores* associated with figurative language, of which birds performing as if they were human forms a striking example (a form of the figure 'prosopopoeia'). On the other, 'colour' in a blazon, the heraldic 'metals' and 'tinctures', forms a statement, not provisional as statements associated with rhetoric are, but of allegedly inherent identity (cf. 420, 430–35, and the extended treatment of the Douglas heart). The blazon, like the drake's green head (210), expresses 'Nature', a fixed relationship (rather than the owl's put-on garments) mirroring inner moral resolve, most strikingly in the poem exemplified in the fidelity and service of James Douglas. Equally, throughout the poem, Holland plays upon the Douglases' connection to generative nature – that they are a 'birth' (406), prolific in their continual success, and true to a genetic inheritance; that equally they 'bear', carry their arms. In the poem, the language of heraldry – which produces another sequence of catalogues – also serves as a language of nature.

In all its variousness, *The Buke of the Howlat* expresses natural capacity. As a careful reader of Chaucer's 'Parliament' and its source in Alain of Lille, Holland is constantly aware of natural plenitude, the profusion of avian species. But, as I have been arguing, plenitude here is equally a rhetorical function, and associated with a poet who names himself and remains the only present human participant in his poem. Indeed, he is the benighted owl's single companion, like the bird 'Withoutin fallowe or feir' (11). However, he early dissociates himself from the bird's quest for beauty and pronounces it a 'bourde', jesting entertainment (87). In contrast to the owl, naturally deprived and ultimately to overreach himself, the poem illustrates its poet's gifts, his originality and rhetorical skills, and his willingness to devote them to a familial tradition of faithful service.

Thus, this panegyric demonstration of the poet's constructive capacity shows, as the owl's career does not, his loyalty and capacity for 'good service' appropriate to a noble house. Indeed, the poem, which predates by perhaps eighteen months the historical evidence linking Holland with Archibald Douglas, might originally have represented a witty plea for preferment. Alternatively, *The Howlat* might function as a 'serviceable' thank-offering for having received such preferment. The mirroring of flashy poetic speaker and ungainly owl gains further purchase because both are involved in stories about changing one's raiment. Appointment in the Douglas household should have conferred on Holland 'livery of service', the promise, semiannually, of a new gown, at least; the poem provides an implicit promise that he knows better, and is more fruitfully committed, than to abuse his position of service.

Other sources of the poem are more local[55] and concern its imbrication in Scottish history. Here the most influential (and perhaps unfortunate) contribution remains Stewart's discussion of the poem as political allegory, or *roman à clef* (1975). In her account, Holland seeks, in fable and poem, to express Douglas antipathy for the ministers of James II's minority, the Livingstones. Men of administrative competence only, the Livingstones gained a prominent position in the kingdom that should have belonged to established lords of honour, like the Douglases faithful servants to Scottish kings for generations. Like the owl, the Livingstones pursued a power and influence not their own, nor proper to their 'natural' social station; like the owl, they merited a fall – which did occur in 1449, shortly after Holland composed the poem. Stewart's narrative has remained a powerful stimulus to criticism (although regularly acknowledged as far from a total account of Holland's work), and indeed routinely appears in historical literature (e.g. Brown 1997, 163–64) as an unproblematised report of Holland's purpose in writing *The Howlat*.

It is certainly the case that the owl falls, and equally certainly so that Holland wishes to applaud 'serviceable' Douglases 'of lang dait' (425), rather than masterful parvenus. But Stewart's view seems to me,

---

[55] Although see the textual note to line 50 for a probable allusion to another European classic, *Le Roman de la rose*.

whatever allowance should be given its claimed 'partialness' as inter-
pretation (after all, all interpretations are such), to distort substantially
the most obvious interests of *The Buke of the Howlat*. As I have already
indicated, in her reading, the peripheral, the poem's frame, becomes its
centre – and it might be argued that reading the work as a rebuke to a
proud over-reacher manages to distort even the frame itself.

First of all, while the poem's owl is the occasion for and the butt of
its moral, that bird could scarcely be described as the unique target of
the poem's satire. One might, for example, consider Nature's response
to the aggrieved birds, when she comes to remove the owl's feathers:

'My first making', quod scho, 'Was vnamendable ...' (928).

The opening *My* alliterates (emphatically, given that the word quite
unusually here bears stress). Implicitly, in Nature's view the other birds
are just as silly as the owl has been. Their desire to 'amend' her crea-
tion, born of misplaced commiseration for a 'colleague', is every bit
as ill-considered (and presumptuous) as the owl's initial attack on the
goddess had been.

Moreover, most critics (and editors) have noticed that, in general,
Holland's birds are scarcely immune to critique, and they have cited
instances of the poet's passing satire of his creations. For example, it
is routine to see the owl's question 'Quha is fader of all foule, pastour
and pape'? (80, cf. further 90–91) as commenting upon the topsy-turvy
contention between variously elected papal candidates during the Great
Schism – and the concomitant loss of papal prestige.[56] Similarly, the
poem's secular lords emerge from 'Babilonis towr' (293), a locale again
associated with less than august activity – man's pride, error, and 'confu-
sion' (the customary medieval etymology for 'Babel'). The poem finds
a broad range of satiric targets (many of them ones only momentarily
present, like the corvine friars of lines 191–95), and the owl is only
the most extravagant instance. Like all fabulists, including Chaucer in
his several essays in this mode, Holland operates by estrangement, the
literal narrative presentation of silly animal activity designed to reveal

---

[56] And of course, as many commentators notice, Holland assigns this role to
the peacock, a bird customarily denigrated for proud extravagance; cf. *PPB*
12.236–63, including a moral resonant with that Holland will apply to the
owl, self-styled *counterpalace to þe pape* (particularly lines 971–75).

to humans that they are just dressed-up animals, and equally risible – or deviantly evil.[57]

Moreover, Holland's moral – that detail in the poem that most closely links him with Odo of Cheriton – emphatically resists Stewart's particularising reading. Obviously enough, fables appeal because the stories are applicable in a broad range of situations, and certainly, like the owl, the Livingstones appear to have been significant examples of getting above one's raising. But the moral here, whilst the falsely high become low, is *not* concerned with social climbing and its ill effects. First, Holland's moral is addressed, and applies to 'all maner of man' (970), with a special proviso, following Odo's account, for the rich, 'princis, prentis of pryde' (lines 970–75, but the address perhaps extending to the end in line 988).

Further, the moral point is the narrow one, that human pride rests on precisely *colores*, engagement with the merely decorative. This is raiment, in the poem specifically and only the owl's 'fetherhame'; following Odo, Holland presents such materials as extracted from non-proper, that is non-personal, sources, the world of nature (e.g. at line 979). Humans are like the owl – and, one could add, the remainder of Holland's flocks – because they pursue impermanent objects, not eternal truths, and pursue objects that do not belong to them, and thus are not spiritually proper. Nature herself makes the point succinctly when she metaphorically describes the owl's borrowed raiment as 'The rent and þe ritches þat þow in rang' (937); feathers obviously are not property but an emblem for it (just as 'mennis' 938 narratively means 'birdis') – and for the world's wealth that departs at death (cf. the evocation of Job 1:21 at lines 976–77, 983 and the surrounding notes).

The one injunction Holland offers in this situation is 'reule þe richtuis' (984). This is a conventional admonition; in a world of impermanence, where all ends in the tomb, one hopes for lasting spiritual good. One achieves this end by a just self-restraint, in more elaborated accounts, frequent in medieval English devotional prose, by self-custody, and the disciplining of desire. But at the poem's end, the subject is revealed – whatever the governing conciliar metaphor of the narrative (which equally provides a figure including 'all maner of man') – not to have been an issue associated with high politics but with a moral life lived in the anticipation of death.

---

[57] The well-known point Henryson makes at *Moral Fables* 43–60 (and in the bumptious reprise, voiced by the enthusiastic narrator at 1398–1404).

Thus, the poem surprisingly undoes its most prominent narrative form in its conclusion. (Indeed, the whole might be considered a plenteous catalogue alluding to various narrative genres.) At this point, Holland replaces one narrative account with another, although one that follows from, and has been carefully occluded since, the opening landscape description.

The entire alliterative tradition from *Beowulf* down represents, to some degree, a sequence of laments over human transience. But some texts engage more explicitly with the theme than others, and one widespread alliterative – and in the main, stanzaic alliterative – tradition forms a powerful background to the frame narrative in *The Buke of the Howlat*. A succession of alliterative poems, many of them customarily invoked as analogues to the poem's *chanson d'aventure* opening, are, as Turville-Petre points out (1974), poems about death and the impermanence of human pride and achievement (which they so[m]berly attack). A list of apposite examples would include 'Summer Sunday' (stanzaic, perhaps cited in line 184 here), *The Parliament of the three ages* (itself a catalogue poem), the first half of *The Awntyrs off Arthure* (stanzaic), 'The Three dead kings' (stanzaic), and, in many respects, 'The Quatrefoil of love' (stanzaic, with a threatening evocation of Last Judgement as an extensive conclusion) and 'Death and Liffe'. Few of these works, it must be said, indulge in quite so apparently extensive a divagation from their moral theme as does *The Howlat*. But all rely for their didactic shocks upon the contrast between that plenitude that man did not make (but has every capacity to pridefully abuse), evoked in the *locus amoenus* opening, and the coming end, the death's head, that, rather than the pursuit of grandeur, should shape responsible human endeavour (the discussion that concludes the poem).[58]

But whether or not one may think satire of the Livingstones central to *The Howlat*, the poem overtly offers a panegyric appreciation of their adversaries, the Douglases, and a more diverse historical allusiveness than Stewart's argument acknowledges. Holland's emphases might imply a rather different, and perhaps 'guilty' historical knowledge. His Douglas panegyric focuses about three prominent moments of family history, a selective presentation that honours persons who could be

---

[58] For further detail on the relationship of *The Howlat* to alliterative 'mortality poems', see the notes to lines 953–70 passim; for suggestions that the topic of mortality is far from absent from the poem's centre, see the notes to 437/445 and 722–23.

construed as resembling the poem's owl – and yet did not perform as that bird does here.

At the centre of Holland's account is James 'the black' Douglas, an obscure Lanarkshire lord elevated by his honourable service to royalty. The other moments honour figures distinctly cadet-ish: James's bastard son, who managed, by luck, violence, and service, to become progenitor of the fifteenth-century Douglas line; and, in turn, this man's younger son, never overtly mentioned in the poem, but a pronounced figure of further violence, service, and natural 'birth' – five surviving sons at the time Holland wrote – who constructed the contemporary success that Holland honours. Douglas narrative here looks to two distanced historical episodes that emphasise moderated ambition in service to princes; in them, the righteous personal self-restraint urged in Holland's concluding *moralitas* becomes conceived as a political tool, more productive than much of the avian conciliar shenanigans Holland also describes. In the third iteration, treating the contemporary sons of James 'the gross' (the enormously obese), 7th earl Douglas, Holland promises the renewal of such service in the poem's present and future. (See the abbreviated family tree at p. xiv.) I here address each of these three Douglas moments in turn.

Holland's account of James 'the black' quite literally is the 'heart' of the entire poem. Not only does James express his fidelity and service by carrying or 'bearing' the heart of his dead lord, Robert Bruce, but through this action, he expresses his own heart, faithful to the death. In turn, the heart stands as public identifier of the Douglases in general, the central device on the family's coat of arms. Rather than simply external 'colour', as are the owl's borrowed feathers, the heart blazon depicts deep inner nature. Moreover, as Mackay's and Alexander's important readings of *The Howlat* indicate, in structural terms, the narrative of James's exploits forms the centre, the heart, of Holland's entire production.[59]

---

59 See Alexander 1983, esp. 17–19; Mackay 1981, 194–200. Both demonstrate that Holland rigorously carries through on the implications of the fairly common linking of a poem's opening lines and concluding ones (here through the words 'middis' and 'May'). If the opening and the end are functionally similar, all parts could be expected to mirror one another across a centre; cf. Spearing 1982. This centre one could well identify with the stanza including lines 495–507, the moment of James's triumphant crusading identification with his king, 'feile feildis he wan, aye worschipand it [Bruce's heart]' (503). Both Alexander and Mackay show another important feature of

35

The central figure is the founder of the line, 'the good Sir James' (1288–1330). His father had died in Edward I's prison in 1299, and, after an initial flirtation with the English, inspired by his desire to regain his lordship of Douglasdale (Lanarkshire), he joined the Bruce in May 1307. As Holland heralds, James was King Robert's constant supporter thenceforth – even after his king's death. The generative account of this relationship, which Holland certainly knew, appears in Barbour's *Bruce*.[60]

Holland's account of James Douglas emphasises his *post mortem* service to his lord and king, and includes original materials. But in the main, it amalgamates two aboriginal, although not altogether homogeneous, narratives of the dying king Robert's request that Douglas carry his heart to Palestine. One of these retellings is, as one would expect, again in Barbour's *Bruce* (20.153–611 passim), which Holland on occasion comes close to citing verbatim (see the notes to 447, 449, 498, 510–11, 521–23). But Holland draws equally upon the account in Froissart's *Croniques*,[61] though this is older still, and manifestly erroneous in detail, Although the Hainault historian had visited Scotland in the 1360s (when he claims to have seen James Douglas, the 2nd earl and slain hero of Otterburn, as a promising youth), his account fundamentally repeats Le Bel's earlier chronicle.

I cite from both accounts of the Bruce's instructions at length, first Froissart (ch. 20; 1:67–68):

Syr William [sic], my dere frend, ye knowe wel that I have had moche ado in my dayes to uphold and susteyn the ryght of this realme. And

Holland's meticulous composition, the numerological symbolism provided by the poem's exactly seventy-seven stanzas and 1001 lines; both agree in associating the first figure with penitential ideas germane to Holland's concluding moral.

60 For the early episodes that initiate this abiding relationship, see *Bruce* 1.407–44, 2.91–174 (and perhaps especially the eight lines that conclude the second passage). Drawn to the Bruce as one equally disinherited by the English, in Barbour's account (which rewrites the documentary record), Douglas meets Bruce on his way to his coronation at Scone and makes his homage *before* the king was actually crowned (and legally merits the gesture as 'rychtwis king', 2.159).

61 Froissart has already (ch. 17; 1:50) identified James Douglas [here misnamed William and his arms also misreported!] as 'the most hardy knyght, and greattest adventurer in al the realme of Scotland'. For the report of young James, see ch. 138, 5:218.

whan I had most ado, I made a solemne vow, the whiche as yet I
have nat accomplysshed, wherof I am right sory. The whiche was, if I
myght acheve and make an ende of al my warres so that I myght ones
haue brought this realme in rest and peace, than I promysed in my
mynd to haue gone and warred on Christis ennemies, aduersaries to
our holy Christen faith. To this purpose my hart hath ever entended,
but our Lorde wolde nat consent therto, for I have had so moche ado
in my dayes and nowe in my last entreprise, I have takyn suche a
malady that I can nat escape. And syth it is so that my body can nat
go nor acheve that my hart desireth, I wyll sende the hart in stede of
the body to accomplysshe myn avowe. And bycause I knowe nat in al
my realme no knyght more valyaunt than ye be, nor of body so well
furnysshed to accomplysshe myn avowe instede of myselfe, therfore
I require you, myn owne dere aspeciall frende, that ye wyll take on
you this voiage for the love of me and to acquite my soule agaynst
my Lord God ... I woll that as soone as I am trepassed out of this
worlde that ye take my harte owte of my body and enbawme it, and
take of my treasoure as ye shall thynke sufficient for that entreprise,
both for yourselfe and suche company as ye wyll take with you, and
present my hart to the Holy Sepulchre whereas our lorde laye, seyng
my body can nat come there. And take with you suche company and
purveyaunce as shal be aparteynyng to your astate, and wheresoever
ye come, let it be knowen howe ye cary with you the harte of kyng
Robert of Scotland at his instaunce and desire to be presented to the
Holy Sepulchre.

And then Barbour:

> For throwch me and my werraying
> Off blud has bene rycht gret spilling,
> Quhar many sakles men war slayn;
> Yarefor yis seknes and yis payn
> I tak in thank for my trespas.
> And myn hart fichyt sekyrly was,
> Quhen I was in prosperite,
> Off my synnys to sauffyt be,
> To trawaill apon Goddis fayis.
> And sen he now me till him tayis,
> Swa yat ye body may na wys
> Fulfill yat ye hart gan dewis,
> I wald ye hart war yidder sent
> Quharin consawit wes yat entent.
> Yarfor I pray ȝou euerilkan
> Yat ȝee amang ȝow chese me ane
> Yat be honest, wis, and wicht

37

And off his hand a noble knycht,
On Goddis fayis my hart to ber,
Quhen saule and cors disseueryt er.
For I wald it war worthily
Brocht yar, sen God will nocht yat I
Haiff pouer yidderwart to ga. (20.178–200)

Both authors report the same event, Bruce's pilgrimage of desire. Now, however, the Bruce's heart must pass as a surrogate for his body and, in his valour, the Douglas is equally a surrogate for his dead lord. Froissart's Bruce requests that his heart be presented at the Holy Sepulcre to show his vow fulfilled (an emblem of himself at another emblem, an empty tomb). And in both accounts, James Douglas's service not only fulfils the responsibility he was assigned but reanimates, as it were, Bruce's heart.

Clear distinctions should be drawn between Froissart's and Barbour's versions of these events. In the former, Bruce's longing will be fulfilled only by his heart's arriving in a particular holy site; even if physically incapable of the act, his desire, what he should have projected as act, had he been capable, will be fulfilled.[62] In contrast, Barbour's Douglas is enjoined, not to an unfulfilled vow, but to an expiatory activity. As penance for possible crimes in the War of Independence, Douglas is to pursue, on Bruce's behalf, a just war, namely a crusade upon Muslim infidels.[63] As a result, in Barbour's account, James's decision to join Spanish forces fighting local Muslims merely fulfils the promise he made his lord and testifies only to his faithful service. Holland, however, adheres to Froissart's account (484–85) in seeing the decision to war upon the infidel as James's individual and distinctly heroic decision:

Than he thought to draw to that partie, thynkyng suerely he could nat bestowe his tyme more nobly than to warre ayenst Goddis ennemies.

---

62 Although both Andrew Wyntoun and Walter Bower explicitly cite Barbour, they are predominantly following Froissart here. Cf. Wyntoun 8.3121–26, who reports that Douglas 'His hart tuk, as fyrst ordande was | For to bere into þe Hali Lande'; Bower (7:64/2–4) says that Bruce 'legavit suum cor mitti Ierosolimis et recondi apud Sepulcrum Domini. Ad cuius lacionem elegit Iacobum de Douglas, in omnibus guerris suis athletam fidissimum'. For an important revisionist account, emphasising that James Douglas probably only intended to 'crusade' in Spain and never to visit Jerusalem, see Cameron 2000.
63 Further emphasised twice in the ensuing narration; cf. *Bruce* 20.249–52, 353–56.

And that entreprise done, than he thought to go forth to Ierusalem and to acheue that he was charged with.

In Holland's account, as we will see, the difficulty that Froissart here implicitly acknowledges, that Douglas's heroic death prevented faithful fulfilment of the task Froissart's Bruce assigned, is obviated.

Although Froissart and Barbour are in general agreement about the remainder of the events leading to James Douglas's death, Holland increasingly relies upon his Scots predecessor. Both historians concur that, while sailing toward the Holy Land, Douglas accepted an appeal for help against the Moors of Granada from King Alfonso of Spain and that, rather than Holland's 'feile feldes' (503), he fell in his first battle in Spain, not Palestine.[64] They further agree, with varying kinds of detail, that with his small retinue of Scots, Douglas became separated from the main force of his Spanish allies and was slain.[65]

Three sets of details, repeated by Holland, differentiate Barbour's account from Froissart's. First, Barbour is responsible for the description of Bruce's heart being encased in an enamelled reliquary of gold, which Douglas carries suspended from his neck. However, Barbour does not mention Holland's important detail that the king's heart rested on Douglas's (*Bruce* 20.313–18, *Howlat* 469–70, 477–78). Second, Barbour alone implies that Douglas might well have escaped his fate, had he not spotted the beleaguered single knight, whom Barbour names William Sinclair, and had he not chosen to die in his support (*Bruce* 20.453–55, *Howlat* 508–28). Finally, Barbour also provides a narrative of the post-battle fate of the Bruce's heart and Douglas's own remains (*Bruce* 20.579–611, *Howlat* 529–33).[66]

---

[64] In Froissart's account, Douglas took ship from Moray, intending to go to Jerusalem, stopped at Sluys, where he would not disembark, but 'kept alwaies his port and behavour with great tryumphe … as though he had been kyng of Scottis hymselfe' (1:69; another fusion of the dead king and his living servant). While there, he heard of the Spanish king's need and sailed to join him. Douglas had Edward III's safe conduct through England in order to crusade, and his death occurred near Seville; see Brown 1998, 27.

[65] In Froissart's account, he charges into his foes with the family battlecry 'Douglas, Douglas', to which Holland alludes at line 402.

[66] Following Barbour, Holland's statement that Douglas was buried near where he fell refers only to his flesh; his bones were returned to Scotland by Sir William Keith and interred at St Bride's, Douglas, in an alabaster tomb built by his bastard son Archibald ('the grim'). According to Barbour, the earl

Unique to Holland's narrative are two important sets of details. First, quite in defiance of documentary history, Holland's James Douglas thoroughly fulfills his promise and quest (and, of course, manages additional heroic feats besides). He ensures that the Bruce's heart is venerated at the place the Bruce commanded, the Holy Sepulchre in Jerusalem (471–76).[67] Yet more striking is James's peculiarly original way of honouring his master, by 'heart-slinging' (490–96). The (fictitious) veneration of the heart in Jerusalem fulfils what Froissart's king Robert regarded as his spiritual needs and commanded his deputy to perform. But Holland's Douglas goes on to achieve deeds the Bruce thought impossible. He literally reanimates his dead lord, restores, in an act of synecdoche (*pars pro toto*, heart for whole) his body as leader of the vanguard – and then preserves that body as a king's loyal champion should, by retrieving it from harm's way (and battering a few 'Saracens' in the process).

We have no idea whether this is Holland's original fantasy. But Holland here emphasises that he follows a written source: 'Reid þe writ of þar werk' (395; see further 507, 534, 536). In context, this comment is ambiguous, since 'their' here might refer either to Douglas and Bruce – and then, of course, simply to Barbour[68] – or to the Douglas line in general. However, Sally Mapstone has recently argued (forthcoming 2) that Holland here is claiming to follow a Douglas chronicle, some variety of family history, probably vernacular. This suggestion might draw further support from three additional observations. First, as I have noted above (see p. 13), the compiler of the *Liber Pluscardensis* (1:263–64) knows an account of Douglas's death 'in nostro wlgari compositam ..., ubi ad longum reperiet'. Whilst Holland's narration is suitably detailed, I doubt that it would qualify as 'lengthy' in the context of chronicle historiography; rather than, as Amours thinks, this reference alluding to *The Howlat* itself, it may gesture at a now-lost family account in Scots, on which Holland draws.

---

of Moray, regent of Scotland, had Bruce's heart buried at the great border monastery Melrose. The Sinclairs may exemplify those 'arms of affinity' Holland describes hanging from the Douglas 'green tree' (608–11). Froissart describes both a John and a Walter Sinclair as companions of James Douglas at Otterburn (ch. 140, 5:221–22), and James 'the gross' married a Sinclair.

[67] While Walter Bower remains vague about the site of the hero's fall, he may also have thought that Douglas had reached Palestine, since he describes the combined Spanish-Scottish force as gathered 'in subsidium Terre Sancte' (7:66/3–4).

[68] The interpretation followed by Brown 1998, 15–16.

Second, the Douglases' great English adversaries, the Percys, special-
ised in this variety of genealogical commemoration (see Holford 2008),
and familial competition may not have been limited simply to battlefield
exploits. Finally, Froissart's report of the two families' nigh legendary
encounter at Otterburn in 1388 involves an episode at least analogous
to Holland's revivified Bruce-heart in the vanguard – the injunctions the
fallen James Douglas gives to ensure that, although dead, he is perceived
as living – and leading his men to victory. So this episode may have
been accommodated to or generated a family chivalric hagiography, on
which Holland here relies.

A second emphasis in Holland's account (413–16, 547–72, 615–20)
concerns the territorial conquests of Archibald 'the grim' (c. 1320–
1400), the true founder of the family dynasty. James's illegitimate son,
he rose, by canniness and ferocity, to become the third earl Douglas.
He apparently consciously strove to replicate with King David II the
relationship his father had maintained with David's father, the Bruce.
After defeating a number of ostensibly better-placed competitor heirs
following the disaster of Otterburn, he became the third earl. In 1362,
he had married 'the lady of Bothwell', Joanna Murray (d. 1408) and
received the whole Murray inheritance, including extensive lands in the
north-east. Owing to this sizable augmentation of the patrimony, the
Douglases carried her arms throughout the fifteenth century.[69] The arms
Holland describes are indeed 'sternis of anenothir strynd' (546), yet not
totally unconnected with the Douglases, who also bore three mullets
(cf. 410); the Douglases and the Murrays were indeed distantly related,
both descendants of mid twelfth-century Flemish incomers (Brown
1998, 12).

Holland's account also heralds a second set of Archibald's territorial
acquisitions. The south-west of Scotland, like the Isles, long remained
unintegrated into the kingdom of the Scots, testimony to this area's
Irish Sea, and Celtic-Norse, heritage. In the early fourteenth century,
these separatist roots were intensified and complicated. These were
lands whose lords were the Balliols, the line of Edward I's puppet-
king, and were frequently subject, not just to anglophile and anti-Bruce
sentiments, but southron occupation. The Douglases from an early date
were engaged in various acts of 'pacification' of the region, and eventu-

---

[69] See Brown 1998, 54–59, 113–14; McGladdery 2005, 161–64. Bothwell and
Threave, which McGladdery describes, surely testify to Archibald as more
than simply 'the grim', but also 'þe honorable in habitacionis' (552).

ally (1364–72) Archibald, as Warden of the West March, was given a free hand at its subjugation. Until the bitter end, in 1455, the Douglases retained their title as 'lords of Galloway', and their imposing castle at Threave, in the heart of the lordship. This conquest is reflected not simply in one quartering of the family's contemporary arms; the 'wild men' supporters of the Douglas blazon (615–19) equally signify this triumph over 'western savages'.[70]

Holland's insistence that these lands were 'heretable ay' (563; the locution also occurs at *Rauf* 761), may reflect contemporary difficulties regarding the status of Galloway. The central Douglas estates had been joined, for a century, in an entail which did not include Galloway. On gaining the earldom in 1440, James 'the gross', Archibald's younger son, made efforts to regain the property and to have it legally included within the entailed remainder of the estate. At that time, the Galloway lands were held as dower, and there was an heiress, Margaret 'the fair maid of Galloway'. After James's death, in 1444, Margaret did marry James's son, William, the 8th earl, and in light of these recent events, Holland was probably insisting that these are lands had been won by honourable conquest and were integral to the family estate.[71]

Holland's final salute to the Douglases concerns the current genera-tion, which he served. These are the sons of James 'the gross', younger son (1370s–1443) of Archibald 'the grim'. He was originally a minor lord, of Abercorn (West Lothian), but made himself a career as persis-tent royal counsellor to James I and II. Through the perfidious judicial murder of his nephews, the 6th earl and his brother ('the black dinner' of 1440), he ascended to the earldom. This ultimate step of disloyalty to the senior line was not unpredictable, since during his career as coun-sellor, James had persistently supported James I's royal initiatives, to the discomfiture of his brothers and nephews, the contemporary earls. His marriage to Beatrice Sinclair, sister of the earl of Orkney, was prolifi-cally successful, to a degree that Nature might have admired; at the time Holland wrote the poem, James had five living sons, among them the poem's co-dedicatee, Archibald, earl of Moray.

One bit of James 'the gross''s politic counsel inflects the poem. Unlike Chaucer's analogous depiction of something resembling an English parliament, Holland presents a version of a fifteenth-century church council (which involved lay lords, as well as ecclesiastical). Moreover,

---

[70] See Brown 1998, 33–34, 46, 60–64; McGladdery 2005, 164–68.
[71] For discussion, see Brown 1998, 263–64, 275–77.

as McDiarmid demonstrates (1969, 278–79), the papal arms described in the poem are those of one papal pretender produced by the conciliar movement. This is the antipope Felix V, actually a lay Savoyard prince. He had been elevated by the Council of Basle in 1440 to counter the unpopular Eugenius IV, and resigned his claims to Nicholas V in 1449.

In the jockeying among various candidates for the mitre, the Douglases, and particularly James 'the gross', stood out as conciliarists (and thus devotees of Felix's cause). James may have pursued this course in hopes that support for the antipope would achieve a secession and a Scottish church independent of the English, or simply to reduce the influence of local clerical adversaries. However, support for the antipope was unpopular in Scotland generally, and certainly the Douglases had retired from active support of Felix by the mid-1440s, before the poem was written – although they may well have retained their conciliarist biases.[72]

A further example of James's exercise of his influence, his effort at carving out an appenage for his younger sons in the north-east, is also important, both within the poem and within family history. It underlies James II's obliteration of the family in 1452–55. Three of James's sons received titles and estates in the area – Archibald in Moray through his marriage to the 'dove of Dunbar', the Murray heiress Elizabeth Dunbar (see 989 and the note); Hugh in 'Ormond' (see 600 and the note); and John in Balvenie (Banffshire). In this process, Douglas expansion ran up against the territorial ambitions of another powerful noble family.

For several generations, the Lords of the Isles, the MacDonalds, whose seat was on Islay, had sought to expand family influence outwith their customary ambit, a south Hebridean/Ulster axis. The family's push into north-east had begun under the 1st Lord of the Isles, John Mór MacDonald/MacDhomnuill of Islay (lord 1334–87), son of a Derry 'princess'. Given a consistent failure of heirs to the earldom of Ross, this interest persisted in his descendants, with resulting 'disruption of the structure of provincial rule in the north'.[73] In 1436, John Mór's grandson, Alexander MacDonald, after two decades of warfare in the area, was acknowledged by James I as earl of Ross; the grant to him also included appointment as sheriff north of the Forth, making him most powerful man in northern Scotland. His interests lay increasingly in the

---

[72] See note to line 338; Brown 1998, 265–66 (and 196–99 for earlier family adherence to conciliar goals); McDiarmid 1969, 278–79.

[73] See Brown 2004, 268–73 and 334.

north-east, not the Isles, and he, with his household of intruded Gaelic magnates, was regularly based at courts in Inverness or Dingwall (and at his death in 1450, he was buried at Rosemarkie, in the Black Isle).

Holland's poem thus was composed at a time when the properties of two of Scotland's most powerful (and belligerent) families directly abutted one another. This was potentially a testy situation; as Brown argues, 'the creation of [Ormond] was a direct affront to Ross, whose chief castle of Dingwall lay close by' (1998, 270). History and Holland's poem record moments both of accommodation (which was to prove fatal to both parties) and of antipathy.

At an indeterminate point the Douglases, MacDonalds, and the earl of Crawford entered a 'bond'. That there was a formal contract of some type we know only by chronicle report and not an actual document.[74] As a result, no fixed terms survive, but the 'bond' apparently stated that each party would respect the territorial integrity of the others, thereby defusing potential conflict in Ross-shire. But there is some likelihood that the three lords may have compacted to withstand any territorial threat posed by James II against any of them. So at least the king interpreted the agreement, and, when William, 8th earl Douglas, refused to repudiate the 'bond' when he came under safe-conduct to Stirling Castle in 1452, James denounced him as a 'traitor' and murdered him.

In essence, James II found a 'trewe' Douglas (cf. 403) to have been compromised by keeping a stronger faith with his north-eastern mates than he was willing to do with the Scottish crown. As a result, not only did he murder William Douglas, but over the next three years, he harried the family and eventually obliterated them as political force at Arkinholme in 1455. One might wish to see Holland's poem, composed well before this calamity, as a form of family assurance that, whatever other agreements might be in place, Douglases remained, as they had always been, the faithful supporters of royalty. There are, however, problems with pressing such an historical reading.

The Munros follow their chronicle source in dating the 'bond' to 1445. But this accord may have postdated the poem and involved John MacDonald, the 4th and last Lord of the Isles. The general, although not unanimous, consensus of Scottish historians would respect something like the chronicle dating and would place the covenant in the mid-late 1440s, thus an event that might influence the poem.[75]

---

[74] See Munro and Munro 1986, lxviii, 68–69; they are citing Balfour's *Annales*.
[75] See Grant 1988, esp. 138 n.61 (dating 1445/6) and 127–29, 131; Brown

However, the poem may not simply allude to the perhaps bristly amity of Douglases and MacDonalds.[76] It may also record the contact in the north-east of specifically western culture, that of the Isles and Ulster, and more cosmopolitan Anglo-French forms. Such at least may offer one explanation for the Gaelic-spouting rook/Irish bard who appears, only in order to be humiliated, at lines 794–827. Not only does this particular bird-identification present the rook as a prideful double of the owl (traditionally this fable features a rook, or its close kin). The bard, in his unpointed and indiscriminate blur of both (foreign/Ulster) gene-alogies and invective, parodies Holland's performance on behalf of the Douglases here. Biographically, given that we first hear of Holland as a MacDonald adherent in Inverness, the episode may signal his (willing-ness to?) exchange of allegiances. Equally, in the historical context I have outlined, Holland may present this episode as another assurance of Douglas commitment to a centralised Scots culture, and its king.

Holland's Verse

Holland's *Howlat* is the oldest surviving alliterative poem in Scots, and probably the first Scots assay in what, from the later fifteenth century, appears a distinctive feature of Scots tradition, the thirteen-line stanza King James VI calls 'rouncefallis' (Craigie 1951–58, 1:81).[77] As such,

1998, esp. 270 (implicitly 1446–48), 291–92 (and cf. 248–49); Macdougall 2000, 251–56. Kingston (2004, 74–82) argues that it was neither Alexander nor John, but the former's nephew, Domnall Ballach of Dunivaig (south Islay) and Ulster (*c.* 1410–76), who was involved, and that this is thus an agreement of the early 1450s.

76 Contemporary with Holland's composition, Alexander MacDonald would have been negotiating to marry his son John to Elizabeth Livingstone, daughter of James, the chamberlain of Scotland (and Stewart's referent for Holland's owl). When Livingstone fell from power almost immediately after the marriage, John rose in retaliation for the loss of the court patronage he had expected; cf. Brown 1998, 291–92.

77 Riddy's suggestion (1986, 1 n.1) that the poem at Skene 1877–80, 1:382–88, represents an earlier alliterative effort is not well taken. This is a Scots rendi-tion ('in lingua Scoticana translata') of French verses affixed to the tomb of Margaret, wife of the French dauphin (*d.* 1445), the translation allegedly requested by her brother, James II. However, the poem is written in abso-lutely regular decasyllabic verse with frequent ornamental alliteration, and it is only with difficulty assimilable to the metrical and syllabic rules normal

the poem exhibits those features that had defined this verse form in ME usage for more than a century. In alliterative poetry, a full verse is characterised by linking two halflines, each with two chief and stressed syllables, by initial rhyme. This rhyme always appears in the two stressed syllables of the first halfline, but, in traditional unrhymed verse, only in the first stressed syllable of the second. The second stressed syllable of this halfline must fall at the line's end, followed by only a single unstressed syllable.

Further, the first halfline, while it may include a third prominent syllable, rhyming or otherwise, is relatively free in its syllabic structure. In contrast, the second halfline is subject to syllabic constraints. Broadly, the line must include one 'strong dip' of two or more syllables, and one 'weak dip' of one or no syllables.[78]

The verses incorporated into the thirteen-line stanza in which Holland composed *The Howlat* follow this general form, but with certain licences. First of all, the coincidence of stress and end-rhyme at the end of the second halfline renders the fourth stress of the line as attractive a site for alliteration as any other stressed syllable. While in traditional unrhymed verse, alliteration cannot occur here, in Holland's poem, as in later Scots usage, many lines show initial rhyme in this position. Hence one regularly finds such variants of the standard form aa/ax as the 'hyperalliterative' aa/aa and aa/xa, but also examples thoroughly impermissible in general tradition, since they occur in the absence of rhymes on one of the stresses in the first halfline, e.g. xa/aa and ax/aa.

In addition, Holland's stanzaic verse regularly admits a variant alien to the general tradition, lines that are constructed with two different rhymes. Most normally, these fulfill the expected function of initial rhyme in this form, to join the two phrasal units that comprise the individual halflines into a single verse; such examples include forms

in either the English or Scots alliterative tradition. At the very best, as the first line of the poem 'The michti makar of the maior munde' shows, the metre resembles a great many stretches of Henryson, Dunbar, and Douglas's poetry, where, following an 'xCxC' opening, the remainder of the line might scan as either (expected) decasyllabic xCxCxC or as some licit alliterative off-verse, e.g. xCxxxC. Cf. in particular the clear allusion to alliterative tradition, and the consequent metrical adjustments, in the lengthy animal catalogue of Henryson's 'The Trial of the Fox', *Moral Fables* 887–915. On the thirteen-line stanza in Scots, see most recently Royan 2010.

[78] For a more extensive account, see *Golagros* xxxix–xli and the references to foundational studies there. On possible syllabic constraints in the first halfline, see Duggan 2000.

of the type ab/ab or ab/ba. But Holland, like subsequent Scots poets, regularly uses forms where this linking function remains only nominal, e.g. the form aa/bb. Lines with two different rhymes occur negligibly in unrhymed alliterative verse (and when they do occur, are frequently corrupt). In English stanzaic contexts, they appear frequently, but rarely in more than 2–3% of all longlines. By this standard, Holland's usage is exceptionally striking. In discussing *Golagros and Gawane*, I noted that poet's reliance on verses with two rhyming sounds in about 5% of all uses as extreme, but Holland's total approaches 70 instances, a whopping 10% of all the poem's longlines.

Moreover, quite a large number of these lines display yet more attenuated patterns, for example, lines 210 and 826:

… With grene almous on hed, Schir Gawane þe drak …
… Ran fast to þe dure and gaif a gret rair …

The first of these apparently rhymes abb/ax, and the second, with an unusual three stressed positions in the second halfline, a(x)x/bba.[79] In both cases, the notion that alliteration need be symmetrically disposed in the halflines is absent. Examples like these imply that Holland may have considered composition in this verse mode in a somewhat idiosyncratic manner. Rather than imagining alliterative practice as the fit of rhyme to phrasal structure, he may have construed alliterative requirements as a simple count, a proper line constituted by four or five stresses in some form of rhyme one with one another.

This perception might interface with a point argued above, Holland's engagement with copiousness of example, and thus copiousness both of linguistic forms and of diction. Holland's sequence of *þylir* join members of a class, most broadly perhaps 'the society of birds', rather than offering various synonyms of the same. Hence the poem proves relatively unengaged with traditional alliterative diction, beyond a number of set half-line phrases, many exemplified in the notes.[80] Indeed, Holland's impressive technical capacity at generating subdivisions of a

---

[79] Some examples resist any definitive analysis, for example line 612: 'Alltherhieast in þe crope, four helmes full fair'. This could represent aax/ax, stressed on *all-* and *-hie-* in the first halfline, the /f/ alliteration of the second halfline decorative only, or the odd ax/bab.

[80] I mainly attend to parallels in other stanzaic poems; Riddy's excellent account offers a more copious selection. On the probably deliberate avoidance of traditional diction, cf. the discussion of 'blyth of blee' in the note to line 3.

class, with consequently diverse lexicon, is joined through a reiterated commonplace diction. This is of a sort generally foreign to alliterative writing, and often requires colourless words to fill emphatic stressed position, e.g. *all, can/couth, cleir, fair, full* (and compounds with *-full* as second element), *gret, man, mony, se.* Given that alliterative collocation exists to facilitate ready generation of set phrasal units that will constitute full verses, the idiosyncratic treatment of alliteration, frequently failing to join the full line, should probably not surprise.

Holland's handling of alliterative rhyme also throws up a number of sports, a variety of them engagingly witty. Holland does not seem, as I have already mentioned, to respect the conventional handling, whereby /s/, /sp/, /st/, and /sk/, and /š/ should alliterate separately from one another. He is also relatively frequently given to 'slant-rhyme', whereby the *-n* of preceding *an* or *in* joins with a following word beginning with a vowel to provide a rhyme in /n/. And relative to the tradition at large, he is fond of letting a single word bear two identical stresses.[81]

But deviations from the norm, as I have already argued of Holland's language, phrasal practice, and diction, are ubiquitous. Alliterative poets are fond of adjusting prefixes, particularly those of romance derivatives, to meet metrical occasion. Holland is no exception, although he may press such variation about as far as it can go. Few poets, even acknowledging that *re-* is etymologically an unstressed prefix (and that modern usage denies it stress), would alliterate *religion* on /l/, as in line 190 here.[82] And one can multiply unusual – but always exceptionally clever – examples, e.g. *prolixt*, rhyming /l/ 34; *expremit*, rhyming /sp/

---

81 For examples of cross-rhymes involving /s/ and /s + second consonant/, see s/š 68, possibly 246 and 442 (both wheel lines), 604, 774; s/sk 373, 485, 542. For 'slant-rhyme', see *a n'owl* 57 (and the line perhaps includes *[n]am* as well); further examples appear at 105, 251, and 254, as well as the reformulated *i'nane* (for *in-ane* < OE on āne) at 47 and 151. For words with double staves, none probably quite so adventurous as Langland's *diapenidion* (*PPB* 5.124), see *cubiculare* and *conclaif* 124, *Babilonis* 293; *principale* 423, and the wonderfully insouciant *rerit* 638.

82 Cf. the exemplary discussion, Borroff 1962, 165–70. As one example, a scan of Holland's treatment of *re*-words, easily assembled from the glossary below, will reveal his breadth of usage, examples of the prefix either stressed or unstressed, either in agreement with or in opposition to later usage, e.g. prefix stressed as in modern usage *rescue* 521 (but see below); prefix stressed but modern usage opposed *reprove* 809 (but cf. *reprovable* 924); prefix unstressed as in modern usage *renew* 4x; prefix unstressed but modern usage opposed *rescue* 433 and 542.

138 (predicated on /ekspr-/ rationalised as /ek-spr-/), or *circumstance*, rhyming /st/ 266.

Yet, as I will note in a moment regarding Holland's handling of some rhyming series, at least part of the poem's wit is to make licence, an expanded set of the norm, like the catalogue, into not exception, but model. In *prolixt*, most vernacular readers, medieval or modern, would probably fail to see the word as combination of prefix + root (*pro*- is, after all, not a particularly generative English morpheme). But having engaged in such parsing, Holland is particularly witty at finding further unexpected rhymes, opening out the full phonetic range – if showing himself oblivious to the conventional rules of alliterative stress – of 'initial' rhyme.[83] Who might have expected *pursewant* 629 to rhyme on /w/, or *metalles* 420 on /t/, or *egill* 313 on /g/? And the ultimate extension of the technique occurs with proper names, for example, *Murray* 'Moray' rhymes on /r/ in 548, and the heroic *Douglas* twice (448, 563) on /g/.

The last example probably demonstrates most thoroughly that Holland pursues such deviations from customary practice with forethought, not as a result of what might appear wilful incompetence. On the one hand, restructuring the family name as if it were 'deGlas(s)' is analogous to the handling of the word 'eagle', the kingly bird, in 313; both nouns are analogously restressed and share the same alliterative rhyme. Thus, through a phonic echo, in which both nouns share the same unusual treatment of syllabic stress and of rhyme, Holland displays the family he serves in its usual posture, as loyal adherents to the (Scottish) throne. Equally, in a poem that will finally present itself to readers as a 'merour' (977), implicitly calling the family Holland honours for its devotion to royalty the 'Glasses' identifies them as the model for emulation (cf. 989n).

If Holland's alliterative practice shows considerable freedom in handling the tradition, the end-rhymes binding the verses of his complex stanza display similar quirks. Only a single example of this feature,

---

[83] Similarly, in a very large number of lines, rhyme is sustained by syllables which, in normal alliterative practice, would not receive stress, much less rhyme. Relevant examples include 113, 119, 184, 239, 432, 449, 452, 485, 515, 535 (a partial list). Such a technique follows from the disjunction, typical everywhere in the stanzaic tradition, of metrical stress and initial rhyme, e.g. 'That was þe 'proper 'pa-peiaye, 'provde in his appar'ale (125). A few other possible oddments are worth passing notice; see the notes to lines 185, 276, and 408.

'bot drowpand and dar' 188, has attracted any editorial attention – in this case unfortunate (see the note there). But features similar to this juxtaposition of participle and infinitive as if grammatically parallel recur, somewhat less problematically, through the whole. In 188, the parallelism between two verb-forms insures that, whatever grammatical form has been written and is necessary for rhyme, it is to be construed as representing the appropriate (unrhyming) grammatical form that fits the construction, here 'darand'. Near analogies, enforced by similar parallelism, include *sure* 85 (for the adverb 'surely'), *duke* 299 (for plural *dukis*), *deir* 439 (for superlative *deirest*), *myth* 693 (adverb, for the adjective *meth*, with revocalisation), *soft* 767 (for the adverb 'softly', although OE *softe* existed and occurs occasionally in ME), and perhaps *schour* 768 (for adverb 'surely'?). More attenuated examples include *on breides* 27 (plural for singular), *part* 387 (singular for plural), *trewe* 523 (adjective for adverb), *renovnis* 548 (plural for singular), *reir* 637 (either *rair* with adjusted vocalism [cf. 13, 826], or for the noun *reird*), perhaps *thingis* 808 (an artificial analogical plural for singular 'nothing'), *our-hie* 932 (adjective for noun), *her-eft* 960 (one adverb for another, 'after'), and, Holland's biggest reach of all, *citharist* 757 (the player for the instrument).

Editing the Text (and deciphering Asloan)

In general, English alliterative tradition is well known for textual survival in *codices unici*. The great majority of the poems seems to have had minimal circulation and perhaps only a local audience. In contrast (and perhaps underlying the extensive early knowledge of the poem I have noted at pp. 13–15), Holland's *Buke of the Howlat* comes to us in two full copies (**A**sloan and **B**annatyne), with fragmentary evidence for a third (**C**hepman and Myllar). This represents an unusual plethora of textual evidence, as well as an editorial problem: which version might provide the most useful copy-text? Which offers the most accurate readings?

The clearest evidence for the state of the text will emerge from examination of those sixty-odd lines (537–99) where all three witnesses (A, B, and C) are present. A full collation of all potentially substantive variants in this textual portion offers twenty-two examples of textual deviation of one or another sort:

> 537 braid AC] bred B; 539 wyis AC] wayis B; 540 gome AC] grome
> B; 541 flang BC] slang A; 542 it AC] *om.* B; 549 had AB] gat C; 550

tresour BC] tressoun A; and AB] et C; 553 wicht AB] with C; 562
couth AC] can'/caus B; 564 on A] of BC; 565 souerane AB] soueranis
C; 566 þar AC] his B; 575 swerd AC] sourd B; 577 þe AC] *om.* B;
schewe AC] sew B; 580 ws occupy AC] *trs.* B; day A] *om.* BC; 581
Referris AC] Refferring B; 589 trewe till attend AC] trewly to tend B;
591 maid AC] *om.* B; 593 fandit AC] fayand \wes fayn/ B.

Some of this recorded variation, particularly in B, may reflect only
spelling, not substance. For example, B *bred* 537 likely indicates only
coalescence of earlier a/ai with e, and B *sourd* 575 probably represents
simply an odd spelling for same reading as appears in the other copies.[84]

Overall, of the twenty-two variant readings here, AC agree fourteen
times in what are manifestly right (or at least, more plausible) readings
and B errs. Particularly clearcut examples include line 591, where B
omits a word necessary for the alliterative rhyme, or line 593, where
Bannatyne failed to recognise OE *fándian* in an archetypal spelling like
faynd. In contrast, C reads in isolation only four times; two of these
examples might represent simple spelling variation, and one a more
explicit rendition of what AB surely intend.[85] The only truly substantial
C variation, clearly erroneous, occurs in line 549, where the verse has
been read in isolation and assimilated to the idiom 'gat ane heir', rather
than attending to the enjambment that shows the statement is 'had ane
heir [to properties]'.

Like C, A varies from the other pair only four times. In one instance,
line 580, where it alone supplies the word *day*, it is surely correct. The
interchange of prepositions in line 564 potentially reflects the three
sources' independent responses to archetypal 'o' (and A provides the
usual idiom, in a set-phrase). However, in one reading (550), A has
either confused *n* and *r*, or one suspension with another (*-n* for *-ur*), and
is manifestly wrong, the other copies correct. A *slang* 541 is potentially
another example of the text in independent error, although the read-
ings here are indifferent (see the textual note). Further, although several
texts in Asloan's anthology appear to have been copied from Chepman
and Myllar's prints, on the basis of C *gat* 549, this would not appear
the case here (although one hesitates to draw firm conclusions from a

[84] Similarly C *with* for *wicht* 553; cf. McIntosh et al. 1986, dot map 334
(1:388).

[85] Line 565; AB either have an unmarked possessive, or transmit a reading
where they are engaged in haplography (souerans **s**aike).

single reading, and the lection might well be the printers' innovation on an archetypal reading shared with A).

This survey would confirm Amours's customarily wise conclusion (1892–97, xxii): 'The superiority of the Asloan text is that it is half a century older than the Bannatyne, and that it is more correct. Against a dozen better readings in the latter there are more than three score in the former; few on either side, however, are of vital importance'. Asloan should form the copy-text for any edition, and will do so here; moreover, its readings appear manifestly superior to those of the only other full copy, the Bannatyne manuscript.

However, the variants in lines 541 and 550, the first certainly an error, the second possibly so, indicate that Asloan does require, in an indeterminate number of instances, the attention associated with critical editing. Moreover, on the showing of the lines surveyed above, this attention cannot be limited to simply examples of textual divergence, lections where Bannatyne offers a different reading. As Amours indicates, few of these variations are apt to offer any substantial improvement to the text communicated in the earlier manuscript.

Moreover, it is the case that all textual situations are unique, and certain aspects of *The Howlat* render some editorial tools of dubious use. My earlier edition of *Golagros and Gawane* could rely upon well-established norms of alliterative practice to identify error (see Hanna 2008, xli–ii). But given the deliberated quirks that mark Holland's presentation, described above, this is a tool of limited applicability (although cf. the emendations in lines 131, 144, and 718, among others).[86]

The absence of a particularly clear sense of how Holland conceived his metre and his customarily inventive distance from traditional lexis have required that I adopt a much more forgiving attitude to the *textus receptus* than I did in the previous edition. As a consequence, in a number of places where I might have emended a line with some confidence, had it appeared in the firmly alliterative context of *Golagros*, I have allowed the text to stand as transmitted. However, discussions in the textual notes, for example to lines 230 and 782 (mentioned above at p. 23), will sufficiently indicate my doubts about what we have received.

At the same time, I have accepted nearly every textual intrusion offered by my distinguished predecessors, Amours and Riddy. Yet

---

[86] This last example was independently intuited by Alasdair MacDonald, who wrote me with the suggestion after I had established my text.

equally, I have performed editorial surgery upon a small number of lines which they have found unproblematic (e.g. the emendation in 487). In general, both understand the text very well indeed; I would feel most critical of their handling (certainly excusable in Amours's case, since he lacked the wonderful resource *DOST* now offers all researchers) of specifically grammatical explanation. Both editors tend to see the poem as composed in something like 'the natural language' of older Scots, rather than what I have been describing here as Holland's acquisitive art of licence.[87] In a poem littered with *hapax legomena* and other nonce-usages, both sometimes make heavy weather of what seem to me reasonably predictable, if unusual, sorts of deliberated variation. Again, the textual notes offer my reformulations of the issues at stake (see for example, that to line 59).

Using the Asloan manuscript as copy-text involves a series of problems, and the transcription offered here might be described as, in a number of instances, 'approximative'.[88] One area of indeterminacy involves the scribe Asloan's intent in his rendition of the sequence vowel + *r*. Asloan's basic form for the letter *r* is a not very embellished descendent of the '2-shaped' form, historically developed for use after letters with a curve or bow to the right. Asloan's generalisation of what had originally been a positional variant is far from unusual and occurs in many late fifteenth-/early sixteenth-century secretary scripts, both English and Scots (and his majuscule *r* is the same basic form but with a head, so that it appears rather ε-shaped).

This form proves to be problematic in a variety of places when trying to transcribe sequences that might represent either *er* or *ir*. The difficulties can be illustrated in the plate of fol. 213ʳ that provides the frontispiece here. One might compare examples like line 9 *erd* or 13 *apperd*. The left extension of the head of the letter *r*, which in these instances must represent the letter *e*, precludes any allusion to upper loop of *e*, in Asloan's hand, frequently represented only by a dot anyhow. As a result, it becomes extremely difficult to decide whether Asloan in such cases meant to indicate *er* or *ir*. Matters remain unresolved because the preceding stroke, which might indicate which vowel was to be read,

---

[87] Similarly, the editors of *DOST*, in their laudable attempt to define 'national usage', often ignore the fact that early Scots is, after all, a form of ME. Here, of course, the blindness is irritatingly mirrored in *MED* (although not *OED*), where the editors fail to survey Scottish texts at all.

[88] With the subsequent account, cf. the earlier discussions, van Buuren 1982, 26–30, 200–7; Houwen 1990, 20–26.

shows significant variation: indifferently slanted '\', which one could construe as 'proper' to the bow of -*e*-, or simply a minim, which would unequivocally represent -*i*-.

The frontispiece will indicate a range of examples, both ambiguous and less so. *bair* 16 and *birdis* 17 seem to me unambiguous examples of -*ir*-, since the head of the 2-shaped *r* begins with a cursive stroke from the foot of the preceding minim. But is the form in line 22 *sekerly* or *sekirly*? And is the word in line 28 (diplomatically) *gerß* or *girß*? The customary appeal to the scribe's general usage is not helpful either. The problem is analogous to an issue to which I turn below, the proper expansion of a form like *vþ'* 573: the spellings in unambiguous full forms prove too various to establish any norm of usage, in this instance, *vþer* 191, 282, 297, etc., but *vthir* 419. Generally editors, perhaps a bit capriciously, have assimilated these ambiguous strokes associated with 2-shaped *r* to 'perceived common spellings'. I follow my predecessors in reading *sekerly* 22 and *girs* 28, but would point out that I see no very ready way to distinguish the vowels in the two words.

Asloan's practice also introduces considerable ambiguity about the transcription of common abbreviated forms – including whether what appear marks of abbreviation might simply constitute socalled 'otiose strokes'.[89] Here some cases admit a definitive resolution, in which my decisions disagree with earlier renditions of the text, while others remain opaque. I take up unproblematic examples first.

I have adjusted some forms familiar from Craigie's transcription. The so-called 'standard mark of abbreviation', a horizontal or curved line to indicate the absence of a nasal (usually *n*), is usually unproblematic. However, when Asloan writes it above the sequence -*on*-, it is ambiguous. Many uses may have been otiose and would reflect a certain amount of inconsistency typical of the script; cf. the contrasting fully written forms -*falcounis* 319 and *falcone* 321. On the basis of a minority of full spellings here (Asloan's full forms are most normally in -*on(e)*), e.g. *felloun* 620 and *falcoune* 679, I have expanded such forms as -*oun*-. However, the same mark, in the same position, must frequently also represent the customary medieval Latin expansion -*ion*-, probably familiar to Asloan from frequent Latin legal copying.[90] Thus,

---

[89] The commonest example of the latter, ubiquitous in later fifteenth- and early sixteenth-century hands, is the loop that adorns virtually every example of -*n*. This is best construed as a positional variant form of the letter, designed to indicate final position, the end of the word.

[90] As also Asloan's only slightly unusual (for the vernacular) abbreviation, *pnt*

I offer forms like *Marchionis* 328 (the full form in this spelling occurs at 685), rather than the -*onn*- Craigie prints universally. Craigie universally expanded *þ'* to represent the modern words 'their' and 'there' as *þair*, but abundant examples of full forms indicate that this decision was shortsighted, and that Asloan's form was in all instances *þar*, which I have used.[91]

With 'their' and 'there', Asloan's reproduction of a vertical above-line loop or stroke to represent -*ar*- introduces another area of ambiguity in the script. Historically (and customarily), this stroke, particularly frequent after the graphs *n* and *u*, represents -*er*-, not -*ar*-. But, in Asloan's practice, this loop appears virtually universally and indicates almost any combination of vowel + *r*. The only regular unambiguous form is the above-line [2] (historically another derivative of 2-shaped *r*) to indicate -*ur*. Thus, the above-line loop/stroke to indicate -*ar*- in 'their' and 'there' also probably occurs in what I expand as *marschale* 677, *marschionis* 685, and *marschalit* 693.

Elsewhere, one is simply forced to rely upon fully written forms, or failing that, etymology to reach a transcriptional decision. The same above-line stroke appears variously, invariably in the word *honorable* to represent *or* (177, 385, 392, etc.);[92] and in *c'cumstance* 266 to represent *ir*. Analogous to the latter, and on the basis of the unique full form in 634, it regularly appears for *ri* in *empriour*; cf. *p'nces* 299, and contrast the unusually unambiguous *p^ecept* 289. This expansion perhaps implies that, in unstressed syllables, e.g. *neu'* 188, the stroke might always represent *ir*. This is especially the case, given that the final loop on a word, usually marking the plural of nouns or the third person in verb forms, certainly represents -*is* (cf. h+loop for *his* 681). Asloan's practice involves an unusual amount of indeterminacy and leaves a good deal to the reader's imagination. (One should perhaps qualify that statement to refer to 'the modern reader'; the book appears to have been produced for the scribe's private recreation, and he will not have been so discomfited.)

with mark above, always for 'present'. This is again a commonplace legal abbreviation ('Know all men by these presents', i.e. 'these present letters', with French plural inflection, still survives).

[91] For the possessive pronoun 'their', see 62, 159, 167, 169, 184, etc.; and for the adverb 'there', see the glossary, s.v. thar(-).

[92] Here one relies on the observations that Asloan preserves [2] for *ur* (although that might be alleged a special positional variant for final positions) and that he has not written a preceding letter *o*.

The last transcriptional problem I raise may be the thorniest, and again involves the presentation of the letter *r*, in this case when it occurs in word-final position. Here, as I have noted above in describing the script, Asloan provides a range of alternative forms – a simple final letter, the unambiguous conclusion *-re*, a final *-r* with an exaggerated loop (written as a full unambiguous stroke, extending back to the left over several graphs), and a final *-r* with a hairline trailing stroke to the right. Craigie meticulously records all these variations in his transcription, as '-r', '-re', '-re', and '-r'', respectively. In spite of a variety of complications, I think that Riddy (1987, 44) wisely throws up her hands here; she simply directs attention to the inconsistency of Asloan's handling.

The major complication here, of which I imagine Craigie to have been well aware, is that historically, in northern English and Scots scripts, whatever practice elsewhere, this feature cannot be construed as analogous to *-n'*, which is simply a word-final form. In these earlier contexts, looped *r* at the end of a word represents *-re*. However, whilst there are a variety of complications, I am inclined, as is Riddy, to consider both the loop and trailing stroke on *-r* as simply otiose and to ignore these in the transcription of the text.

First of all, it is apparent that, for Asloan, all these terminations are equivalents. One might note situations in which they occur indiscriminately in rhyme and in brief compass, e.g. lines 907–9 and 920–22. In the second example, *Natur* ends with trailing stroke, but *iniur* has the full loop, and *bure* an explicitly written *-e*. But the example only illustrates the dilemma: if all are equivalent, and one has fully written *-e*, should not all of them have it?

Against such a view one can provide a range of variously compelling examples. Not to range overly far afield from my last example, both uses of the adjective *bair* in line 976 are marked with a trailing stroke. In neither case can this have any meaning at all, since the etymon, OE bær, has no final *-e*,[93] and in the inflection of adjectives in ME, this form, the nominative, is distinguished from others by lacking *-e* as well. Other certainly otiose instances occur with some frequency, e.g. *for'* 183 (OE for), or as termination to three of the six uses of 'therefore' in the text.

Indeed, there is a considerable, if sometimes murky, amount of evidence to suggest that strokes attached to *-r* are, for Asloan, simply

---

93 The long a here is derived from lengthening in forms like plural bāre < bære.

word-terminal. For example, whatever one is to make of *for'* 183, Asloan never elaborates simple *r* in medial position in words like *forsaid, forsicht, forsuth, forþi,* and *forthocht.* Similarly, *quhar-* has unelaborated *r* on the two occasions it occurs in compounds, but simple 'where' is ubiquitously (13x) *quhar'.* Yet even in instances like this, anomalies occur; *thar-/þar-* 'there' routinely occurs without any extra stroke at the end of the first element in compounds – except for *thar'with* (460, 497, 927, 942). The verb form *war* 'were', which could have final *-e* (OE wǣre, wǣron), never appears as fully written *ware,* and uses are about evenly split between examples of *war* (34x) and *war'* (33x).

I would conclude that these, mainly terminal, strokes are to be ignored. They seem simply to reflect Asloan's shifting sense of when to offer various ornament to the letter *r,* particularly when that letter falls in final position. Perhaps the best proof for the proposition is that, ignoring the strokes, various as they are, produces virtually no spellings one would characterise as strange or objectionable. Perhaps the most unsightly examples would be *natur,* although this *e*-less spelling twice appears as the full and unelaborated form in any case (862, 867), and *towr* 293.

Finally, in my transcription, I ignore Scots final *ß* as a positional variant and transcribe it as *s.* Similarly (for this is historically a doubled letter-form), I render both majuscule *Ff* and the equivalent *-ff* following a majuscule as *F* or *f,* as appropriate. I would note in passing that Asloan writes majuscule thorn only once (line 650) at the head of a line, preferring positional *Th-* instead. In general, *th-* occurs only occasionally within the line (e.g. 105 *thus,* 460 *tham*), but regularly with the word 'through'. Use of the majuscule for *yogh* is, however, not so limited. As is customary, I have provided my transcription of the text with modern word-division and punctuation. Editorial activity on the text is marked with square brackets (for emendations and additions) and the sign '+' for omissions, and all alterations are discussed in the textual notes.

The Buke of the Howlat: The Text

In þe myddis of May at morne as I ment,   [fol. 213]
Throwe myrth markit on mold till a grene meid,
The bemes, blythest of ble, fro þe son blent
That all brichtnyt about þe bordouris on breid.
With alkyn herbes of air þat war in erd lent,   5
The feldis flurist and fret full of fairhed.
So soft was þe sessoun our souerane dovne sent
Throw þe greable gift of his godhed
That all was amyable owr þe air and þe erd.
Thus throw þir cliftis so cleir,   10
Withoutin fallowe or feir,
I raikit till ane reveir
That ryally [rei]rd.

This riche rever dovn ran, but resting or ruf,
Throwe ane forest on fold þat farly was fair.   15
All þe brays of þe brym bair branchis abuf,
And birdis blythest of ble on blossomes bair.
The land lowne was and le, with lyking and luf,
And for to lende by þat laike thocht me levar
Becaus þat þir hartes in heirdis couth huf,   20
Pransand and prunȝeand be pair and be pair.
Thus sat I in solace, sekerly and sure,
Content of þe fair firth,
Mekle mair of þe mirth,
Als blyth of þe birth   25
Þat þe ground bure.

The birth þat þe ground bure was browdin on breidis
With girs gaye as þe gold and granes of grace,
Mendis and medicyne for mennis all neidis,
Helpe to hert and to hurt heilfull it was.   30
Vnder þe cerkill solar þir sauorus seidis   [fol. 213ᵛ]
War nurist be Dame Natur, þat noble mastres.
Bot all þar names to nevyn as now it nocht neidis;

It war prolixt and lang and lenthing of space,
And I haue mekle mater in meter to glos   35
Of anenothir sentence,
And waike is my eloquence.
Tharfor in haist will I hens
To þe purpos.

Of þat purpos in þe place be pryme of þe day   40
I herd ane petuos appele with ane pur mane,
Solpit in sorowe þat sadly couth say,
'Wa is me, wretche, in þis warld wilsome of wane,
With mair murnyng in mynd þan I meyne may';
Rolpit, reuthfully ro[c]h, in a rude rane.   45
Of þat ferly on fold I fell in affray.
Nerar þat noys in nest I nechit in-ane;
I saw ane howlat in haist vnder ane holyne,
Lukand þe laike throwe
And saw his awne schadowe,   50
At þe quhilk he couth growe
And maid gowlyne.

He grat grysly grym and gaif a gret ȝowle,
Cheuerand and chydand with churliche cheir.
'Quhy is my fax', quod þe fyle, 'Fassonit so foule,   55
My forme and my fetherem vnfrely but feir?
My neb is netherit as a nok – I am bot ane owle.
Aganis natur in þe nicht I walk into weir;
I dar do nocht on þe day bot droupe as a dovle,
Nocht for schame of my schape in pert till appeir.   60
Thus all þir fowlis for my filth has me at feid.
That be I seyne in þar sicht,
To luke out on daylicht,   [fol. 214]
Sum will me dulfully dicht;
Sum dyng me to deid.   65

Sum bird will bay at my beike, and sum will me byte;
Sum skripe me with scorne; sum skrym at myn e.
I se be my schadowe my schape has þe wyte.
Quhom sall I blame in þis breth a bysyn þat I be?
Is nane bot Dame Natur – I bid nocht to nyte –   70
Till a[c]us of þis caise, in case þat I de.

Bot quha sall mak me ane mendis of hir worth a myte,
That þus has maid on þe mold ane monstour of me?
I will appele to þe pape and pas till him plane,
For happin þat his halynace   75
Throw prayer may purchace
To reforme my foule face,
And þan war I fane.

'Fayne wald I wyte', quod þe fyle, 'Or I furth fure,
Quha is fader of all foule, pastour and pape?   80
That is þe plesant pacok, precious and pure,
Constant and kirklyk vnder his cler cape,
Mi[teri]t as þe maner is, manswet and mure,
Schroude in his schene weid, schand in his schap,
Sad in his sanctitud sekerly and sure.   85
I will go to þat gud, his grace for to grap'.
Of þat bourde I was blyth and bade to behald.
The howlet, wylest in wyce,
Raikit vnder þe rys
To þe pacoke of pryce   90
That was pape cald.

Befor þe pape quhen þe pur present him had,
With sic courtassy as he couth, on kneis he fell;
Said, 'Aue, Raby! Be þe rud, I am richt rad
For to behald ȝour halynes or my tale tell.   95 [fol. 214ᵛ]
I may nocht suffys to se ȝour sanctitud sad'.
The pape, wyslie iwis, of worschipe þe well,
Gaif him his braid benesoun and baldly him bad
That he suld spedely speike and spair nocht to spell.
'I come to speir', quod þe spreit, 'Into speciall   100
Quhy I am formed so fowle,
Ay to ȝowt and to ȝowle
As ane horrible owle,
Wgsum our-all.

'I am netherit ane owll thus be Natur,   105
Lykar a fule than a fowle in figur and face,
Bysyn of all birdis þat euer body bure,
Withoutin caus or cryme kend in þis case.
I haue appelit to ȝour presence, precious and pur;

61

Askis helpe intill haist at ȝour halynes,   110
That ȝe wald cry apon Crist þat all has in cur
To schape me a schand bird in a schort space
And till accus Natur – þis is no nay.
Thus throw ȝour halynes may ȝe
Make a fair foule of me,   115
Or elles, dredles, I de
Or myne end-day'.

'Of þi [plicht]', quod þe pape, 'Pite I haife,
Bot apon Natur to pleyne it is perell.
I can nocht say sudanelye, so me Crist saif,   120
Bot I sall call my cardinallis and my counsall,
Patriarkis and prophetis, of lerit þe laif;
Thai sal be semblit full sone – þat þow se sall'.
He callit on his cubicular within his conclaif –
That was þe proper papeiaye, provde in his apparale –,   125
Bad send for his secretar and his sele sone.
That was þe turtour trewest,   [fol. 215]
Ferme, faithfull, and fast,
That bure þat office honest
And enterit but hone.   130

The pape [hecht] but hone to wryte in all landis
Be þe said secretar þat þe sele ȝemyt,
For all statis of kirk þat wnder Crist standis
To semble to his summondis, as it wele semyt.
The trewe turtour has tane with þe tythandis;   135
Done dewlie his det as þe deir demyt;
Syne belyf send þe letteris into seir landis
With þe swallowe so swyft in speciale expremit,
The papis harrald at poynt into present.
For he is forthwart to fle   140
And ay will haue entre
In hous and in hall hie
To tell his entent.

Quhat suld I [m]ell ony mair of þir materis,
Bot þir lordis belyf þe letteris has tane,   145
Resauit þaim with reuerence to reid as efferis,
And richely þe harraldis rewardit ilkane?

Than busk þai but blyn mony bewschyris,
Grathis þam but gru[c]hing þat gait for to gane.
All þe statis of þe kirk out of steid steris,   150
And I sall not ȝow richt now þar names in ane,
How þai apperit to þe pape and present þaim aye –
Fair-farrand and fre,
In a gudly degre
And manlyke, as thocht me,   155
In myddis of May.

All þus in May, as I ment in a mornyng,
Come four fasandis full fair in þe first front,
Present þam as partriarkis in þar appering,
Benyng of obedience and blyth in þe bront.   160 [fol. 215ᵛ]
A college of cardinalis come syne in a lyng,
That war crannis of kynd, gif I richt compt,
With red hattis on hed, in haile takynnyng
Of þat deir dignite, with worschipe ay wont.
Thir ar fowlis of effect, but fellony or feid,   165
Spirituale in all thing,
Leile in þar leving.
Tharfor in dignite digne
Thai dure to þar deid.

Ȝit endurand þe daye, to þat deir drewe   170
Swannis suowchand ful swyth, swetest of swar,
In quhyte rocatis arrayd; as I richt knewe
That þai war bischopis blist, I was þe blythar.
Stable and steidfast, tender and trewe,
Of fewe wordis, full wys and worthy þai war.   175
Thar was pyotis and partrikis and pluwaris ynewe
As abbotis of all ordouris þat honorable ar.
The se-mawis war monkis, þe blak and þe quhyte;
The goule was a gryntar;
The suerthbak a sellerar;   180
The scarth a fische-fangar,
And þat a parfyte.

Parfytlye þir pik-mawis, as for priouris
With þar party habitis, present þam þar;
Herounis contemplatif, clene Charterouris,   185

63

With toppit hudis on hed and clething of hair,
Ay sorowfull and sad at evinsang and houris –
Was neuir leid saw þaim lauch bot drowpand and dar;
Alkyn chennonis eik of vþer ordouris;
All maner of religioun, þe les and þe mair;   190
Cryand crawis and cais þat cravis þe corne
War pure freris forthward,
That with þe leif of þe lard   [fol. 216]
Will cum to þe corne-ȝard
At ewyn and at morn.   195

Ȝit or ewyn enterit, come þat bur office,
Obeyand þir bischoppis and bydand þam by:
Gret ganeris on ground in gudly awys
That war demyt, but dowt, denys douchty.
Thai mak residence raith and airly will rys   200
To kepe þe college clene and þe clergye.
The cok in his cleir cape þat crawis and cryis
Was chosyn chantour full cheif in þe channonry.
Thar come þe curlewe, a clerk and þat full cunnand,
Chargit as chancillar,   205
For he couth wryte wounder fair
With his neb for mistar
Apon þe se-sand.

Apon þe sand ȝit I sawe as thesaurer tane,
With grene almous on hed, Schir Gawane þe drak.   210
The archedene, þat our-man, ay prechand in plane,
Correker of kirkmen, was clepit þe claik.
The martoune, þe murcoke, þe myresnype in ane
Lichtit as lerit men law by þat laike.
The ravyne, rolpand rudly in a roche ran,   215
Was dene rurale to reid, rank as a raike.
Quhill þe lardner was laid, held he na hous,
Bot in wplandis townis
At vicaris and persounis,
For þe procuracionis   220
Cryand full crows.

The crovs capone, a clerk vnder cleir weidis,
Full of cherite, chast and vnchangeable,

Was officiale, but les, þat þe law leidis
In causs consistoriale þat ar coursable.   225 [fol. 216ᵛ]
The sparrowe, Wenus [sone], he wesit for his vyle deidis,
Lyand in lichory, laith, vnloveable.
The feldefer in þe forest, þat febilly him feidis,
Be ordour ane hospitular was, ordanit full able.
The cowschotis war personis in þar apparale;   230
The dow, Noyis messinger,
Rownand aye with his feir,
Was a corate to heir
Confessionis hale.

Confes cleir can I nocht nor kyth all þe cas,   235
The kynd of þar cummyng, þar companys eike,
The maner nor þe multitud – so mony þar was.
All se-fowle and seid-fowle was nocht for to seike;
Thir ar na fowlis of reif nor of r[et]hn[a]s,
Bot mansweit, but malice, manerit and meike.   240
And all apperit to þe pape in þat ilk place,
Salust his sanctitud with spirituale speike.
The pape gaf his benesoun and blissit þaim all.
Quhen þai war rangit on rawis,
Of þar come þe haile caus   245
Was said into schort sawis,
As ʒe heir sall.

The pape said to þe owle, 'Propone þin appele,
Thy lamentable langage, as lykis þe best'.
'I am deformed', quod þe fyle, 'With faltis full feile,   250
Be Natur netherit ane owle, noyus in nest,
Wre[c]he of all wretches, fra worschipe and wele'.
All this trety has he tald be termes in test.
'It neidis nocht to renewe all myn vnhele,
Sen it was menyt to ʒour mynd and maid manifest'.   255
Bot to þe poynt: petuos he prayit þe pape
To call þe clergy with cure   [fol. 217]
And se gif þat Nature
Mycht reforme his figour
In a fair schaipe.   260

Than fairlie þe fader þir fowlis he franyt

Of þar counsall in þis cais, sen þe richt þai knewe,
Gif þai þe howlat mycht helpe þat was so hard paynit,
And þai weraly awysit, full of wertewe.
The maner, þe mater, and how it remanyt,   265
The circumstance, and þe stait – all couth þai argewe.
Mony allegiance leile, in leid nocht to layne it,
Of Arestotill and ald men scharplie þai schewe.
The prelatis þar apperans proponit generale.
Sum said to and sum fra,   270
Sum nay and sum ʒa,
Baith pro and contra;
Thus argewe þai all.

Thus argewe þai ernistly wounder oft-sys;
Syne samyn, forsuth, þai assent haile   275
That sen it nechit Natur, þar alleris [nu]ris,
Thai couth nocht trete but entent of þe temporale.
Tharfor þai counsall þe pape to writ in þis wys
To þe athile empriour, souerane in saile,
To adres to þat dyet to deme his awys –   280
With dukis and with digne lordis, darrest in dale,
Erlles of ancestry, and vþeris ynewe –
So þat þe spirituale staite
And þe secular consait
Mycht all gang in a gait,   285
Tender and trewe.

The trewe turtour and traist, as I eir tauld,
Wrait þir letteris at lenth, lelest in leid;
Syne throw þe papis precept planly þaim ʒald   [fol. 217ᵛ]
To þe swallowe so swyft, harrald in hed,   290
To ettill to þe empriour of ancestry auld.
He wald nocht spair for to spring on a gud speid,
Fand him in Babilonis towr with bernis so bald,
Cruell kingis with crovne and dukis but dreid.
He gaf þir lordis belyve þe letteris to luke,   295
Quhilk þe riche empriour
And all vþer in þe hour
Ressauit with honour,
Bath princis and duke.

66

Quhen þai consauit had þe cais and þe credence 300
Be þe harrald in hall, hove þai nocht ellis
Bot bownis out of Babulone with all obediens,
Seikis our þe salt se fro þe south fellis,
Enteris in Ewrope, fre but offens,
Walis wyslie þe wayis be woddis and wellis, 305
Quhill þai approche to þe pape in his presence
At þe forsaid trist quhar þe trete tellis.
Thai fand him in a forest, frely and fair;
Thai halsit his halynas,
And ȝe sall heir in schort space 310
Quhat worthy lordis þar was,
Gif ȝour willis war.

Thar was þe egill so grym, gretest on groundis,
Athill empriour our-all, most awfull in erd.
Ernes ancient of air, kingis þat crovnd is 315
Nixt his celsitud, forsuth, secoundlie apperd,
Quhilk in þe firmament throu fors of þar flicht foundis,
Perses þe sone with þar sicht, selcouth to herd.
Geirfalcounis, þat gentilly in bewte haboundis,
War deir dukis and digne, to deme as efferd. 320 [fol. 218]
The falcone, farest on flicht formed on fold,
Was ane erll of honour,
Marschell to þe empriour,
Boith in hall and in bowr
Hende to behold. 325

Goishalkis war governouris of þe gret oist,
Chosin chiftanis chevalrus in charg[is] of weris,
Marchionis in þe mapamond and of mychtis most,
Nixt dukis in dignite, quhom na dreid deris.
Sparhalkis, þat spedely will compas þe cost, 330
War kene knychtis of kynd, clene of maneris,
Blyth-bodyit and beld, but baret or boist,
With eyne celestiale to se, circulit as sapheris.
The specht was a pursevant provde till apper,
That raid befor þe empriour 335
In a cot-armour
Of all kynd of colour
Cumly and cleir.

67

He bure, cumly to knawe be connysaunce cleir,
Thre crovnis and a crucifix, all of cler gold,   340
The burde with orient perle plantit till apper,
Dicht as a dyademe digne – deir to behold –
Circulit on ilk syde with þe sapheir,
The iaspis ioynit in gem and rubyis inrold.
Syne twa keyis our croce of siluer so cleir   345
In a feild of asure flammit on fold:
The papis armes at poynt to blason and beir,
As feris for a pursewant
That will wayage awant,
Active and awenant   350
Armes to weir.

Syne in a feild of siluer, secoundlie he beris   [fol. 218ᵛ]
Ane egill ardent of air þat etlis so hie,
The memberis of þe samyn foull displait, as efferis,
Ferme formyt on fold, ay set for to fle,   355
All of sable þe self – quha þe suth leris –
The beke bypartit breme, of þat ilk ble.
The empriour of Almane þe armes he weris
As signifer souerane. And syne couth I se
Thre flour de lycis of Fraunce all of fyne gold   360
In a feld of asure,
The thrid armes in honour
The said pursevant bure
That bl[enk]it so bold.

Tharwith lynkit in a lyng, be lerit men approvit,   365
He bure a lyon as lord of gowlis full gay,
Maid maikles of mycht on mold quhar he movit,
Rich[t] rampand, as roye ryke of array.
Of pure gold was þe ground quhar þe grym hovit
[With dowble tressour about, flowrit in fay,   370
And flour de lycis on loft – that mony leid lovit –]
Of gowlis sygnit and set to schawe in assay,
Our souerane of Scotland his [sign]es to knawe,
Quhilk sall be lord and ledar
Our braid Brettane all-quhar   375
As sanct Margaretis air,
And þe signe schawe.

68

Next þe souerane signe was sekerly sene
That seruit his serenite, euer seruabile,
The armes of þe Dowglas, douchty bedene,   380
Knawin throw all Cristindome by conysance able,
Of Scotland þe wer-wall – wit ʒe but wene –
Our fais force to defend and vnfalʒeable,
Baith barmekyn and bar to Scottis blud bene,
Our lois and our lyking þat lyne honorable.   385 [fol. 219]
That word is so wonder warme and euer ʒit was
It synkis sone in all part
Of a trewe Scottis hart,
Reiosand ws inwart
To heir of Dowglas.   390

Of þe douchty Dowglas to dyte I me dres,
Thar armes of ancestry honorable ay,
Quhilk oft blythit þe Bruse in his distres;
Tharfor he blissit þat blud, bald in assay.
Reid þe writ of þar werk to ʒour witnes;   395
Furth on my mater to muse I mufe as I may.
The said pursevantis gyde was grathit, I ges,
Brusit with ane grene tre, gudly and gay,
That bure branchis on breid, blythest of hewe.
On ilk beugh till embrace   400
Writtin in a bill was,
'O Douglas! O Douglas'!
Tender and trewe.

Syne schir schapyn to schawe, mony schene scheld
With tuscheis of trast silk tichit to þe tre.   405
Ilk branche had þe birth burly and beld,
Four flurist our all, gretest of gre.
Ane in þe crope hiegh as cheif I beheld,
Quhilk bure intill asure, blythest of ble,
Siluer sternis so fair, and part of þe feld,   410
Was siluer, set with ane hert, heirly and hie,
Of gowlis full gracious, þat glemyt so gay.
Syne in asure þe mold
A lyoun, crovnit with gold,
Of siluer ʒe se shold   415
To ramp in array.

69

Quhilk cassyn be cognoscence quarterly was.   [fol. 219ᵛ]
With barris of best gold, it brynt as þe fyr;
And vthir signes, forsuth, syndry, I ges,
Of metallis and colouris in tentfull atyr.   420
It war tyrefull to tell, dyte or addres,
All þar deir armes in dewlye desyre,
Bot part of þe principale neuerþeles
I sall haist me to hewe, hartlie but hyre.
Thar lois and þar lordschipe of sa lang dait   425
That be[r]e cot-armouris of eild,
Tharin to harrald I held,
Bot sen þai þe Brus beld
I wryt as I wait:

In þe takinnyng of treuth and constance kend,   430
The colour of asure, ane hevinliche hewe,
Forþi to þe Dowglas þat senȝe was send,
As lelest, all Scotland fra scaith to reskewe.
The siluer in þe samyn half, trewly to tend,
Is cleir corage in armes, quha þe richt knewe.   435
The bludy hart þat þai bere þe Brus at his end,
With his estatis in þe steid and nobillis ynewe,
Addit in þar armes for honorable caus,
As his tenderest and deir
In his mast misteir,   440
As sal be said to ȝow heir
Into schort sawis.

The roye Robert þe Brus þe rayke he awowit
With all þe hart þat he had to þe Haly Graif.
Syne quhen þe dait of his deid [was] derfly him dowit,   445
With lordis of Scotland, lerit, and þe laif,
As worthy wysest to waile in worschipe allowit,
To Iames, lord Dowglas, þ[ai] þe gre gaif,   [fol. 220]
To ga with þe kingis hart. Þarwith he nocht growit,
Bot said to his souerane, 'So me God saif,   450
Ȝour gret giftis and grant ay gracious I fand,
Bot now it movis allthermaist
That ȝour hart nobillast
To me is closit and cast
Throw ȝour command.   455

70

'I love ȝou mair for þat lois ȝe lippyn me till
Than ony lordschipe or land, so me our Lord leid.
I sall waynd for no wye to wirk as ȝe will,
At wis, gif my werd wald, with ȝou to þe deid'.
Tharwith he lowtit full lawe; tham lykit full ill   460
Baith lordis and ladyis þat stude in þe steid.
Of commoun nature the cours be kynd to fulfill,
The gud king gaif þe gaist to God for to reid;
In Cardros þat crownit closit his end.
Now God for his gret grace   465
Set his saull in solace,
And we will speike of Dowglace
Quhat way he couth wend.

The hert costlye he couth clos in a cler cace
And held all hale þe behest he hecht to þe king: 470
Come to þe Haly Graf, throw Goddis gret grace,
With offerandis and vrisounis and all vþer thing,
Our saluatouris sepultur and þe samyn place
Quhar he rais, as we reid, richtuis to ryng.
With all þe relykis raith þat in þat rovme was,   475
He gart hallowe þe hart and syne couth it hyng
About his hals full hende and on his awne hart.
Oft wald he kis it and cry,
'O flour of all chewalry!
Quhy leif I, allace, quhy   480
And þow deid art?

'My deir', quod þe Douglas, 'Art þow [to] deid dicht,   [fol. 220ᵛ]
My singulir souerane, of Saxonis þe wand?
Now bot I semble for þi saull with Sarazenis mycht,
Sall I never sene be into Scotland'!   485
Thus in defence of þe faith, he fure to þe fecht
With knychtis of Cristindome to kepe his con[n]and.
And quhen þe battallis so brym, brathly and bricht,
War ioyned, thraly in thrang mony thousand,
Amang þe hethin men þe hert hardely he slang.   490
Said, 'Wend on as þou was wont
Throw þe batell in bront,
Ay formast in þe front
Thy fays amang!

71

'And I sall followe þe in faith, or feye to be fellit.   495
As þi legeman leile, my lyking þow art'.
Tharwith on Mahownis men manly he mellit,
Braid throw þe batallis in bront and bur þaim bakwart.
The wyis quhar þe wicht went war in wa wellit;
Was nane so stur in þe steid micht stand him a start.   500
Thus frayis he þe fals folk, trewly to tell it,
Aye quhill he cowerit and come to þe kingis hart;
Thus feile feildis he wan, aye worschipand it.
Throwout Cristindome kid
War þe deidis þat he did,   505
Till on a tyme it betid,
As tellis þe writ.

He bownyt till a batall and þe beld wan,
Ourset all þe Sathanas syde, Sarazenis mycht.
Syne followit fast on þe chace, quhen þai fle can;   510
Full ferly feile has he feld and slane in þe flicht.
As he relevit, iwis, so was he war þan
Of ane wy him allane, worthy and wicht,
Circulit with Sarazenis, mony sad man,   [fol. 221]
That tranoyntit with a trayne apon þat trewe knycht.   515
'Thow sall nocht de þe allane' [sai]d þe Dowglas;
'Sen I se þe ourset,
To fecht for þe faith fete,
I sall devoid þe of det
Or de in þe place'.   520

He ruschit in þe gret rowte þe knycht to reskewe.
Feile of þe fals folk, þat fled of befor,
Relevit in on þir twa, for to tell trewe,
That þai war samyn ourset; þarfor I murn sore.
Thus in defence of þe faith, as fermes ynewe,   525
And pite of þe prys knycht þat was in [perell] þore,
The douchty Dowglas is deid and adewe
With los and with lyking þat lestis evirmor.
His hardy men tuke þe hart syne vpon hand;
Quhen þai had beryit þar lord   530
With mekle mane to remord,
Thai maid it hame be restord
Into Scotland.

Be þis ressoun we reid, and as oure roy levit,
The Dowglas in armes þe bludy hart beris.   535
For it bled he his blud, as þe bill brevit,
And in battallis full braid vnder baneris
Throw full chevalrus chance, he þis hert chevit
Fra walit wyis and wicht, worthy in weris.
Mony galiard gome was on þe ground levit   540
Quhen he it slang in þe feld, felloun of feris;
Syne reskewand it agane, þe hethin + men harmes.
This hert red to behald
Throw þir ressonis ald
The bludy hart it is cald   545 [fol. 221ᵛ]
In Dowglas armes.

The sternis of anenothir strynd steris so fair.
Ane callit Murray þe riche, lord of renovnis,
Deit, and a douchter had till his deir air
Of all his tressou[r] vntald, towris and townis.   550
The Dowglas in þai dayis, douchty all-quhar,
Archebald, þe honorable in habitacionis,
Weddit þat wlonk wicht, worthy of ware,
With rent and with riches; and be þai ressonis,
He bure þe sternis of estait in his stele-weidis,   555
Blyth, blomand, and bricht
Throw þe Murrayis micht.
And sa throw Goddis forsicht
The Douglas succedis.

The lyon lansand on loft, lord in effeir,   560
For gud caus, as I ges, is of Galloway.
Quhen þai rebellit þe crovne and couth þe kyng deir,
He gaif it to þe Douglas, heretable ay
On þis wys: gif he couth wyn it on weir.
Quhilk for his souerane saike, he set till assay;   565
Kelit dovne þar capitanis and couth it conquer,
Maid it ferme, as we fynd, till our Scottis fay.
Tharfor þe lyoun he bure, with loving and lois,
Of siluer semely and sure
In a feild of asure,   570
Crovnit with gold pur
To þe purpos.

73

The forest of Ettrik and vþer ynewe,
The landis of Lawder and lordschipis sere,
With dynt of his derf swerd þe Dowglas so dewe 575
Wan wichtly of weir – wit ȝe but weir – [fol. 222]
Fra sonnis of þe Saxonis. Now gif I sall schewe
The order of þar armes, it war to tell teir
The barris of best gold; þocht I þaim hale knewe,
It suld ws occupy all day. Þarfor I end heir; 580
Referris me to harraldis to tell ȝow þe hale.
Of other scheldis so schene
Sum part will I mene
That war on þe tre grene
Worthy to vale. 585

Secund syne, in a feld of siluer certane
Of a kynde colour thre coddis I kend,
With dowble tressur about, burely and bane,
And flour de lycis so fair, trewe till attend,
The tane and þe toþer of gowlis full gane. 590
He bure quarterly maid, þat nane micht amend
The armes of þe Dowglas – þarof was I fayne –,
Quhilk oft fandit with force his fa till offend.
Of honorable ancestry, þir armes of eld
Bure þe erll of Murray 595
As sad signe of assay
His fell fais till affray
In a fair feld.

Anenothir erll, of Ormond, also he bure
The said Dowglas armes with a differens, 600
And richt so did þe ferd quhar he furth fure,
Ȝaipe, þocht he ȝong was, to faynd his offens;
It semyt þat þai sib war, forsuth I assure.
Thir four scheldis of pryce into presence
War chenȝeit so chevalrus þat no creatur 605
Of lokis nor lynis mycht lous worth a lence. [fol. 222ᵛ]
Syne ilk braunche and beugh bowit þaim till,
And ilk scheld in þat place,
Thar tennend or man was
Or ellis thar allyas 610
At þar awn will.

Alltherhieast in þe crope, four helmes full fair,
And in þar tymeralis tryid trewly þai bere
The plesand povne in apart, provde to repair.
And als kepit ilk armes þat I said eir   615
The rouch wodwys wyld þat bastounis bare
Ourgrowin, grysly and growe, grym in effeir,
Mair awfull in all thing saw I never air,
Baith to walk and to ward, as watchis in weir.
That terrible felloun my spreit affrayd;   620
So ferdfull of fantasy,
I durst nocht kyth to copy
All other armes þarby
Of renkis arayd.

Tharfor of þe said tre I tell nocht þe teynd,   625
The birth and þe branchis þat blomyt so brayd.
Quhat fele armes on loft, louely to lend,
Of lordingis and sere landis, gudly and glad,
The said pursewant bure quhar he away wend
On his garment so gay of ane hie haid,   630
I leif þaim blasonde to be with harraldis hende.
And I will to my [era]st mater, as I eir maid,
And begyn quhar I left at lordingis deir,
The court of þe empriour,
How þai come in honour,   635
Thire fowlis of rigour
With a gret reir.

Than rerit þir merlȝeonis þat mountis so hie   [fol. 223]
Furth borne bacheleris, bald on þe bordouris;
Busardis and beld-kytis, as it mycht be   640
Soldiouris and sumptermen to þai senȝeouris.
The pitill and þe pype-gled, cryand pewewe,
Befor þir princis ay past as pert purviouris,
For þai couth chewis chikinnis and purches pultre,
To cleke fra þe commonis as kingis caytouris,   645
Syne hufe, hover, and behald þe herbery place.
Robyn redbrest nocht ran
Bot raid as a hensman,
And þe litill we wran
Þe wretchit dorche was.   650

75

Thar was þe har[oun]is fa, þe hobby, but fable;
Stanchalis steropis strecht to þai stern lordis,
With alkyn officeris in erd, awenand and able;
So mekle was þe multitud no mynd it remordis.
Thus assemblit thir segis, syris senȝourable,   655
All þat war fowlis of reif, þe richt quha recordis,
For þe temporalite tretit in table.
The stern empriouris style þus staitly restord is.
The pape and þe patriarkis, prelatis, iwist,
Welcummit þaim wynly, but weir,   660
With haly sermonis seir,
Pardoun and prayer,
And blythly þam blist.

The blissit pape in þe place prayit þaim ilkane
To remayne to þe meit at þe mydday,   665
And þai grantit þat gud but gru[c]hing to gane.
Than till a wortheliche wane went þai þar way,
Past till a palace of pryce, plesand all ane,
Was erekit rially, ryke of array,   [fol. 223ᵛ]
Pantit and apparalit proudly in pane,   670
Sylit semely with silk, suthly to say:
Braid burdis and benkis ourbeld with bancouris of gold,
Cled our with clene clathis,
Railit full of richas.
The esiast was arras   675
That ȝe se shold.

All þus þai mufe to þe meit, and þe marschale
Gart bring watter to wesche of a well cleir.
That was þe falcoune so fair, frely but fale,
Bad birnis burdis vp braid with a blyth cheir.   680
The pape passit till his place in + pontificale;
The athill empriour anone nechit him neir.
Kyngis and patriarkis kend with cardinalis hale
Addressit þaim to þat deis, and dukis so deir.
Bischopis bovnis to þe burd and marschionis of mychtis,   685
Erllis of hono[ur]is,
Abbotis of ordouris,
Prowestis and priouris,
And mony kene knychtis,

Denys and digniteis, as I eir demyt,   690
Scutiferis and sqwyeris and bachilleris blyth.
I pres nocht all to report – ȝe hard þaim expremit –
Bot all war marschalit to meit, meikly and myth;
Syne seruit semely in saile, forsuth as it semyt,
With all curis of cost þat cukis couth kyth   695
In flesche-tyme, quhen þe fische war away flemyt.
Quha was stewart bot þe stork, stallwart and styth?
Syne all þe Lentryne, but leis, and þe lang reid
And als in þe Adwent,
The soland stewart was sent,   700 [fol. 224]
For he couth fro þe firmament
Fang þe fische deid.

The boytour callit was cuke, þat him weile kend
In craftis of þe ketchyne, costlyk of curis.
Mony sawouris sals with sewaris he send   705
And confectionis on force þat phisik furth furis,
Mony man[er] metis. Gif I suld mak end,
It neidis nocht to renewe all þar naturis;
Quhar sic statis will steir þar stylis till ostend,
ȝe wait all worschip and welth dayly induris.   710
Syne at þe myddis of þe meit, in com þe menstralis;
The mavis and þe merle syngis,
Osillis and stirlingis,
The blyth lark þat begynnis,
And þe nychtgalis.   715

And þar notis anone, gif I richt newyne,
War of Mary þe myld, þis maner iwis:
'Hale! temple of þe Trinite, [tro]nit in hevin;
Haile! Moder of our maker and medicyn of mys;
Haile! Succour and salf for þe synnis sevyne;   720
Haile! Bute of our baret and beld of our blis.
Haile! Grane full of grace þat growis so ewyn,
Ferme our seid to þe set quhar þi son is.
Haile! Lady of all ladyis, lichtest of leme.
Haile! Chalmer of chastite;   725
Haile! Charbunkle of cherite;
Haile! Blissit mot þow be
For þi barneteme.

77

'Haile! Blist throw þe bodword of blyth angellis;
Haile! Princes þat completis all prophecis pur;   730
Haile! Blythar of þe Baptist within þ[e] bowallis
Of Elizebeth þi ant aganis natur.   [fol. 224ᵛ]
Haile! Speciose, most specifyet with + spiritualis;
Haile! Ordanyt or Adam and ay till indur;
Haile! Our hope and our helpe quhen þat harme alis;   735
Haile! Alterar of Eua in Aue, but vre;
Haile! Well of our weilfair. We wait nocht of ellis,
Bot all committis to þe,
Saull and lyf, ladye.
Now for þi frute mak ws fre   740
Fro fendis þat fell is.

'Fro þi gre to þis ground, lat þi grace glyde,
As þow art grantar þarof and þe gevar.
Now souerane, quhar þow sittis be þi sonnis syd,
Send sum succour dovne sone to þe synner.   745
The fende is our felloune fa; in þe we confide,
Thow moder of all mercy and þe menar
For ws wappit in wo in þis warld wyde.
To þi son mak þi mane and þi maker.
Now lady, luke to þe leid þat þe so leile lufis,   750
Thow seker trone of Salamon,
Thow worthy wand of Aaron,
Thow ioyus fleis of Gedion,
Ws help þe behufis'.

All þus Our Lady þai lovit with lyking and lyst   755
Menstralis and musicianis mo þan I mene may:
The psaltery, þe sytholis, þe soft sytharist,
The crovde and þe monycordis, þe gittyrnis gay,
The rote and þe recordour, þe rivupe, þe rist,
The trumpe and þe talburn, þe tympane but tray,   760
The lilt-pype and þe lute, þe fydill in fist,
The dulset, þe dulsacordis, þe schalme of assay,
The amyable organis vsit full oft;
Claryonis lowde knellis,   [fol. 225]
Portatiuis and bellis;   765
Cymbaclauis in þe cellis
That soundis so soft.

Quhen þai had songyn and said softly an[e] schour
And playit as of paradys it a poynt war,
In com iapand þe ia as a iuglour,   770
With castis and with cawtelis a quaynt caryar.
He gart þaim se as it semyt, in þe samyn hour,
Huntyng at herdis in holtis so hair,
Sound saland on þe se schippis of towr,
Bernes batalland on burde, brym as a bair.   775
He couth cary þe cowpe of þe kingis des,
Syne leve in þe sted
Bot a blak bunwed.
He couth of a hennis hed
Make a mane mes.   780

He gart þe empriour trowe and trewly behald
That þe cornecrake, þe pundar at hand,
Had pyndit all his prys hors in a pundfald,
For caus þai ete of þe corne in þe kirkland.
He couth wirk wounderis, quhat way þat he wald: 785
Mak of a gray gus a gold garland,
A lang sper of a betill for a berne bald,
Nobillis of nutschellis, and siluer of sand.
Thus iowkit with iuperdys þe iangland ia.
Fair ladyis in ryngis,   790
Knyghtis in caralyngis
Boith dansis and syngis –
It semyt as sa.

Sa come þe ruke with a rerd and a rane roch,
A bard owt of Irland with banachadee;   795
Said, 'Gluntow guk dynyd dach hala mischy doch;   [fol. 225ᵛ]
Raike hir a rug of þe rost, or scho sall ryme the.
Mich macmory ach mach mometir moch loch;
Set hir dovne; gif hir drink; quhat dele alis ȝhe?
O'Deremyne, O'Donnall, O'Dochardy droch.   800
Thir ar hi[r] Irland kingis of þe Irischerye:
O'Knewlyn, O'Conochor, O'Gregre Makgrane,
The schenachy, þe claischach,
The benschene, þe ballach,
The crekery, þe corach.   805
Scho kennis þaim ilkane'.

79

Mony lesingis he maid, wald let for no man
To speike quhill he spokin had, sparit no thingis.
The dene rurale, þe ravyn, reprovit him þan,
Bad him his lesingis leif befor þai lordingis.   810
The barde worth brane-wod and bitterly couth ban,
'How! Corby messinger', quod he, 'With sorowe now syngis!
Thow ischit owt of Noyes ark and to þe erd wan,
Taryit as a tratour and brocht na tythingis.
I sall ryme þe, ravyne, baith guttis and gall'.   815
The dene rurale worthit reid,
Stawe for schame of þe steid;
The barde held a gret pleid
In þe hie hall.

In come twa flyrand fulis with a fonde fair,   820
The tuchet and þe gukkit golk, and ȝeid hiddy-giddy.
Ruschit baith to þe bard and ruggit his hair,
Callit him thrys 'Thevis-nek to thrawe in a widdy';
Thai fylit fra þe fortope to þe fut þar.
The barde smaddit lyke a smaik smorit in a smedy,   825
Ran fast to þe dure and gaif a gret rair,   [fol. 226]
Socht watter to wesche him þarout in ane ydy.
The lordis leuch apon loft and lyking þai had
That þe barde was so bet.
The fulis fonde in þe flet   830
And mony mowis at mete
On þe flure maid.

Syne for ane figonale of frut þai straif in þe steid.
The tuchet gird to þe golk and gaif him a fall,
Raif his taile fra his rig with a rath pleid.   835
The golk gat wpe agane in þe gret hall,
Tit þe tuchet be þe tope, ourtirvit his hed,
Flang him flat in þe fyre, fetheris and all.
He cryid 'Allace', with ane rair, 'Revyn is my reid;
I am vngraciously gorrit, baith guttis and gall';   840
Ȝit he lap fra þe lowe richt in a lyne.
Quhen þai had remelis raucht,
Thai forthocht þat þai faucht,
Kissit samyn, and saucht,
And sat dovne syne.   845

All þus þir hathillis in hall heirly remanit
With all welthis at wis and worschipe to vale.
The pape begynnis þe grace, as greably ganit,
Wosche with þir worthyis and went to counsall.
The pure howlatis appele completly was planyt,   850
His falt and his foule forme vnfrely, but faile,
For þe quhilk þir lordis, in leid nocht to layne it,
He besocht of sucour, as souerane in saile,
That þai wald pray Natur his prent to renewe.
For it was haile his behest   855
At þar alleris request
Mycht Dame Natur arrest
Of him for to rewe.

Than rewit þir riallis of þat rath mane,   [fol. 226ᵛ]
Baith spirituale and temporale þat kend þe case,   860
And considerand þe caus, concludit in ane
That þai wald Natur beseike of hir gret grace
To discend þat samyn hour as þar souerane,
At þar allaris instance in þat ilk place.
The pape and þe patriarkis, þe prelatis ilkane,   865
Thus pray þai as penitentis, and all þat þar was,
Quharthrow Dame Natur þe trast discendit þat tyde
At þar haile instance;
Quhom þai ressaif with reuerens
And bowsome obeysance   870
As goddes and gyde.

'It nedis nocht', quod Natur, 'To renewe oucht
Of ȝour entent in þis tyde or forther to tell.
I wait ȝour will and quhat way ȝe wald þat I wrocht,
To reforme þe howlot of faltis full fell.   875
It sall be done as ȝe deme, dreid ȝe richt nocht.
I consent in þis caise to ȝour counsall;
Sen myself for ȝour saike hiddir has socht,
Ʒe sall be specialy sped or ȝe mayr spell.
Now ilka foull of þe firth a fedder sall ta   880
And len þe howlat, sen ȝe
Of him haue sic pete,
And I sall gar þaim samyn be
To growe, or I ga.

81

Than ilk foule of his flicht a fedder has tane 885
And lent to þe howlat in hast, hartlie but hone.
Dame Natur þe nobillest nechit in-ane
For to ferme þis federem, and dewly has done,
Gart it ground and growe gayly agane
On <þe> samyn howlat, semely and sone. 890
Than was he schand of his schape and his schroude schane [fol. 227]
Of alkyn colour most cleir, beldit abone,
The farest foule of þe firth and hendest of hewes,
So clene and so colourlyke
That no bird was him lyke 895
Fro Burone to Berwike
Wnder þe bewes.

Thus was þe howlat in herde herely at hicht,
Flour of all fowlis throw fedderis so fair.
He lukit to his lykame þat lemyt so licht, 900
So propir plesand of prent, provde to repar.
He thocht him maid on þe mold makles of mycht,
As souerane him awne self throw bewte he bair,
Counterpalace to þe pape, our princis i' plicht.
So hiely he hyit him in Luciferis lair 905
That all þe fowlis of þe firth he defowlit syne.
Thus leit he no man his peir;
Gif ony nech wald him neir,
He bad þam, 'Rebaldis orere'
With a [quh]ruyne. 910

'The pape and þe patriarkis and princis of prow –
I am cummyn of þar kyn, be cosingage knawin.
So fair is my fetherem – I haf no falowe –
My schrowde and my schene weid schir to be schawin'.
All birdis he rebalkit þat wald him nocht bowe, 915
In breth as a batall-wricht full of bost blawin,
With vnloveable latis nocht till allow.
Thus wycit he þe walentyne thraly and thrawin
That all þe fowlis with assent assemblit agane
And plenʒeit to Natur 920
Of þis intollerable iniur,
How þe howlat him bure
So hie and so haltane,

So pompos, importinat, and reprovable,   [fol. 227ᵛ]
In exces our-arrogant. Þir birdis ilkane   925
Besocht Natur to ces þat vnsufferable.
Tharwith þat lady a lyte leuch hir allane,
'My first making', quod scho 'Was vnamendable,
Þocht I alterit as 3e all askit in ane.
3it sall I preif 3ow to pleis, sen it is possible'.   930
Scho callit þe howlat in haist þat was so haltane;
'Thy pryde', quod þe princes, 'Approchis our-hie
Lyke Lucifer in estaite.
And sen þow art so elate,
As þe Ewangelist wrait,   935
Thow sall lawe be.

'The rent and þe ritches þat þow in rang
Was of othir mennis all, and nocht of þi awne.
Now ilk fowle his awne fedder sall agane fang
And mak þe catif of kynd till himself knawin'.   940
As scho has demyt þai haf done, thraly in thrang;
Tharwith Dame Natur has to þe hevin drawin,
Ascendit sone in my sicht with solace and sang.
And ilk fowle tuke þe flicht, schortly to schawin,
Held hame to þar hant and þar herbery,   945
Quhar þai war wont to remane.
All þir gudly ar gane,
And þar levit allane
The howlat and I.

Than þis howlat, hidowis of hair and of hyde,   950
Put first fro poverte to pryce and princis awne per,
Syne degradit fra grace for his gret pryde,
Bannyt bitterly his birth, bailefull in beir.
He welterit, he wrythit, he waryit þe tyde
That he was wrocht in þis warld, wofull in weir.   955
He crepillit, he crengit, he carfully cryd;   [fol. 228]
He solpit, he sorowit in sighingis seir.
He said, 'Allace, I am lost, lathest of all;
By syn in baile beft,
I may be sampill her-eft   960
Þat pryde neuer 3it left
His feir but a fall.

'I couth nocht won into welth, wre[c]h [vsit to] wast;
I was so wantoun of will, my werdis ar wan.
Thus for my hicht I am hurt and harmit in haist,   965
Cairfull and caytif for craft þat I can.
Quhen I was hewit as heir alltherhieast,
Fra rule, ressoun, and richt redles I ran;
Tharfor I ly in þe lyme, lympit lathast.
Now maik зour merour be me, all maner of man,   970
зe princis, prentis of pryde, for penneis and prowe
That pullis þe pure ay,
зe sall syng as I say.
All зour welth will away;
Thus I warn зow.   975

'Think how bair þow was borne and bair ay will be
For ouch þat sedis of þiself in ony sessoun.
Thy cude, þi claithis, nor þi cost cummis nocht of þe,
Bot of þe frute of þe erd and Godis fusoun.
Quhen ilk thing has þe awne, suthly we se,   980
Thy nakit cors bot of clay a foule carioun,
Hatit and hawles. Quharof art þow hie?
We cum pure; we gang pure, baith king and commoun.
Bot þow reule þe richtuis, þi rovme sall orere'.
Thus said þe howlat on hicht;   985
Now God for his gret micht   [fol. 228ᵛ]
Set our sawlis in sicht
Of sanctis so sere.

Thus for ane dow of Dunbar drewe I þis dyte,
Dowit with ane Dowglas, and boith war þai dow<is>,   990
In þe forest forsaid, frely parfyte,
Of Terneway tender and tryde, quhoso trast trowis.
War my wit as my will, þan suld I wele wryt<e>,
Bot gif I lak in my leid þat nocht till allow is,
зe wyse for зour worschipe wryth me no wyte.   995
Now blyth ws þe blist barne þat all berne bowis;
He len ws lyking and lyf euerlestand.
In mirthfull moneth of May
In myddis of Murraye,
Thus on a tyme be Ternway   1000
Happinnit Holland.

Heir endis þe buke of þe howlat
Per manum Iohannis Asloan.

Collation of the Witnesses

The following corpus of variants includes only substantive variations; however, they include the marginal finding notes Bannatyne appended to his copy. Thus 'lemma] B' indicates only that B has the same reading, and offers no information on its spelling. These transcriptions follow the conventions of the text, with modern word-division and capitalisation, e.g. final -ß appears as '-s'. The witnesses are presented with the same sigla as used in the introduction: A = Asloan, B = Bannatyne, C = Chepman and Myllar. Readings are presented in stanza-long paragraphs, and emendations to the text are starred and in bold.

rubric: *The Houlate maid be Holland* B
3 blythest] blywe est B   10 þir] þei B   11 Withoutin] Alone but B   ***13 reird**] B; apperd A
14 ruf] rove, *corr. from* rowe B   16 þe²] that B   20 huf] muif (*canc.*) huf A   25 Als] \Als/ (*marg.*) was B
29 mennis all] *trs.* B neidis] meidis \leydis (lerdis?)/ (*the first word also corrected later*) B   33 þar] \þer/ B   34 prolixt] prolixit B
40 þe¹] that B   ***45 roch**] B; roth A   a] a \rouch/ B   47 noys] noyus B   52 maid] maid a B
54 Cheuerand] Hedand B   55 fax] face B   65 to] to my B
69 bysyn] besym B   ***71 acus**] B, agus A   of] in B   caise] caus B   72 ane mendis] amendis B
82 kirklyk] clene (*canc.*) kirklyk B   ***83 Miterit**] B, Micht A   mure] demure B   84 weid] weid and B   85 sanctitud] sanc\cti/tud B   86 grap] get (*canc.*) grap A   88 wylest in] violent of B
92 þe²] þat B   95 For to] To B   halynes] hellynes B   99 spedely] speanlie (?) B   103 As] Ay B
107 Bysyn] Byssym B   116 de] will (*canc.*) dee B
*118 plicht] deid AB   119 apon] of B   122 of … laif] ourelerit all the lawe B   125 papeiaye] Papingo \Pape io (*marg.*)/ B
*131 hecht] commandit AB
144 suld] sall   ***mell**] tell AB   145 þe] thir   ***149 gruching**] B, gruthing A   150 þe²] *om.*
159 Present] Presentit B   163 red] ride B   169 dure] *originally* dine, *partly altered and* \dure/ *later* B
170 daye] tarding, *corr. later int.* B   173 blythar] blyvare B   176 ynewe] anew B   179 gryntare] garintar B

87

185 Charterouris] chertouris B   186 clething] cleir, *corr. to* clethit
B   187 evinsang and] all B   191 cais] kais, *perhaps a corr.*, \kais/
[*marg.*] B   cravis] crewis B

196 ewyn] he (*canc.*) \evin/ B   come] *om.* B   200 raith] reth
B   204 a] and (*canc.*) a B   full] a B   207 neb for mistar] b *of first
word and* M *of third corrs.*, \neb for mystar/ (*marg.*) B

211 archedene] arsdene B   212 Correkere] Correctour B   217 laid]
led (*canc.*) laid B

*226 sone] *om.* AB   wesit] vesyit B

*239 rethnas] richnes A, rethna*n*s (i.e. rethnas *with apparent common
mark*) B   245 come] cuming (*canc. and then rewritten in marg.*) B

249 lykis] like B   250 fyle] foull B   ***252 wreche**] B, wrethe A

262 þai] *after* sen B   265 manere ... matere] *trs. sbs.* B   270 and]
om. B

275 Syne samyn] And syne ^ \?/ \to the (*marg., later*)/ samyn
B   haile] all (*canc.*) hale B   276 nechit] ne<w?>it (*canc.*) \nychlit
(*marg.*)/ B   ***276 nuris**] mastris AB   278 in] on B   281 digne] dili-
gente (*canc.*) digne B   282 vþeris] vþer B   283 þe] *om.* B

287 eir] heir \ar/ B

306 Quhill] Till B

316 secoundlie] secound B   318 Perses] Percying B   to] in erd (*all
canc.*) to B   319 gentilly] generalle (*canc.*) \gentille/ B   321 on¹] of
B   formed] fermyt B

326 þe] þat (*canc.*) \þe/ B   ***327 chargis**] B, charge A   328
Marchionis] Marchions *but also* \marquisis (*marg.*)/ B   mychtis] mycht
B   330 Spar-] Sperk- B   333 as] with B   336 cot-] cote of B

339 He] *marginal note:* The armes B   connysaunce] conscience
B   340 cler] clene B   341 plantit] plant B   343 þe] a B   344 in] the
B   346 In] *marginal note:* 1 Papis armes B

352 Syne] *marginal note:* 2 Empriouris armes B   secoundlie]
secound B   357 bypartit] bypertitit B   breme] bryme B   358 þe] ?the,
altered from tha B   359 As] *marginal note:* 3 France armes B   ***364
blenkit**] B, bloutit A

366 He] *marginal note:* Scotlandis arms B   366 gowlis] gold (*canc.*)
\gowlis/ B   ***368 Richt**] B, Riche A   ryke] ryell B   ***370–71** *lines om.*
A, *supplied from* B, *in its spellings*   372 gowlis] gold \gowlis/ B   to]
?on (*canc.*) to B   373 his] -is B   ***signes**] armes AB   375 Our] Our,
corr. from On B

378 Next] *marginal note:* The discriptioun of the Dowglas armes
B   379 seruabile] seruiable B   381 conysance] cognoscence B   383
vnfalȝeable] vnselȝeable B

393 his] *om.* B   397 The] *marginal note:* The grene tre B   grathit]
ch (*canc.*) grathit   402 Douglas O] duchty (*canc.*) \dowglas/ B

406 birth] beild (*canc.*) birth B   408 Ane] *marginal note:* Four bran-
chis of the tre B   408 as ... I] ^ \as cheif/ I chiefly (*canc.*) B   410 so]
int. corr. B   412 so] full B

417 cassyn] ^ \o/ was (*canc.*) \cassin (*marg.*)/ B   congnoscence]
conysance B   419 syndry] sindre B   421 tyrefull] lere for B   422
dewlye] dolie B   424 hewe] have (*canc.*) \hew/ B   425 dait] dace *or*
date (*canc.*) \dake (*marg.*)/ B   ***426 bere**] bene AB   429 wait] *appar-
ently* wake B

430 takinnyng] takin B   431 asure ane] *apparently* azure of (*canc.*)
\asure an/, \azure (*marg.*)/ *by 432* B   434 The] *marginal note:* <Th>e
azure The siluer B   trewly] *repeats, first use canc.* B   436 The]
marginal note: Bludy hairt B   437 and] *supplied marg., following an
illeg. canc.* B

443 þe³] to B   ***445 was**] *om.* AB   447 to waile] of weir (*canc.*) \to
wale/ B   ***448 þai**] as thay B, þow A

456 ȝe ... till] *corr. from* I lippyn ȝow till A   458 wye] way B   462
be] þe (*canc.*), \be/ B

472 thing] *corr. from* thingis B   479 O] Of (*canc.*) o B   all] *om.* B
*482 to deid] B, deid A   484 saull] sawlis B   486 Thus] Than
B   ***487 connand**] command AB   489 in] and (*canc.*) \in (*canc.*)/ \in/
B   491 was] *om.* B

495 feye to] or \with/ fayis to (*canc.*) be B   499 wyis] wayis B   503
feile] fell B   505 þat] *om.* B

509 all] on B   511 þe flicht] ficht B   512 iwis] was B   513 wy]
wycht B   514 mony] mony a B   515 apon] mony (*canc.*) \vponn/
B   ***516 said**] quod AB   520 þe] this B

524 samyn] \boith/ samyn (*later corr.*) B   525 ynewe] anew B   526
prys] pretius B   ***perell**] pane B, *om.* A   527 and] doun B   529 þe]
his (*canc.*) þe B

534 and] ar (*canc.*) \and/   **C is present for lines 537–99**   537
braid] bred B   539 wyis] wayis B   540 gome] grome   541 slang]
flang BC   542 it] *om.* B   ***men**] mennis ABC

550 Of] *marginal note:* The sternis B   ***550 tressour**] BC, tressoun
A   554 riches] ressounis (*canc.*) riches B   and] et C   553 wicht] with
C

561 For] *marginal note:* The lyoun B   562 couth] caus B   564 on]
of BC   565 souerane] soueranis B?C   566 Kelit] Killis B   þar] his B
575 swerd] sourd B   577 þe] *om.* B   schewe] sew B   580 ws
occupy] *trs.* B   day] *om.* BC   581 Referris] Reffering B

586 Secund] *marginal note:* The coddis B   587 coddis] kyndis
(*canc.*) koddis B   589 trewe till attend] trewly to tend B   591 maid]
om. B   593 fandit] fayand \wes fayn (*canc.*)/ B

C ends at 599   604 into] forsuth (*canc.*) into B   605 chenӡeit]
changit B   606 lynis] linkkis B

612 Allther] Als B   613 tymeralis] tynnerallis B   614 apart] aport
B   616 The] *marginal note:* The powyn B   wyld] wale B   bastounis]
bustomis? B   617 growe] *cancelled* B   618 never air] nevair B

628 and[1]] and (*canc.*) \in/ B   630 On] Of B   of] *repeated, first use*
canc. B   haid] hede B   ***632 erast**] frist A, *om.* B

641 sumpter-] subiett B   642 pewewe] pewe B   643 pert] pairt of
B   644 chewis] cheires B   650 And blythly thame blist (*canc.*, cf. 653)
precedes B   Þe] That B

*651 harounis] haraldis AB   652 þai] þair B   656 þe richt quha]
quha richtly B   657 tretit] trctit B   659 prelatis] the prelattis B   660
wynly] wysalie B

*666 gruching] B, gruthing A   667 went] thay (*canc.*) went B   669
erekit] erectit B   670 proudly] peir (*canc.*) prowdly B   675 was] was
the B

677 All] *marginal note*: falcone marchell A   ***681 in**] in his AB   683
hale] all B   ***686 honouris**] B, hono + *loop* A

690 I eir] are B   695 curis] curies B   697 Quha] *marginal note:*
*s*tewartis B

704 In] *marginal note:* cuke B   706 on] of B   furis] *repeated, first*
use canc. B   ***707 maner**] man AB   suld] sall B   709 stylis] styll
B   710 worschip and welth] *trs. sbs.* B   711 Syne] *marginal note:*
menstralis The maveis The merle The osill The Lark B

716 anone] in ane B   717 *at the end of the preceding line* B   ***718**
tronit] crovnit AB   721 Haile] *marginal note:* Thair song B   728
-teme] tyme (*canc.*) teme B

731 within] of (*canc.*) \within/ B   ***731 þe**] þi AB   ***733 with**] with
þe AB   736 alterare] altare B

753 Thow] *marginal note:* end of the sang B

755 þai] lad (*canc.*) þai B   lovit] lofe B   757 The] *marginal note:*
The kyndis of instrumentis B   758 gittyrnis] gythornis B   759 rivupe]
ribup B 762 þe[2]] and the B   766 Cymbaclauis] Symbacllis, *corr. from*
Symbacllauis B   767 soft] oft B

*768 ane] a B, and A   770 In] *marginal note:* The sportaris B
783 pyndit] poyndit B   784 For] Be- B   786 of] *int. later?* B
795 A] *marginal note:* The ruke callit the bard B   796 dach] each *or*

rach B   797 Raike] Reke B   ryme] ryve B   798 mometir] momi'tir
B   **801 hir**] his A, the B   803 claischach] clarschach B

808 To] *marginal note:* dene rurall B   811 worth] wox B   814 a]
om. B   Tythingis] tadingis B   815 ryme] rywe B   816 The] Than the
B   worthit] worth B

821 The] *marginal note:* The fulis B   tuchet] tuquheit (*also* 834,
837) B   822 Ruschit] \R/Wischit B   824 fylit] *adds* him B

833 ane] a *interlined* B   835 rig] heid B   837 tope] tope and
B   840 vngraciously] vngretiouslye B   841 lowe] \low/ (*marg.*),
earlier reading canc. B   richt] lycht B   a] *om.* B   842 remelis] revin
his (*all canc.*) remyllis B

846 hathillis] athillis B   848 þe²] to B   854 prent] present B

860 kend] kennit B   866 penitentis] penitent B   871 obeysance]
adds as god (*canc.*) B

872 oucht] nocht (*canc.*) oucht A   875 reforme] reasoun B   879
ȝe²] I B   882 haue sic] hes B

886 to] *om.* B   hartlie] hurtly B   888 þis] this fe (*canc.*) this B   889
a-] and B   890 þe] *illegible* A   891 he] þe B   892 -kyn] *om.* B   894
colourlyke] colourike B   896 Burone] byron B

900 þat] *om.* B   902 him] *om.* B   904 to] with B   **910** quhryne]
ruyne AB

911 and²] *interlined later* B   912 kyn] blud B   knawin] of blud (*all
canc.*) knawin B   917 vnloveable] vnlowable B   918 wycit] vicut B

924 importinat] impertinax B   925 exces] excessis B   926 vn-] in-
B   927 Thar-] Þat B   a lyte] allyt B   929 alterit] allerit (?) B   932
princes] princens (?) B

940 him-] thy- B   944 flicht] flicht and B   schawin] sawin (*canc.*)
schawin A   945 and] and to B   947 ar] and B

953 bailefull] belfully B   957 he²] and B   959 Bysyn] Bysym
B   961 neuer ȝit] *trs., the second word a misplaced marginal addition*
B

963 wrech ... wast] wreth wast A, wrech wayest B   964 of] in
B   967 hewit] of hevit B   -ther-] -thill- B   968 rule] rewll and (*canc.*)
B   969 lyme] lymb B   lympit] *adds* the B   970 maik] mek B   971
prentes] prelettis B

978 nor] *om.* B   979 frute] fruitis B   984 orere] ourrere B   986
his] thy B

990 dowis] -is *under old adhesive* B   992 Terneway] terway B   993
wryte] *final letter illegible* B   994 I] *om.* B   1000 on] in B
colophon: *Explicit* B

Textual Commentary

1–39 Riddy's excellent note on this *chanson d'aventure* opening compares the scenes at the heads of 'Winner and Waster', *PPB* (also note the deliberate reprise at 8.62–69), *PTA*, and *SS*. To these examples, one should add *Quat*, where most of the poem forms an address delivered from a tree by a talking bird, a turtle-dove, 'faire foulle full of lufe, so mylde and so swete' (40); and *DL* 22–36. *PTA* begins with the activities of a poaching huntsman, an image of Death as stalker, germane to Holland's concluding moralisation. Similar hunting scenes appear at the openings of *AA*, *TDK*, and *SS*.

2 *markit*: As the continuing alliterative rhyme of the distych implies, the verb is parallel to *ment*. Thus, whilst *on mold* is quite frequently in alliterative poetry a pleonasm (cf. *on fold* 15), here it has its full force, and *markit on mold* means 'I passed over the ground'.

3 *blythest of ble*: The phrase, a stock collocation for Holland (cf. 17, 409, more distantly 399), provides an early signal indicating the poet's deliberated distance from the central alliterative tradition. Contrast the formulaic 'brightest of blee' (and variants), e.g. *GG* 134, 212, 317 (and cf. *Rauf* 551 'in that bricht hew' with 399).

4 *That*: Introducing a clause of result 'So that'. Thus, the first quatrain implicitly parallels the construction in lines 7–9, with more explicit *So ... That*.

6 *flurist*: 'Were' is implicit; the example in the preceding line is taken to govern this line as well. Amours compares Dunbar *TMW* 27.

9 *That all was amyable owr*: The subject of the statement comes at the end, *þe aire and þe erd*; these phrases form the off-verse, the customary end of a line with three on-verse stresses, and the cesura must precede them. One then must choose how to construe the remainder. The more straightforward option would connect *all* with the materials of the off-verse; this requires seeing *owr* as representing OE āhwær 'everywhere', not OE ofer. Alternatively, *all ... owr* could represent the compound *owrall*, with more or less identical sense. Given that *owr* is a rhyming stress, the first alternative may be preferable; translate 'That all the air and the earth were everywhere pleasant'.

10 Cf. *Pearl* 74, *AA* 44.

13 *reird*: I follow Amours in preferring the more pointed reading of B, 'resounded'. One might perhaps see this usage, in the specific context

93

where streams are usually musical, as expressive of a 'Scottish differ-ence'. See further 637n.

14 *but resting or ruf*: Cf. *DOST* ruve n. and *MED* ro n.⁴, sense b, a widespread collocation (although not in alliterative verse).

16–17 Cf. *Susan* 79–80, as Amours suggests, although note the fortunate *occupatio* of line 33, which precludes reproducing *Susan*'s surrounding catalogue of flowers. The subject of *bair* 17 is probably *branchis*, i.e. 'The banks bore (trees with) branches, and they, in turn, bore birds among their flowers'. Cf. the Douglas arms, and their fruitful tree, in 399, and the deliberate echo at 976.

21 *prunȝeand*: Because Prunȝe v.¹ usually refers to birds preening their feathers, *DOST* presents this use as a unique Prunȝe v.². The editors hypothesise that the transmitted form misrepresents an otherwise unre-corded *punȝeand* 'galloping, charging'. The use here predates by a long stretch any other example of *prunȝe* in Scots. But *MED* proinen v. is fairly widely recorded, and 'prik and proin' a set phrase (cf. *Susan* 81). Since in ME, as later Scots, the verb regularly is used of persons in a sense like 'spruce or smarten oneself up', *Pransand and prunȝeand* probably should be translated, 'strutting proudly about' (given the off-verse, as mating behaviour).

22 Ostensibly, the rhymeword presents the adjective form with adverbial sense 'surely, securely'. But one cannot dismiss the possi-bility of rather ornate grammatical parallelism, parsing the full line, 'I sat sekerly in solace sure'. Like many alliterative constructions, the last might be further ambiguous: is the speaker 'sure' in his (soon to be interrupted) delight ('sure in solace'), or is the delight itself constant, 'in sure solace'? The construction recurs at 85.

25 *Als*: Translate 'As a person who was'.

27 *The birth*: While *of grace* 28 speaks to spiritual delight, the following lines return to the physical, alluding to the medicinal value of herb simples.

29 *mennis all neides*: B offers the more direct *all mennis* 'all men's needs', but the form in A may seek to imply the translation, 'every need pertaining to man'.

30 *to hert and to hurt*: Translate the line 'that growth assuaged the heart and cured evils'.

32 *dame Natur*: Just as in Chaucer's evocation of the figure from Alain of Lille's *De planctu naturae,* the goddess represents the crea-tive principle of generation and plenitude; in addition to the discus-sions by Curtius, Bennett, and Lewis that Riddy cites, see Economou 1972. 31 *Vnder þe cerkill solar* may only mean something like 'In this

bright landscape', but probably alludes, a little inexactly, to the limits of Nature's control, usually described as sublunary.

38 *will I hens*: With unexpressed verb of motion, 'pass'.

45 *Rolpit*: The implicit rhyme with *Solpit* 42 is slightly misleading. That is a participle, modifying *ane petuos* 41, whilst *Rolpit* is the verb of an independent clause. '(And) he' is implicit at the head of this line.

roch: Amours identifies (xxi) the AB agreement in *roth* (but cf. 215, 794) as an example of both sources in common error; Riddy follows his suggestion, and also emends. The phrase conveys something like 'he was so hoarse that I pitied him'.

47 *noys in nest*: Amours, followed by Riddy, emends the text to accord with B *noyus* and thus assimilates the line to the usage in 251. But the A reading *noys* explains the outcry Holland's speaker in previous lines says he has heard and identifies it as coming from a bird (the witty implication of the prepositional phrase). Only in the following line does the speaker discover that the complainer is a *noyus* owl. Amours and Riddy may respond over-literally, since the owl is not in a nest, but, as line 48 says, *vnder ane holyne*. But that detail only reinforces what is everywhere else characteristic of the portrait, the owl's out-of-place-ness, his unnaturalness.

in-ane: I regularly distinguish, so far as possible, this form (OE an āne, 'anon, i.e. immediately') from phrasal *in ane* (OE in āne, 'as one, unanimously'). Asloan writes *anone* itself at midline in 682 and 716, but *in-ane* in rhyme.

48 *ane howlat*: Wise old owls do not figure prominently in medieval portrayals, and the bird is a nigh proverbial example of evil; for discussion, see Mann 2009, 157–62. Cf. Dunbar, 'Against Donald Owyr' (Bawcutt's poem 27) 7–12 'And he evir odious as ane owle, | The falt sa filthy is and fowle: | Horrible to natour | Is ane tratour, | As feind in fratour | Vndir a cowle' (cf. Bawcutt's note on owl-lore 2:349–50 and McDiarmid 1969, 281–82). For a comparable charge of treachery against the owl, see *O&N* 157–70. For further examples of Dunbar using the bird's name as an insult, see 53n, 58n, 251n.

Most of Holland's depiction can be paralleled in the grand compendium of commonplace medieval owl-lore gathered in the first 200-odd lines of the thirteenth-century *O&N*. The admission of lines 58–59 underlies all the negative depictions, 'Aganis natur in þe nicht I walk … | I dar do nocht on þe day'. Unlike a 'natural bird', active in daylight hours, the owl hunts in the dark, and this habit defines it as the *bysyn* and *monstour* (69, 73) to which Holland's owl ruefully alludes. Cf. *O&N*'s *vnwiȝt* 'miscreated thing' 33 (the nightingale's very first address to its adversary-bird), 90, 218; and Chaucer's evocation of the topic: 'Thow farst by love as oules don by lyght: | The day hem blent, ful wel they se by nyght. | Thy kynde is of so low a wrechednesse | That what love is, thow canst nouther seen ne gesse' (*PF* 599–602), a citation from Boethius, in Chaucer's translation 4 p4/186–87. As a result of its aversion to daylight ('tenebras amat magis quam lucem'), the *Physiologus*, for example, associates the owl with the recalcitrant Jews, who, in this account, refused the light of true faith offered by Jesus (Carmody 1939, ch. 7 [19]). This last detail may interface with the perception, the most positive detail most medieval writers adduce about the owl, that it is a bird of funereal lament (see further 53n), and it may be implicit in Holland's moralising conclusion.

Equally, as Alain of Lille points out (see the Introduction, pp. 26–27), the night-owl ('noctua') is 'deformed', ill-shaped, a perception underlying Holland's owl's persistent restiveness about its *fax* and *schape* (55, 60). First of all, its head, in relation to those of other birds, is distinctly disproportionate and outsized (see *O&N* 71–78, and more generally, the nightingale's charge that the owl is so ugly that her corpse makes an effective scarecrow, *O&N* 1122–44). Second, the owl is characterised by its large and staring eyes – it is the only bird with binocular vision, associated with its nocturnal hunting habits. In a passage seminal in the tradition of discussing the bird, Ambrose draws attention to this feature:

> Noctua ipsa quemadmodum magnis et glaucis oculorum pupillis nocturnarum tenebrarum caligentem non sentit horrorem. (The owl itself does not feel at all the dark horror of the shadows of night because of its eyes' large, grey pupils.) (*O&N*, p. 96)

Finally, as Holland's bird says, 'My neb is netherit as a nok' (57; cf. *O&N* 79–80, with a punning connection with an *awl*). The owl's short hooked beak contrasts with those of common perching birds (although not, as the exemplar of the species points out at *O&N* 1673–88, with those of nobler birds of prey). It is at least worth noting that *O&N* implicitly associates the owl with northern regions, including Galloway and Scotland, either because of the greater need for penance there (again, potentially germane to Holland's moral, as well as to the Marian lyric at 718–54) or because these lands provide savage habitats in keeping with the owl's habits, in *O&N* avianised alternative views that depend on which bird is speaking (see 905–32, 995–1030).

in haist: Functionally a temporal adverb, modifying *saw*, i.e. 'I immediately saw'.

48 *vnder ane holyne*: The appearance of the bird here, whilst others

are cavorting in the branches (16–17), recalls the initial description of *O&N* 13–28. There whilst the nightingale sits on a flowery bough amidst a hedge, the owl is on 'on old stoc ... mid iui al bigrowe'. It is not clear why this should be a fixed contrast, or why it should be appropriately echoed by Dunbar's narrator in *TMW* skulking in a hollybush.

50 *his awne schadowe*: This provides the first mirror-reference in the poem, answered by an equally evocative one at the conclusion. It may be read trenchantly against Henryson's later depiction of the similarly abjected Cresseid and her looking glass ('Testament' 347–50), but animating both depictions is the central 'mirror of Narcissus' scene in *Le Roman de la rose* 1425–1510. There Narcissus stares into a fountain and falls in love with his own glorious (and naturally provided) image. In the *Roman*, his fate is presented as just punishment for his converting a natural gift into unnatural self-affection, exemplified in his proud and scornful rebuff of the nymph Echo's love. Jean de Meun's reprise, at *Roman* 20405–30, in a passage responding, as does *The Howlat*, to Alain's *De planctu naturae*, emphasises Narcissus's unnaturalness, his turning to self-love, rather than natural generative desire (cf. the contrast of pine and olive trees, implicitly onanism and generative sexuality). Holland's owl, but only partially, parodies Narcissus's experience, since his face is unlovable, even to himself. *Rauf* is perhaps the deliberate antitype to Holland's poem, since there demonstrable virtue is found in insalubrious surroundings.

51 *growe*: The verb also occurs when the 'three dead kings' make their horrifying appearance in that poem: 'Now al my gladchip is gone, I grue and am agast' (57).

53 *grysly grym*: Perhaps hendiadys, 'terrifying and fierce'; in any event, *grym* is an adjective modifying *He* and *grysly* its adverbial modifier.

a gret ʒowle: Unlike 'proper' birds, with their melodious song (cf. 711–16 et seq.), the owl only hoots. This failure at song forms a major strand of in the 'plait' of *O&N*, and the nightingale persistently uses, like Holland, the root *ʒowl-* (again at 102) to describe this outcry, e.g. 40, 219–24, 971–94, 1643. Traditionally, this mournful hoot is associated with lamentation and keening the dead, for example at the head of Walter Map's 'Dissuasio Valerii', '[O]di ... vocem ulule, bubonem et aves ceteras, que lutose hiemis gravitatem luctuose preululant' (with contrasting 'Lusciniam amo et merulam ... et potissimum Philomenam') (*O&N*, p. 98). Cf. *AA* 86–87 (describing a ghost, and see further *AA* 127–30 for the effect of this outcry on birds); and Dunbar, *Flyting* 236, 'Oule, rare and ʒowle, I sall defowll thy pryd'.

54 The off-verse is metrical on the assumption that *churliche* has the sounded *-e* of the dative (after a preposition). This phrase plays on the paradox 'cheerless cheerfulness'.

55 *fax*: *Fax ... foule* (again at 77) inverts the usual alliterative panegyric, e.g. *GG* 354, 'Fayr of fell and of face'.

57 *am*: Given the tendency in the poem to hyperalliteration, one might wish to read *n'am*, re-enforcing the 'slant-alliteration' of *a n(e)'owle*.

58 *Aganis natur*: Dunbar persists in associating Kennedy with 'owlish' behaviour (cf. 53n). Early in *Flyting* (161–68), and relevant to the conclusion of Holland's poem, he evokes the language of death-lyrics to describe his adversary. As Parkinson 1986 notices, his description of the outlander Kennedy attracting derision in Edinburgh relies on descriptions of other birds 'mobbing the owl', described in the subsequent lines here, 'Than fleis thow lyk an howlat chest with crawis' (219). Like Holland's owl, Kennedy is an unnatural being, 'Baird rehator, theif of nator, fals tratour, feyindis gett' (244).

59 *dovle*: The word appears in *DOST* as a *hapax legomenon* and has inspired a certain amount of etymological conjecture. All these discussions assume that the rhyme here is exact and that Holland reproduces a word with Scots long u. It is much simpler, however, to see the form as a 'half-rhyme' (short u with long u; cf. the analogous *hald:cald* 87–91, 543–45), and to associate it with the adjective 'dull'. The spelling then reflects either Holland's frequent analogical forms in rhyme (see the Introduction, pp. 49–50), with adjective for noun (perhaps signalling a form like *dullard*?), or simply the common alliterative 'absolute use' of an adjective.

66 *at my beike*: 'if I stick my nose/face out'. For 'mobbing the owl', see the discussions at *O&N* 61–70, 277–80, 1653–66; and Parkinson 1986.

69 *bysyn*: Amours and Riddy, guided by *monstour* 73, gloss the word 'monster' (ultimately from an ON cognate of OE besēon). But a least a strong echo to this reading is the word *forbisen* 'example' (i.e. 'why am I being singled out in this way?'). Ironically enough, the owl sees itself as an unfair example, and its efforts at escaping this status ensure that it will become the subject of a true example, an *exemplum*, and one that vindicates fully the treatment it receives. In this regard, one might compare the owl's lonely skulking to avoid combat, being 'mobbed', with James Douglas's death scene, the product of selflessly putting oneself at risk (512–28).

70 Translate the off-verse 'I'm not asking/seeking to deny it'; cf. *GG* 902.

71 *acus*: Amours's emendation of A *agus*, followed also by Riddy.

72 *ane mendis*: Amours compares Lyndsay, 'Dream' 877 'Quha may mak mendis of this myscheif'. As *DOST* Mendis n., sense 2 points out, both A and B represent the functionally identical 'amends'.

80 *Quha is fader*: Perhaps an amusingly loaded question, given the poem's conciliar background – and the presentation of papal arms as those of an antipope (see 339n). Cf. *was pape cald* 91. The 'pride of the peacock' remains proverbial today, but see also Introduction n.56, and from the alliterative tradition, Dunbar *TMW* 379: 'payntit me as pako, proudest of fedderis'.

82 *cape*: The form, which appears again in 202 (within the line) is ambiguous, and might represent either 'cap' (with artificially lengthened vowel) or 'cape'. It thus might refer to the birds' resplendent plumage, or their 'headgear' – here the mitre of the next line, in 202 the cockerel's comb.

83 *Miterit*: The B reading, appropriately adopted by Amours and Riddy to restore *Micht* A. Asloan has either missed the suspension for *er*, or confused its appearance with simple *miᵗ* , i.e. *micht*.

84 *schand*: The adjective is unique to this poem and presented as a *hapax legomenon* in *DOST*. However, both sense and etymon are fairly obvious; the form reflects an adjectival use of the past participle of OE scǣnan 'to cause to shine, be resplendent'. The verb appears in OE at least once in the sense '? to render brilliant'. The phrase s*chand in his schap* looks ahead to the poem's end (891), when the owl has been transformed so that he resembles the colourful tail of the peacock (or the absurdly overintricate and variegated papal arms of 339–46) and his claim to be the pope's *counterpalace* 904.

85 *sure*: See 22n. Here it is unclear whether the off-verse use is parallel to the earlier adjective *Sad*, in which case one might translate the line 'Truly, confident in his constant holiness'.

88 *wyce*: Probably representing *DOST* (Vis), Wyce, Wais n. 'face', cited twice from Hay's *Alexander*, but with extensive ME citations at *MED* vis n.². Alternatively, one could associate the form with *DOST* Vic(e, Vice n.1 'counsel'. Certainly, the former supports Holland's entire 'device': appearances are real (and provide the logic for assigning birds offices on the basis of their appearance), and a bad *vise* communicates moral turpitude absolutely.

94 *Aue Raby*: See Matt. 26:49 and Mark 14:45, spoken by Judas at the betrayal in Gethsemane, and thus comically appropriate in a context

that calls attention both to *With sic courtassy as he couth* (93) and to the potentially questionable status of the pope. Contrast the repeated *Ha(i)le* 719ff., representing another biblical *Ave*, that of Luke 1:28.

106 Cf. *AA* 137 'I was of figure and flesh fairest of alle'.

110 *Askis*: '(And I) ask ...'

118 *plicht*: The line is the first of a distich rhyming /p/, the rhyme quite emphatic, given that 119 stresses the normally subordinate *-pon*. Yet this line does not bear sufficient alliteration. AB agree in offering *deid*, which may seem mandated by stanza-linking (answering *de* in 116, just as 103 *owle* is echoed at 105 in the succeeding stanza). However, stanza-linking in the poem is considerably less regular than is alliterative rhyme; it either fails to occur, or might be described as fortuitously anaemic, at 247–48, 260–61, 299–300, 312–13, 325–26, 351–52, 364–65, 403–4, 416–17, 429–30, etc. Moreover, *deid* here seems to me unconvincing (and thus potentially scribal supply), since, the dire event not having occurred, the off-verse verb should display subjunctive forms (minimally *suld I haife* or the like). The roughly synonymous *plicht* would fulfill metrical requirements, and one must assume that here and at 144 a scribal effort to emphasise stanza-linking has occurred somewhere in the tradition underlying the manuscript texts.

This represents the first of a series of emendations I offer to repair the poem's alliterative rhymes (cf. 131, 373, 632, etc.). All these answer the same general logic. A very substantial portion of the errors in any text are purely mechanical, e.g. the dropped distych at 370–71, the provision of *c* instead of *t* at 718. But perhaps just as prominent are various forms of substitution, most frequently the scribal provision of synonymous readings. Across the alliterative tradition, as Duggan first demonstrated (1986), transmission offers up hundreds of analogous examples where scribes copied more or less accurately for sense, while not always respecting poetic rhyme.

122 I have punctuated in order to avoid various confusions enunciated by past editors. Lines 121–22 provide an extended series, all of it fundamentally a specifying variation for the central phrase *my counsall*. The series involves four groups, cardinals, either orthodox Christian 'patriarchs' or figures taken as metaphorical descendants of Old Testament wise men, prophets (again, perhaps a metaphorical title?), and *of lerit þe laif*, 'all the remainder/residue of learned men'. Cf. the parallel locution in 446, to be translated: 'secular lords, learned men/clerics, and everyone else'. That line shows that the difficulty here reflects Holland's awkward, but metrically necessary, placement of 121 *and*; logically, the conjunction should appear at the opening of the off-verse in 122 (where

it would be unmetrical). Similarly, the conjunction of nouns in 121 is disconcerting, because it is too reminiscent of a much more limited gathering, the 'college of cardinals'.

125 *papeiaye, provde in his apparale*: At Dunbar *TMW* 382, after coercing finery from her husband and obtaining a lover, the widow says 'I thoght myself a papingay and him a plukit herle'. The parrot resembles the peacock/pope birds in its gaudily colourful plumage, a true 'bird of paradise' central to the two early sixteenth-century poems, Skelton's 'Speak Parrot' and Lindsay's 'The Testament of the papyngo'.

127 *turtour trewest*: Of course, proverbially so, cf. Whiting T 542, and the frequent examples in alliterative tradition, e.g. *Quat* 132, *SJE* 91; cf. further *GG* 293, 755, 1177; *Susan* 187.

130 *but hone*: cf. *Rauf* 575 '... he hynt withoutin hone'.

131 *hecht*: As in 118, the verse lacks sufficient rhyme, and I have supplied the alliterating synonymous verb for AB *commandit*. *all* provides the answering stave in the off-verse. I am further suspicious about the rhyme-word, the original now unrecoverable; *landis* is unduly colourless and repeated later in the stanza (where it also rhymes initially), an unusual procedure in this poem.

135 *tane with*: For the sense, see *DOST* ta v., sense 74.

136 *as þe deir demyt*: As frequently in alliterative poetry, the antecedent is unclear. Has the turtle-dove done exactly as the one dear to him, the pope, had judged it should be done? Or has he, the dear one, carried out his orders dutifully, as he saw fit? 170 *deir* clearly refers to the pope.

138 For the swift swallow, Riddy cites Whiting S 923. At 'The Thrissil and the rois' (Bawcutt's poem 52) 80, Dunbar perhaps recalls *The Howlat*, when he describes Nature sending a swallow as messenger to summon the other birds to her presence (cf. Bawcutt's notes 2:397–99 passim).

144 *mell*: Just as in 117 above, a form responding to imperatives of stanza-linking disrupts the initial rhymes of the line. Here it is relatively easy to find verbs in /m/ with the sense 'tell, relate'. I adopt *mell* simply because palaeographically convenient; Holland's usual relevant form is *me(y)ne*.

146 *as efferis*: The adverbial phrase presumably modifies either *Resauit* or *reuerence*, in the latter case with fundamentally adjectival force 'appropriate'.

147 The alliterative pattern is ambiguous. Either *harraldis* alliterates /r/ on the second syllable to form a normal aa/ax line (cf. the rhyme at 581), or the line rhymes ab/ab on /r/ and /vowel-h/ (*har-:ilk-*).

155 *manlyke*: 'courteous', but with a whimsical allusion to the characters described being birds, not men; cf. 162 *of kynd* for another instance of 'baring the device'.

157 *as I ment in a mornyng*: One of several moments when Holland implies that all his birds are available for observation at Darnaway; cf. *þat ilk place* 291 and similar locutions, e.g. 209, 214, 308, 338.

163 *compt*: The rhyme requires the Norman form *acunt*.

164 *þat*: Perhaps for *þar*, although the reading of the textus acceptus links the *deir dignite* associated with *cardinalis* with their sign (*takyn-nyng*), the red hat/red crown of European cranes. Translate the off-verse, '(office), always accustomed to/invested in honour'.

165 Amours aptly compares with the on-verse Dunbar, *Flyting* 289 'Na fowlis of effect'.

170 Translate the on-verse: 'While it was still day …'; similarly the echoing construction in line 196: 'But before dusk …'

171 *suowchand ful swyth*: The phrase appears several times to describe swans in Douglas, *Aeneis*; cf. in addition to Amours's citation of 2.44.1 (reproducing Virgil's 'stridentibus alis', 1.401), 7.11.153 or 12.Prol.152.

177 *þat honorable ar*: Probably modifies *abbotis*, not *ordouris*.

178 *monkis, þe blak and þe quhyte*: Referring to the two traditional monastic orders, the Benedictines, with their black habits, and the Cistercians, with their white ones. The line appears to have defective rhyme, aa/xx only, and, as the monastic reference indicates, its off-verse must be considered fixed. It is just plausible that *war* and *quhyt* rhyme, forming the pattern aba/xb. However, this rhyme would be distinctly 'southron English', reflecting the coalescence of earlier /w/ and /hw/.

182 *parfyte*: For the rhyme here and at 992, see the Introduction, n.43.

183 *pik-mawis*: The word is presented in *DOST* as a *hapax legomenon*, but it is a fairly transparent coinage, from OE pic 'pitch, tar (i.e. black)' + mǣw, mēw 'gull'. The birds' black heads render them 'party'-habited, as the next line says.

as for: Translate 'as if (they were)'.

184 *þar party habitis*: As transmitted, the line appears to alliterate on the two examples of *þar*.

185 *clene Charterouris*: Carthusian monk-hermits, as Holland notes, given to extreme devotions. This line probably alliterates ab/ab, with the rhyming syllables *con* /k/-*tem* /t/ … *clene* /k/ … -*ter* /t/, although the second stress of the off-verse falls, as customary, on the rhyming syllable -*rour(i)s*. However, Holland may rely on a rhyme extending a

traditional historical license associated with early ME and Middle Scots end-rhyme. Any stop may rhyme with another having the same 'voice', i.e. any of /p/, /t/, /k/ with one another. Cf. Hay's *Alexander* 5633–34 (*lap* 'leapt':*gat* 'gotten'), 5786–87 (*clekis* 'seizes':*fletis* 'floats'), and cf. the more distant examples cited Introduction n.38.

188 Amours xxi (followed by Riddy) cites this line, which should, he believes, read 'drowp + and dar' with dittography, as an example of AB in common error. The suggestion is sensible, and certainly, in grammatical terms, both verbs should be in a parallel construction dependent upon *saw*. Cf. *AA* 52 'Þei durken and dares'. However, the scribes here appear wiser than the editors, since they perceive that Amours's emended form would not be metrical. The closer parallel, from a text Holland may have known, is provided by *SS* 132–33 'A bare body in a bed, a bere ibrouth | A duk drawe to þe deþ wiþ *drouping and dare*'. The rhyme involves, as frequently (see Introduction, pp. 49–50), a form technically nongrammatical in a construction, here parallelism, where its actual grammatical force is easily intuited. Translate as if the final word were *darand*: 'No one saw them laugh, but rather saw them skulking and lying hidden'. Not only were Carthusians enclosed, but members of the order followed a private life of contemplation in their cells, rather than the fully common life of traditional monastic orders.

189 Like the monks in 178, *Alkyn chennonis* would minimally include those 'black and white', the Augustinian and the Premonstratensian canons, respectively. But the term 'canon' is more inclusive, extending to cathedral clergy, described in 196ff., for example; those are prebendary canons, the holders of prebends, the income of designated parishes. Unlike enclosed monks, canons were supposed to engage actively in the *cura animarum*, to attend to the spiritual needs of the laity, even in parish churches. The cathedral chapters at St Andrews and Whithorn were comprised of black and white canons, respectively; the remaining Scottish chapters, of 'secular canons' (see Cowan 1960, 19–20).

190 The line rhymes ab/ba with *religioun* parsed *re-ligioun* and answering *les*.

191–95 *pure freris forthward*: Friars were, at least theoretically, devoted to the literal enactment of apostolic poverty and thus, uniquely among 'regular clergy', bound to rules of mendicancy and non-ownership. This ideal included such injunctions as Luke 10:4 'Carry neither purse, nor scrip, nor shoes' (thus to beg only for the day's food, cf. Matt. 6:34), and like the apostles and disciples, they were 'to preach the kingdom of God, and to heal the sick' (the last understood as encouragement of penance). Typically, friars sought the charity of well-off benefactors and frequently traversed established 'limits' seeking their support. But their twice-daily appearance as reapers/gleaners here has an ironic sting; cf. Luke 10:2 'The harvest indeed is great, but the labourers are few. Pray ye therefore the Lord of the harvest, that he *send labourers into the harvest*' (my emphasis).

196 *þat bur office*: As Holland indicates, the officials of a cathedral chapter, the *familia* of a bishop. Holland names these *principales personae* in the conventional order (cf. Cowan 1960, 20–21): the dean, the chief adminstrative head of the chapter (199); the chanter (203); the chancellor, responsible for chapter muniments and other documents (205); and the treasurer (209). The last was responsible not only for finance, but also the ornaments of the church.

198 Amours xxi cites the line, which he wished to emend to read a[m]yss ('amice'), as another example of AB in common error. However, the scribes probably have the word *avys*, with *w* for usual *v*; cf. *awysit* 264. Translate 'of good counsel'.

200 *raith*: Amours points out that the B spelling *reth* indicates that this is the adjective meaning 'severe, strict'. (Riddy emends the spelling for the sake of clarity.) Asloan again has difficulty rendering this root in 239. Even if Holland's Scots predated the coalescence of older *a, ai,* and *e*, this was normal by Asloan's time, and he provides a back-spelling, not requiring emendation.

203 *chantour full chief*: A calque translation of Latin *pre-centor*, the title given the choir-master (and customarily the chapter's librarian as well). Here *channonry* probably has a sense not noted in *DOST*, 'the whole collection of canons, the cathedral chapter'; cf. *MED* canonie, cited once as a scribal variant at Chaucer, 'Canon Yeoman's Tale' 992.

205 *Chargit*: With implicit 'Who was'. The curlew, like other shore-birds, uses its long curved beak to dig for food in the sand.

210 *grene almous*: As Riddy points out, an allusion to the green heads of several varieties of duck, not just the mallard. I have no real idea why a duck (or a chapter's treasurer) should be called 'Gawain/ Gavin'. Possibly Scots ducks are alleged to sound 'Gaw' (rather than the Chaucerian 'quek quek' of *PF* 499), or as the apparent echo at 605 might suggest, Holland is recalling another (and differently situated) piece of cloth in *GGK*. The line alliterates abb/ax.

211 Holland follows the strict hierarchy, an order of precedence, that he will repeat in introducing 'the secular estate' at 313. Here he passes from the bishop's household, his *familia* of canons, and its officials,

to those administrators who manage the delivery of spiritual care and discipline throughout the diocese.

212 Translate the off-verse: 'The goose was appointed'; his office as archdeacon, which opens the sentence, is the direct object. Here the apt fit between bird and vocation relies upon the same learned allusion that underlies Chaucer's epithet 'the waker [vigilant] goos' (*PF* 358). In an episode widely known through Virgil's *Æneid* 8.655–58 (and commentaries upon the passage), cackling geese awoke the defenders of the Capitoline hill and saved the Romans from invasion.

As Thompson points out at length (1943), in the later Middle Ages, the office of archdeacon – typically more than one in a diocese – had developed from that of the dean of the cathedral chapter (cf. 196n). Such a figure engaged in public perambulations of his archdeaconry and was responsible for all matters of discipline relating to the cure of souls, both lay misbehaviour and clerical sloppiness. Traditionally, depictions of the office emphasise the opportunities it afforded for extortive behaviours and self-enrichment, activities Holland associates with the 'dene rurale' later in the stanza (cf. Thompson 1943:153–56 and 225n).

213 *martoune*: *DOST* Mortoun n. has only three uses, and the editors connect the word with a modern dialect term for the guillemot. Certainly, the context implies that Holland does not intend the house martin here. *MED* martinet n.[1] offers one citation which may refer to the kingfisher (OF martinet, ML martineta); while *OED* martinet n.[1] considers this to be a martin, it cites a naturalist, writing in 1544, who describes 'Tertium genus [of martin], quod in ripis nidulatur, Angli *a bank martnet* nominant'. However, the remaining *DOST* citations indicate that this should be some variety of edible upland game bird.

215 *The ravyne*: His speech resembles the owl's (cf. 45), and he will ultimately run afoul of yet another *ran*-nish speaker, the rook/Irish bard, at 809–17. Cf. further 231n, for his antitype, the dove, associated with the bard's insult. In the later Middle Ages, archdeaconries were divided into deaneries, their deans traditionally elected from among their number by the local clergy. This dean supervised only this group of priests, attending to their morals and spiritual leadership; unlike the archdeacon, he had no judicial powers (cf. Thompson 1943, 185).

216 *rank*: *DOST* cites this usage as the unique Rank adj.[2], but the editors' interpretation depends on connecting the usage with the modern proverbial 'lean/thin as a rake' or 'rake-thin'. Amours provides parallels that suggest that a rake is a type of overbearing rigour, and the normal sense of ME/Middle Scots *rank* reinforces this suggestion.

218 *Bot in*: The verb of the preceding line continues to govern the

construction, but with a small quibble: 'he did not keep a household, but hung about (lit. held himself)'. *For* 220 complements *Cryand* 221; translate: 'confidently demanding his in-lieu-of-hospitality payments (from rural priests)'.

225 *causs consistoriale þat ar coursable*: It was customary to periodically read in churches 'the great sentence of curse', an extensive listing of behaviours worthy of anathema. For discussion, see Pickering 1981. The primary business of ecclesiastical courts, in which the *crovs capone* presides as judge, was hearing cases of sexual misconduct (cf. Chaucer's Summoner, a minor official of such an institution, 'General Prologue' 622–68). *coursable* 'deserving anathema' has no analogues in either ME or Scots; *DOST* coursable adj. unconvincingly associates the usage here with the set legalism *coursable breves* 'current [i.e. 'running', valid] writs (allowing entry to a property)'.

226 *Wenus sone*: I follow Riddy's suggestion (in a text-note, not the text). She connects the reference to *Wenus* with the phrase at *PF* 351. In antiquity, the sparrow was sacred to Venus (and conventionally alleged to be devoted to Venerian activities).

229 *hospitular*: Given Holland's hierarchical order of presentation and the phrase *in þe forest*, this describes the keeper of a hospital (i.e. hospice or hostel). In the Middle Ages, these were not usually establishments dedicated to treating the sick, but rather devoted to eleemosynary works, like supporting the poor and travellers. There were more than one hundred such institutions, with varying specialities, in Scotland during the Middle Ages.

Chaucer's description of the bird whom Holland makes its keeper, 'the frosty feldefare' (*PF* 364), seems apposite. The fieldfare is primarily a winter migrant in Britain and thus has to forage widely, hence perhaps the second element of its compound name, as if from OE faru 'travel'. The phrase 'farewell, feldfare', i.e. 'the game's up', may also be relevant to the identification; *OED* feldfare n. cites Lydgate apparently glossing the locution 'As man forsake in euery place'. Higgins 2008's firm identification with a member of order of St John of Jerusalem is unconvincing (and avowedly offered tendentiously *argumenti causa*). Translate the line, '(The) capable (fieldfare) was appointed to the rank of hospitaller'.

230 *cowschotis*: The line, with a common Scots poetic word for a dove or pigeon, does not alliterate, whilst the synonymous 'pudʒeoun' would do so. *DOST* first cites 'pudʒeoun' from a 1513 account, but the word is widely attested in fifteenth-century ME. I let the text stand, although I suspect that Holland's reliance here on English diction

may have been subjected to intervention in transmission. For a similar example, see 782n.

231 *Noyis messinger*: Cf. Gen. 8:11 (cf. 215n, 813).

234 *confessionis hale*: A technical term; among the customary conditions attached to a proper confession, and to be enforced by a conscientious priest, is completeness; cf. Chaucer, 'The Parson's Tale' I 318–20, 1006–11; and Millett 1999.

236 *cummyng*: Perhaps for *come*, as in 245 (although B there reads *coming*). Cf. *SJ* 348, 495.

239 *rethnas*: Amours prefers to A *richnes* the reading signalled in B *rethna(n)s*, *rethnas* 'ferocity, cruelty'. This is the only Scots usage offered in *DOST*; Amours cites as parallel the northern English *Cursor Mundi* 22667, nearly as isolated in ME. Like Riddy, I follow this suggestion; the error is another example of Asloan's rather persistent confusion over the similar graphs *c* and *t*, e.g. *roch* 45, *gruching* 149 and 666. The line probably alliterates, a little limply, ab/ba, *na* rhyming with *-nas*. *reif* 'robbery' represents a vernacular calque translation of Latin *raptor*; the usage is analogous to Chaucer's OF-derived 'foules of ravyne' (*PF* 323, 527; < Latin rapina 'theft'), echoed at Dunbar, 'The Thrissil and the rois' 125 (cf. 313–14n).

243 The line probably alliterates, as Holland's frequent ab/ba. The form transmitted as Northern ME/Scots *gaf* in its Southern form *yaf* probably can alliterate with vowels (and thus with *all* at the line's end). One might, however, notice the resemblance of the on-verse to that of 98, with the unproblematically alliterating phrase *braid benison*.

251 *noyus in nest*: Unlike the earlier, somewhat unpointed example in B 47 (see the note there), in this context the phrase alludes to a standard bit of (un)natural history concerning the owl. Probably on the basis of its being classified among 'unclean' birds at Deut. 14:15, the owl is alleged to have a particularly foul nest, smeared with the droppings of its young. Cf. *O&N* 91–100 (with the suggestion that the owl is the source of the proverb, 'Don't shit in your own nest', i.e. 'Don't do something disgraceful near home, where your neighbours can discover it'); and Dunbar *Flyting* 36–37: 'Ignorant elf, aip, owll irregular, | Skaldit skaitbird and commoun skamelar' (see Bawcutt's note to 37, 2:431; although *skait* lexically is 'scold', it is difficult to suppress the echo of *skyte*).

252 At the head of the line, Asloan again confused the graphs *c* and *t*. The off-verse depends upon *netherit* in the preceding line; translate 'abased ... from (a position of) honour and prosperity'. The owl's pitying self-identification as 'Wre[c]he of all wretches' is particularly inept; after all, the pope is traditionally (and honourably) known as 'servus servorum Dei' (cf. Chaucer, *Troilus* 1.15).

253 Translate the off-verse, 'Putting forth his evidence precisely'.

254 Both off-verse stresses fall on the final word, which also displays Holland's frequent 'slant alliteration', i.e. *my n'vnhele*.

256 *Bot to þe poynt*: Echoing that moment in Chaucer's *PF* when a difficult case is put to judgement, line 372.

266 *all couth þai argewe*: Probably to be translated 'they knew how to debate (about) all these things'. As usual in the poem, it is difficult to distinguish the 'hard' use of *couth* (past of the auxiliary *can*) from the 'soft' use (a pleonastic stand-in for the verb, which follows as infinitive, a construction generally used to fulfill metrical requirements). The line alliterates abb/ax on '-cum-', 'stance', 'stait', and 'couth'.

267 *in leid nocht to layne it*: For other examples of this common-place off-verse (it appears again at 852), see *AA* 82, more distantly *Quat* 270, *Susan* 282, *Rauf* 313.

268 *Arestotill*: Citing Aristotle here may be particularly pointed. In the Middle Ages, his biological works formed the pinnacle of that science (the three originally separate Greek texts circulated as a combined single Latin *De animalibus*, translated by Michael Scot), and they were particularly influential in describing the nature and diverse behaviours of birds (cf. the offhand reference of *PPB* 12.268). But equally, scholarly debate from the mid-thirteenth century was dependent upon Aristotelian logic, with its interest in innate being (substance), and the relation of that to observed detail and behaviour (accident), surely relevant to the case the owl proposes, and to its outcome. Cf. Henryson's possible reminiscence, *Moral Fables* 45–46.

269 *generale*: Although perhaps awkwardly, the word appears the modifier of *apperans* (as Amours sees).

270 *to ... fro*: The prepositional adverbs certainly convey the sense 'some moved toward (accepting the owl's proposal) while others moved away from (accepting) it'. But this sense is qualified by the randomness customarily associated with the phrase *to and fro*, e.g. Chaucer, *Troilus* 4.484–85.

276 *nuris*: Not only does the line not alliterate, but at least on the basis of Holland's usual practice (see Introduction, pp. 21–22), it does not rhyme. Elsewhere in the poem, 'mistress' and similar words rhyme /a(:)s/, not the /i(:)s/ necessary here. On the basis of 32, I have supplied the rhyming *DOST* Nuris n. (cf. further the entry for Nuris(s)har n.). See, in particular, the uses at Henryson, 'Testament' 171, 199 'fostering one'; and Alexander Scott 1.221 'Noblest Natour, nurice to nurtour'.

However, traditionally in Scots verse, /n/ and /m/ serve as equivalents in end-rhyme. Cf. *Wallace* 7.153–54 (tane:hame) and similar rhymes at 7.453–54, 1075–76; *Legends of Saints* Eugenia 215–16, 423–24, 675–76. Holland may have extended this perceived equivalence from word-final position to word-initial, although the unusual vocalism of *mastris* would remain problematic.

278 Again the line does not alliterate, and a plethora of choices might be suggested. For example, a form of *visen/avisen* 'to counsel', with crossrhyme of /v/ and /w/, would be acceptable (and might explain the putative scribal handling as dissimilation from the rhyme-words here and in 280). But a word sustaining the rhyme in /p/, e.g. *prayit*, would serve equally well.

279 *souerane in saile*: With this halfline (and that at 853), cf. *GG* 133 'the syre in the saill'; more distantly *AA* 339.

281 *With dukis and with digne lordis*: Cf. *GG* 9, 184; *Rauf* 753 (and more distantly, 320 below).

282 *vperis*: Although both AB report the word (and one could compare 297 or 472), I doubt that any alliterative poet, persons given to the multiplication of terms of this sort, would provide such a substitute for a specific title. Perhaps Holland wrote something like *alderes*.

287 *The trewe turtour and traist*: Cf. 127n. *as I eire tauld* presumably modifies the adjectives *trewe ... and traist*.

288 *lelest in leid*: Probably, given the implicit carryover of the subject at the head of the next line, the phrase describes the turtle-dove secretary. His scrupulous report of the discussion is 'most faithful in (his) language'. Of course, the phrase might equally, understood in those terms, modify *letteris*.

293 *bernis so bald*: Cf. *GG* 345, 736, 1281, 1319 (of forty considerably varied uses, an indication of commitment to metonymic variation); *AA* 40, cf. 145, 367, 490, 670. For *Babilonis towr*, see p. 32.

301 *hove*: The spelling might equally be an effort to reproduce *hone* 'delay'.

303 *fro þe south fellis*: This offhand, apparently geographical term appears to have no parallel, in either ME or Scots. Holland here seems to be relying on the rather unusual sense of *MED* fel n.[2], 'wasteland' (not 'mountain'). Presumably the phrase is intended to mean something like 'the Middle Eastern desert'.

308 *frely and fair*: Cf. *Susan* 17, 331; the owl is, of course, *vnfrely* 56.

313–14 Similarly, at Dunbar, 'The Thrissil and the rois' 120–26, the eagle is crowned the just lord of the birds. While the two poets' identi-

fication is commonplace, it may be resonant, given the details discussed
at 138n.

315 *ancient*: The adjective probably modifies *kingis* in the off-verse,
i.e. 'The (high)flying eagles, kings long-crowned'.

318 *Perses þe sone with þar sicht*: Chaucer's introduction of the bird
evokes the same details: 'There myghte men the royal egle fynde, | That
with his sharpe lok perseth the sonne' (*PF* 330–31). Cf. Carmody 1939,
ch. 8 (19); the *Physiologus* reports that when eagles age and their wings
weaken and sight fails, they fly to the sun, which burns away their old
wings and the *caligo* afflicting their eyes. They then bathe in a fountain
and are revived.

herd: i.e. 'hear it'. Like nearly all early Scots poets, Holland regu-
larly alternates between voiced /d/ and voiceless /t/, when necessary in
rhyme.

327 *chargis*: The off-verse in A, unusually in the transmission of
the poem, is a syllable short. I have filled it out with B's plural; Asloan
may have been attracted to the idiom, 'be in charge of', rather than the
specific implied sense of fulfilling stated plans (and thus responsibili-
ties). However, in the immediate context, there seems a scribal tendency
to dissimilate some of the repeated plurals; note that B reads singular
for *mychtis* 328.

328 The word-order appears entirely artificial, largely an effort to
fit an elaborate(ly inflated) statement into the framework of the line. In
prose order, the statement would be 'And marchionis of mychtis most
in þe mapamond', i.e. 'As well as marqueses, the most powerful in the
entire world'.

329 *Nixt dukis in dignite*: 'Nearest/Next in honourable status to/after
dukes'; cf. 316. In the slippery grammar of alliterative poetry, *quhome*
might have any number of antecedents, e.g. *chiftanis, marchonis, dukis*.

332 *but baret or boist*: Rather than referring to the knightly spar-
rowhawks, the phrase forms the usual emphatic asseveration, 'it is not
a matter of contentious discussion', more bluntly 'truly, certainly'.

332 *beld*: In this construction, the adjective (which appears again
at 406) parallels *-bodyit*, as if it were *blyth-beld. DOST* s.v. Beld adj.[2],
finds the word difficult, 'Perhaps the pp. of Belde v., used vaguely for
alliteration and rhyme', and offers no definition. More probably, one
should associate the word with Beild v. and translate 'built, i.e. (well-)
shaped'.

333 *circulit as sapheris*: The locution echoes *AA* 21–22, more
distantly *Rauf* 475 and the mordant (but relevant to Holland's conclu-
sion) *AA* 120 'Serkeled with serpentes' (i.e. worms). The halfline follows

from *Blyth-bodyit and beld* 'of a body and shape that impresses with its beauty'. Sparrowhawks are blue-grey above ('circulit'), but their eyes themselves are yellow or red, with white eye-stripes. In such a reading, the on-verse would be independent, meaning 'With heavenly eyes to look about', or (construing *celestiale* as quasi-adverbial) 'With eyes to look about from the sky' (in allusion to hawks' customary hunting, and answering the description of eagles in 318).

338 *Cumly and cleir*: The line presumably modifies either *colour* or *cot-armour*. Cf. *Rauf* 194.

339 At this point, when he comes to describe the pursuivant's coat, Holland begins a lengthy demonstration (whatever the rhetorical apologies of 421–29, 577–81) of his capacities as herald. He describes in accurate detail two groups of blazons, first those of great powers, next those of the contemporary Douglases (see 380n). All these are symmetrically displayed as three sets (two of them Douglas) of four blazons each. The general armorial begins here with the contemporary papal arms, succeeded at 352 by the imperial arms, and followed by those of France (359) and of Scotland (365).

On the politics involved in presenting here arms of the antipope Felix V, see the Introduction, p. 43. Lines 345–46 make it clear that, so far as blazon is concerned, Holland is describing, with some inaccuracy (cf. Riddy 1986, esp. 3–4 n.17), the shield as depicted in Galbreath 1972, figure 147 (83). This blazon, as was conventional in fifteenth-century papal arms, adds papal insignia to pre-existing family arms (see Galbreath 45). Amadeus/Felix accomplished this by 'add[ing] an azure chief with gold keys' (Galbreath 47). Then, *our croce of siluer* 345 must be construed as a single grammatical unit (i.e. 'of siluer' does not describe the keys, represented in a different 'metal'), and refers to the Savoy arms beneath the blazon's chief, 'gules a cross silver', the so-called 'cross of Savoy' (Galbreath 83).

However, as Riddy sees, there remain problems. The description never identifies the tincture of the blazon proper, which is gules. The 'thre crovnis' are not separate images, but a reference to the triple papal tiara, *Dicht as a dyademe digne* 342, here replacing a helm above the shield and surmounted by its own cross, distinct from that cross described in subsequent lines as part of the blazon proper. The intervening lines 341–44 presumably describe these materials above the blazon, rather than the device itself, and refer to a background (*The burde*), and to the banderoles Galbreath's figure 147 show rising from the upper corners of the blazon proper. The latter could well be described, from the perspective of the tiara, as *Circulit on ilk syde*. In Holland's account (Galbreath offers no description), these ribbons are presumably azure, with a decorative, jewel-like semy gules. For discussion, see Galbreath 1972, 45–49 (particularly 48, figure 100), 83 (and figure 147), and Riddy's comments.

cumly to knawe: *GG* has the same locution, although with *kythen*, at 159, 490 (and *cumly ... to kyth* at 673). The complex syntax here is signalled by the fact that this line and the next form a monorhyming distych. The adjective *cumly* modifies either or both of *Thre crownis and a crucifix* (and perhaps also *gold*, as if 'clear and comely'). Similarly, the infinitive *to knawe* is basically adjectival 'recognisable'. The language here is particularly ornate, perhaps as befitting its subject, and all topped off by the additional quibble of *cleir/cler* – both 'transparent/ easily legible' and 'shining'. Further elaborations continue throughout these descriptions, here, for example, the 'envelope' formed by *He bure* at the opening in 339 and *to ... beir* 347.

340 *cler*: Here B reads *clene*. The readings are probably indifferent, but either A has assimilated the adjective to the rhyme in the preceding line, or B has attempted to dissimilate the readings.

344 *inrold*: *DOST*'s explanation of this *hapax legomenon*, s.v. In-rold adj., as 'secured by rolling' is impossible. The editors offer a similarly unconvincing account of the related Henryson, *Moral Fables* 874–75 'A croun ... | With iaspis ionit and royall rubeis rold'; see Roll v., sense 6, 'smoothed with a roller'. Rather, both locutions reflect a ME alliterative stock-phrase, 'railed with rubies' (*MED* railen v.[1], 'to ornament or adorn'). For the phrase, see *AA* 17, *PTA* 128, *SJ* 1250, *Winner and Waster* 343. This explanation, reported by Riddy, relies upon Fox's notes explaining Henryson's usage (pp. 237–38).

The real difficulty posed by *inrold* then is not lexical, but formal, the nature of the rhyme. In Scots, the diphthong of the ME word had coalesced with the vowel /a:/, and the contemporary form in Scots was presumably /ra:ld/. This vocalism allowed both Holland and Henryson to rely for rhyme on the regular equivalence between northern ME *-ald* and southern ME *-old*, both reflexes of OE -áld . See the discussion, Introduction, pp. 15–16, and note particularly the examples cited there of Holland's frequent rhymes between derivatives of OE -áld and OE -óld.

352 *secoundlie he beris*: The imperial arms are 'Or, a double-headed eagle displayed sable, beaked, langued, and clawed gules'. Here, however, as Riddy points out (1986), although described as arms of *the empriour of Almane* (358), the single-headed eagle is appropriate to the arms of the king of the Romans. Frederick III, the Hapsburg duke

of Styria, became heir to the empire in 1440 and was elected emperor in 1442, but not crowned until 1452. Thus, at the time Holland wrote, he still bore his earlier arms. Although customarily in alliterative verse *feild* should receive both stress and rhyme, here *Syne* alliterates (cf. 359, where, however, rhyme on *syne* is not necessary for the verse to be metrical).

353 The line crossrhymes /s/ with /sp/ (*samen:-splay*). The eagle's 'displayed' members are its wings, and conceivably Holland wrote *pennes*, to rhyme with *-plait*, which would form an ab/ab line.

360 *Thre flour de lycis of Fraunce*: The arms known as 'France modern', 'azure, three fleurs-de-lis or'.

364 *blenkit*: A *bloutit* is not sensible; the only similar root in *DOST* is the certainly inappropriate Blout adj. 'bleak, bare'. Mindful of *lynkit* 365 and of the potential for stanza-linking, Amours (followed by Riddy) adapts B *blenkit*. Aslaon apparently did not recognise the word here and offered a homoeograph.

365 *Tharwith lynkit in a lyng*: Presumably a reference to the 'auld alliaunce' between Scotland and France, designed to withstand English aggression. Archibald 'the grim' Douglas's son and grandson both were French, as well as Scottish peers, and the former was slain fighting the English in France; see Brown 1998, 203–26 passim.

366 *He bure a lyon*: The arms of Scotland described here represent those used by Robert II and Robert III, 'Or, a red lion rampant, with double tressure red, flory' (see McAndrew 2006, 208 on 'the royal tressure', a heraldic bearing distinctive to the Scottish crown, and the images at 176 [chart 9.5]). The flowers of the encircling 'dowble tressure', a double bordering fillet, are indeed, as Holland says, *flour de lycis* (371).

as lord modifies *He*. For 'gay goules' (cf. 413 and more distantly 590), see *Rauf* 667.

368 *Richt*: I follow Amours in adapting the B reading; the word, here meaning 'upright', offers specific detail supporting the heraldic *rampand*. Aslaon has probably assimilated the adverb to *rike* later in the line. With the off-verse (and that of 669), cf. the variously formulaic *GG* 15, 133; *Rauf* 478, 480, 550, etc.

370 *dowble*: Holland apparently rhymes the second syllable, with *a-'bout*. For such rhymes, see the Introduction, p. 49. Aslaon's omitted distych can be paralleled elsewhere in stanzaic poetry and often simply results from a scribe's losing his place in a form characterised by repetitive rhyme. Here Aslaon's omission may have been stimulated by memorial contamination, forgetting whether *of ... gold* 369 was the phrase he had just copied or the one he should take up next for copying, and seizing on the similar *Of gowlis* 372.

373 *signes*: The line does not alliterate, and I have replaced *armes*, to create a cross-rhyme of /s/ and /sk/ (a similar rhyme involving *Scotland* also occurs in 485). *armes* may have intruded as a way of reducing repetition here; cf. *signe* 377 and 378 and note the echoic uses of *schawe* 373 and 377.

374 *sanct Margaretis heir*: She (1046–93) was queen to Malcolm Canmore (and a Wessex princess). Margaret was indeed a mighty Scottish progenetrix, three of her sons ruling Scotland in succession, 1093–1124. Equally, she was a woman of great faith and devotion – a Lanfrancian reformer of the Scottish church, founder of Dumfermline abbey (which housed her tomb/relics until the Reformation), and patron of an elaborately decorated gospel book (Bodleian Library, MS Lat. liturg. f.5). She was canonised in 1250.

380 With the off-verse, cf. *AA* 305.

The armes of þe Dowglas: The pursuivant bears not simply royal arms, but those of Holland's patrons, the Douglases, associated with the preceding discussion by their staunch support of Scottish kings. Amours explains clearly Holland's slightly confusing presentation; the poet describes two partly overlapping groups of four coats each. First, at 407, he refers to *Four flurist our all*; these arms, in the account mainly reserved for (much) later discussion, represent those associated with the contemporary line, the sons of James 'the gross': (1) the arms of Douglas at the time of the poem (408); (2) those of Holland's patron, Archibald, earl of Moray (586), (3) those of Hugh, earl of Ormond (599–602, with the next), and (4) those of John, lord of Balvenie. The depiction, however, is complicated by a second, and more extensively discussed, quartet, presented in 408–18, 547–79. These are the quarters (cf. *cassyn þe cognoscence quarterly* 417) of the mid-fifteenth-century family arms, borne by the earl Douglas, at the time of the poem James's son William. The whole is introduced (398–409) by a prominent element in the family's full 'achievement of arms', the green tree, an element which Holland has carefully integrated with his depiction of natural growth and plenty elsewhere in the poem.

As Amours also shows, probably the fullest surviving analogue to Holland's account appears on James 'the gross''s tomb in St Bride church, Douglas. This, just as does the poem, presents the family's full 'achievement of arms', including a crest, the peacock, and supporters, wild men with clubs (cf. 612–19). As a blazon, James's tomb displays the same arms as does Holland, 'quarterly 1st, Douglas; 2nd, Galloway;

3rd, Murray of Bothwell; 4th, Lauderdale'. These were the arms not only of James 'the gross', but also of his two older sons, the eighth and ninth earls. (The latter revised the blazon at least twice after 1455; see the form recorded in the oldest Scots roll of arms [c. 1455–58, with later additions], Campbell 1995, 18–19, and 612n below.) In his section of photographs, following 150, Brown 1998 provides images of Douglas heraldry, including two seals with some heraldic detail, including the green tree, and a partial depiction of James's tomb. See further the drawings of James's tomb and its heraldry, Fraser 1885, 1:441–42.

381 *Knawin throw all Cristindome*: This is not an exaggeration (as it might be for many an English noble of comparable status), and Brown exports the poem's locution as title for his chapter discussing the early fifteenth-century earls (1998, 203–26). The Douglases' lofty status continued well after James's crusade, which provides Holland's central episode (443–553; see the Introduction, pp. 35–41). Archibald 'the grim' was a notable combatant, opposing the Black Prince at Poitiers in 1356 (although he is unmentioned in Froissart's account); the fourth earl was also duke of Touraine in the Loire valley (and died in battle at Verneuil in 1424); and so late as 1450, William, the eighth earl, made a triumphant pilgrimage to the Roman jubilee. The underlying construction of the line is 'Knawin able be conysance', i.e. 'Recognised, from his cognisance, as capable ...'

382 *þe wer-wall*, 384 *barmekyn and bar*: The first of these lines (made the title of a chapter, Brown 1998, 132–56) is reminiscent of Bower's epithet 'defensive wall': 'antemurale tuum [Scotland's] contra Anglorum insultus' (7:42/14–15, as well as 'solidum ... fulcimentum' 42/23). However, Bower here describes, not Douglas, but the Bruce; cf. 483n for the complementary exchange of epithets, in which King Robert I receives a cognomen that, in Bower, is associated with his most faithful servant. With the off-verse (and the variant at 576), cf. *GG* 98.

384 *bene*: This form is most sensible as a postposited adjective; in ME alliterative poetry, see *Pearl* 110, *GGK* 2475, *WA* 1715. But the word is more common in Scots, and frequently postposited in verse, e.g. *Rauf* 679. Here *bene* probably does not modify the juxtaposed *blud*, but rather one of the Douglases' two epithets, i.e. 'both noble battlement and barrier for (all of) Scots blood'. In any event, the rules governing assignment of stress in an alliterative longline indicate that this probably cannot be the present plural *bene*.

391–93 The initial distich rebuffs modern punctuation. Fundamentally, *Thar* at the head of the second line rephrases the opening of the preceding one. Translate 'I turn to compose (about) the arms of the ever honourable bold Douglases (who) ...' Equally, *Dowglas* remains ambiguous in grammatical number. The arms pertain to the entire family line, as line 385 asserts (and *Thar* 392 implicitly reiterates). Yet *Quhilk* 393 focuses the account upon but a single Douglas, the head of the line, James 'the black', 'the doughty Douglas' indeed.

393 The line should probably to be construed to rhyme as abb/ax, with nominal stresses on *oft* and *in*.

395 *Reid þe writ of þar werk*: See the Introduction, pp. 40–41.

398 *Brusit*: The word certainly means 'embroidered', but it also conveys 'assimilated to the Bruce' (as well as – in an echoic technique typical of alliterative poetry – accumulating the connotations of other proximate words of similar phonetic form, e.g. *blissit* 394, more distantly *blyth-* 393 and 399).

ane grene tre: Brown 1986, following 150, provides an image of the seal of William, first earl Douglas (*d.* 1384), with his arms and a crest pendant from the green tree (cf. 405), and additional paired trees in the background. Cf. McAndrew, who describes the 'shield suspended by a guige in front of a tree' (2006, 141). The 'guige', a strap or lanyard (originally to support the shield in battle), appears in the poem as *tuscheis* 405. For further images of Douglas heraldry, including the green tree and the full achievement of family arms with wild man supporters, see Fraser 1885, 1:190, 199, 291, 354, 450, 476; and the verbal descriptions, Stevenson and Wood 1940, 2:316–20.

402 *O Douglas O Douglas*: Recorded as the family, and thus Scots, war-cry from an early date, apparently first in a successful night assault upon Edward III in 1327; and again in the pyrrhic triumph over the Percys at Otterburn (1388); cf. *Bruce* 5.335–66; Brown 1998, 21, 85, 128. McDiarmid (1969, 290 n.47) construes 'tender and true' – as he points out, repeated at 286 and 992 (cf. further 439), as part of the motto as well.

404 With the off-verse, cf. *Rauf* 459; *AA* 503, more distantly 569, 588.

405 *tuscheis*: The word probably also occurs at *AA* 355, printed as 'The *tasselles* were of topas', but with the variants *tasses, tasee*, and *lace*.

406 With the off-verse here (and in 588), cf. *Susan* 195.

408 *as chief*: Holland's phrase is just a little too clever, and confusingly seems to communicate three different (yet integrally related) statements. Most obviously, and normatively, it identifies the shield to be described as 'the chief', slightly redundantly identifying it as the top one of four. Equally, and appropriately, it is the blazon borne by the head

of the Douglas family and retinue, as if progenitor of the remainder. However, this sense is inflected against two differing heraldic uses of the word *chief.*

The phrase may, especially given the subsequent *Syne* 413 (perhaps coordinated with the use in 404), refer to the more specific 'dexter chief quarter'. The phrase describes those arms displayed in a shield's upper left quarter (as seen by an observer). This is the 'most honourable' quarter and customarily reserved for the patrinomial arms, whilst the other quarters present honours of later acquisition.

However, the ongoing grammar of the poem presupposes a second heraldic sense of *chief.* In an heraldic account, *chief* refers to a differently tinctured horizontal rectangle at the top of the blazon. And Holland's developing sense is 'I beheld one on high that bore, as (an heraldic) chief, in azure, ... silver stars ...'

Lines 409–12 indeed describe the original family arms, with the single augmentation earned by 'James the black'/'the good Sir James', its origins to be narrated in 436–533. The earliest Douglas arms, described here, are 'Argent, on a chief azure, three mullets argent'; a heraldic 'mullet' is a six-pointed star (for the stars' symbolic value, see 430–35). To this coat, the descendants of 'James the black' (apparently first recorded from Hugh 'the dull', s. xiv$^{2/4}$) *Addit in þar armes* (438) a red heart. See McAndrew 2006, 140–41 and Brown 1998, 76, 122–24.

The line probably rhymes on *Ane ... heigh ... -held.* However, the line's emphasis would imply that greater prominence should be given to *crope* in /k/ and *cheif* in /tš/, thus an ab/ab pattern. This would represent, not a phonic rhyme, but apparently an 'eye-rhyme' of /k/, spelled *c*, and /tš/, spelled *ch*. A further example may occur at 605 'War **chen**ȝeit so **che**valrus þat no **crea**tur', although Holland here may rhyme aa/ xa, i.e. /kre:a-**tšy:r**/, with both off-verse stresses on this concluding word. Although one would regard rhyme of /k/ and /tš/ as 'strained', apparent examples occur in *AA*, e.g. 680 'Als the cheualrous knyghte has chalanchede as ayere' (a number of further ambiguous instances, e.g. 269), and cf. *DL* 207. Analogously, in *MA*, most lines with apparent alliteration on the infrequent sound /tš/ and its voiced counterpart /dž/ are in some respect defective and may rely on similar licence; see examples with /tš/ at 172, 208, 531, 682; with /dž/ at 245, 340, 372–75, 612.

410 *part of þe feld*: This seems to be another small (and confusing) heraldic quibble. Rather than the description I have provided in the preceding note, the trick for the device in chief might be described as 'three mullets of the field', i.e. in the same 'metal' as the ground of the blazon. Thus translate *part of* as the adjectival 'sharing with'; this

reading requires translating the on-verse of 411 as implicitly (and redundantly in heraldic terms) '(Which) was also silver (and) set …' The line cross-rhymes /s/ and /st/ and shows the rhyme-pattern aab/xb.

411 *heirly*: The entry in *DOST* provides only the three uses in this poem, and the word does not appear in *MED*. As Amours sees, its derivation, and thus sense, is unproblematic; cf. OE herrlic.

413 *Syne in … þe mold*: 'Afterwards, in the earth'. Were one to coordinate *Syne* here with the usage in 404, it introduces a blazon lower in position; in these terms, the description moves vertically, from top/chief to bottom/mould. However, this usage is figurative only, for the arms described here are those of the Douglases' second quarter, that immediately to the right of the patrinomial arms. It is equally the case that *mold* here must also mean 'the (heraldic) field'. These are the arms of Galloway, to which Holland will return at 560 and redescribe at 568–72: 'Azure, a lion rampant argent, langued gules, crowned or' (McAndrew 2006, 206; cf. 183–84, 267, and 134 [chart 7.8], the second shield from the left at the foot).

In spite of the later repetition, Holland here describes the customary mid-fifteenth-century Douglas arms, which quarter, first, Douglas; and second, Galloway separately. But it is possible that the stanza seeks to depict the arms of the progenitor of the fifteenth-century line, Archibald 'the grim' (d. 1400), third earl Douglas, who bore 'impaled arms of Dexter, Douglas; Sinister, Galloway'. 'Impaled' means the two figures are side by side; cf. *samyn half* 434, which may be intended as heraldically specific.

417 *Quhilk*: Rather confusingly, coordinated with the word's earlier appearance in line 409.

418 *With barris of best gold*: Cf. the repetition at 579 and the note there.

420 *Of metallis and colouris*: A set phrase, indicating a basic heraldic distinction, between 'natural' colours and those representing metals. In a line rhyming on /t/, Holland probably intends that one stress the second syllable *me-'tall-is*.

tentfull: The word appears as a hapax legomenon in *DOST*. But cf. *MED* tentfulli 'attentively', with two citations, once from Robert Manning, once as a scribal variant at Chaucer, 'The Clerk's Tale' E 334.

422 *in dewlye desyre*: 'in a measure appropriate to what I would wish'.

424 *hartlie but hyre*: i.e. 'I am doing this sincerely, not in hope of reward'.

425–29 Both Amours and Riddy, correctly, I believe, put a full stop at the end of 424. They see the central difficulty in parsing the remainder of the stanza as 427 *Tharin to harrald I held*, which they agree in translating 'I leave to heralds'. But this interpretation, first, does not explain *Tharin*, and second, as neither editor realises, probably requires at least one active emendation, construing *held* as *yheld* or *ȝeld* or *'eld* (and perhaps a second emendation to *harrald[s]*?).

While this line is far from pellucid, past editors may overlook the real difficulty here. This is a locution that seems perfectly simple and straightforward (an immediate reason for suspecting that it may be scribal), *That bene* 426. The Midland English plural *bene* never appears in the poem (as noted above, in 384 the form must represent an adjective); Holland regularly uses the expected *ar*. The passage would make reasonable sense (424 and 427 would seem to contradict one another in any interpretation), were one to emend *bene* to *be(i)re* (cf. 436). One might recall that Asloan's single certain error in the passage discussed in the Introduction (p. 51) involves writing *n* where *r* was intended in 550.

I would translate the lines loosely: 'I would avoid formally enunciating the full historical sweep (*lang dait*) of honour and leadership associated with those bearing these arms. However, because they (either the bearers of the arms or the arms themselves) emboldened the Bruce, I will write about that, as well as I know how'. The contrast, partly obviating the apparent *non sequitur* of 424 and 427, is between a full historical account and a *pars pro toto*, a single illustrative episode, in Holland's words *part of þe principale* 423, not the whole. At the centre of this interpretation (and perhaps elegantly skirted in my translation) is a reading of line 427 differing from that of my predecessors.

I take *harrald* to be an infinitive, 'to perform/provide information like a herald'. *held*, then, must be the auxiliary controlling this form, which I would translate literally as 'I turn aside'. This is a reflex of OE *héldan* 'bend, bow'. I would see *Tharin* 427 as a loose restatement of the preceding two lines, which, as my translation indicates, provide the object of the verb *harrald*. Whilst still not altogether comfortable with this reading (and it is possible that *bene* is not the single problem of transmission here), this account of the lines appears to me more plausible than my predecessors' suggestions.

430 *constance*: The line may be a syllable short of a metrical off-verse; as a result, this spelling must be understood to represent 'constancy', or one must assume that both scribes have dropped a metrically necessary but grammatically otiose repetition of the preposition, reading *and of*. The latter may be preferable, since neither *DOST* nor *OED* records the

word 'constancy' before the sixteenth century (although it may always be available as a nonce-reflex of Latin *constantia*).

432 *Forþi*: The sentence unfolds in reverse of the expected order; its centre is 'Therefore this sign, the azure ground ..., was sent ... in tokening ... since he was the most loyal/faithful ...'. I see no very ready way to supply this line with adequate alliteration.

433 *all Scotland*: Cf. 382–85, the claim instantiated by concentration on properties in the peripheries of the realm, from the Middle March with England (Ettrick) to the far southwest (Galloway) and the northeast (Moray).

434 *trewly to tend*: Cf. *GG* 344 'I rede ye tente treuly'.

436 *bludy*: Answers *Of gowlis full gracious* 412, and is probably intended to suggest a connection with the Sacred Heart, into whose 'presence' at the Holy Sepulchre James Douglas is alleged to have carried Bruce's heart.

437 *in þe steid*: At Cardross, mentioned in 464, a detail probably derived from Barbour. Similarly, both Froissart (ch. 20; 1:67) and Barbour mention the weeping lords and ladies. Holland probably expects one to notice the contrastive parallelism between the historical event, the death that befalls even heroes, and the conclave convened to hear the owl's case, a debate over prideful apparel (cf. 122n).

443 For *roy* and *rayken* (the verb) in collocation, see *GG* 1073, 1275.

444 *With all þe hart þat he had*: For king Robert's pilgrimage of desire, see the Introduction, pp. 36–38.

445 *was ... dowit*: *DOST* takes *dowit* to be a *hapax legomenon*; the editors gloss the word 'oppressed?' and associate it with Dutch *duwen*. (Cf. *OED* dow v.[4], cited only from Caxton, where it is a direct borrowing from a source-text in Dutch.) It would seem more sensible to identify the form as an extended (and ironic) use of the verb *dowen* 'endow' (*DOST* dow v.[2], 'gave/bestowed entry [to a property]; enriched'). This reading requires a slightly different construction than the scribes report, and I have inserted the necessary *was*.

Predictably, Holland's account of James Douglas's heroic devotion is that point in the poem where he must engage most directly with traditional alliterative diction. Here he alludes – but only alludes – to the commonplace *derf deid*, e.g. *GGK* 1047, *MA* 3778. However, in such contexts, the spelling *deid* represents the heroic 'deed', not the powerless 'death'. As the transforming echo (not to mention the insistence of 462–63) indicates, for Holland 'the paths of glory lead but to the grave'. Whilst this perception forms the motive of all heroic poetry, it equally gestures at the logic underlying natural plenitude, replenishment of the attrition brought by death – and offers a powerful prolepsis of Holland's moralising conclusion. References to 'derf deaths' do appear elsewhere in the tradition, but are rhetorical effects just as calculated as Holland's, e.g. Arthur's 'A! dowttouse derfe dede' (*MA* 3967) or Jesus's 'Full derfely my dede schall be dight' (the York *Gethsemane* 131; cf. 482 and the note).

447 Translate the line: 'As that worthy man praised for honourable deeds and the one whom it was (thus) most wise to choose' (although *wysest* might equally well be construed with *worthy*). The line paraphrases Bruce's instructions, as Barbour reports them at 20.193–96 (cited in the Introduction, pp. 37–38). But equally cf. the numerous parallels, *GG* 198, 211, 363, 513, 551, 787, 1099.

The prominence of *worthy* here may be intended to evoke the Nine Worthies, the greatest warriors of history (three each Jewish, classical, and Christian). Such an allusion might be particularly pregnant here, given the existence of a Scottish tradition with ten worthies – the added figure the Bruce himself (see *GG* 1236ff.n). Here the king's honour is displaced, or perhaps more accurately, doubled in Douglas's actions.

448 *þai*: I follow Amours and Riddy in preferring this B reading to A *þow*.

449 *To ga with þe kingis hart*: The halfline specifies the *gre* 'prize' in the preceding, and one understands implicit 'Namely'. The line presumably rhymes ab/ba, a bit limply, with the subsidiary rhymes on the two uses of *with*.

growit: A word of infrequent occurrence, here probably a reminiscence or citation from Barbour's praise of James Douglas's antipathy to treason:

> Our all thing luffit he lawte,
> At treasoun growyt he sa gretly
> Yat na traytour mycht be him by,
> Yat he mycht wyt yat he ne suld be
> Weill punyst off his cruelte. (20.526–31)

One might recall that the owl shows a subheroic inability – Barbour compares Douglas here with Fabius (the cunctator) – to maintain such courage (see 51 and note). See further 48n for citations associating the owl and treachery.

450–59 Holland reformulates the speech Barbour assigns Douglas at this juncture:

I thank ȝow gretly, lord ...
Off mony larges and gret bounte
That yhe haff done mee fel sys
Sen fyrst I come to ȝour seruice.
But our all thing, I mak thanking
Yat ȝe sa dyng and worthy thing
As ȝour hart, yat enlumynyt wes
Off all bounte and all prowes,
Will yat I in my ȝemsall tak.
For ȝou, schyr, I will blythly mak
Yis trawaill, gif God will mee gif
Layser and space swa lang to liff. (20.233–44)

452 'Me' is implicit, signalled by the use two lines later.

456 Cf. *GG* 1081, describing the subheroic man who 'mare luffis his life than lois'; the echo at 528, enveloping the full account, demonstrates Douglas's fulfillment of his words.

458 Cf. *WA* 1411, *Pearl* 153–54, *Cln* 855, *MA* 3494.

459 *at wis*: '(Even) at your wish, were it my destiny, (to pass) to the (point of) death with you'.

460 With the on-verse, cf. *AA* 175, *GG* 994.

469 *clos ... clene*: Like *clos ... clere*, a set-phrase, although most usually of a knight in his armour, e.g. *GG* 870–71, *WA* 1378 and 3034, but also *Pearl* 2 (cf. *GGK* 1298).

473–74 This proximate mapping of holy sites is a commonplace; cf. *The Prick of Conscience* 4601–3, 5129–32, 5183–90. *richtuis to ryng*, another locution anticipating Holland's conclusion (cf. 984), plays off of the more usual 'with richese to ring' (*GG* 497); for other analogues, see *GG* 1044, 1239, 1292; *Susan* 4.

475 Cf. *SJ* 264.

482 *to deid*: I follow Amours's insertion of B's preposition; the A reading, implying the compound *deid-dicht*, does not resemble most of Holland's repertoire. Cf. *AA* 154, 160; *GG* 603, 735. Asloan has probably dropped the preposition through haplography after the similar *þow*. The subject-verb inversion, implying a question here, is slightly peculiar. It seems to signal Douglas's longing for a living Bruce, a longing achieved in the surrogate life of the king's heart being flung amidst enemies.

483 *of Saxonis þe wand*: Cf. Bower's similar epithet for Douglas, an exchange of honorifics set in train in 382 above (see the note): 'Iste nobilis Iacobus diebus suis fortis malliator fuit Anglicorum' (7:68/16–17). Douglas was for Bower a 'hammerer', analogous to Bruce as a

wand, this word recalling the common Latin usage of *virga* 'scourge/ flail'. Given the subsequent narrative, one should note the further exchange of attributes in Bower's praise of James Douglas, 'Nobilis hic vixit, in Christo *cor* bene fixit, | Ut scriptor dixit, miles similis sibi vixit'; and 'Flos armatorum, dum vixit' (7.68/36–37, 46).

487 *connand*: I rather doubt, whatever Amours and Riddy think, that *command* is at all sensible. The scribes have simply mishandled an ambiguous, perhaps abbreviated, sequence of minims, and the proper form appears frequently in *Rauf*, e.g. at 538, 545. As always, Douglas 'keeps his word', carries through on what he had promised to do (cf. *þe behest* 470). But the covenant or pledge here is not that discussed to this point in the poem, Froissart's journey to the Sepulchre; rather, this marks Holland's switch from that narrative to the crusading account provided by Barbour.

488 *Breme*, *brath*, and *battal* routinely are collocated in alliterative verse; cf. *Destruction of Troy* 6905 and 9632, *William of Palerne* 1157.

489 *thraly in thrang*: Another anticipation of the conclusion (cf. 918, 941); for parallels, cf. *Cln* 180, 504, 754; *MA* 1150, 2217, 3755–56.

491–94 Cf. the late interpolation into Barbour, following 20.430 (where this is described as Douglas's customary behaviour), in part:

> Now pas thow furth befoir,
> As thow was wont in feild to be,
> And I sall follow, or ellis die.

495 *to be*: *be* would be expected, but *to* is metrically necessary. Douglas here envisions two alternatives, that (a) (as always in my life) I will follow you, (b) unless I am prevented by my doom. Cf. 459: here Douglas's fidelity extends to not just awaiting Bruce's will, but voluntarily anticipating what his dead lord would wish, to the point (540) that bloody Bruce heart and Douglas's own blood mingle. B simply misunderstands *feye* 'doomed to death'.

498 *bur þaim bakwart*: Perhaps recalling *Bruce* 20.437–38 'Pressyt ye Sarazynys swa | Yat yai hali ye bak gan ta'.

499 *wellit*: Although presented in *DOST* as a unique usage (for sense), see *MED* wellen v., sense 6, perhaps significantly, most usually of the pains of hell, but not citing any passive uses.

510–11 Recalling *Bruce* 20.439–40: 'And yai chassit with all yar mayn | And mony in ye chas has slayn'.

514 *Circulit with Sarazenis*: Cf. *Bruce* 20.455: 'With a gret rout enweround was'.

516 *said*: The line does not rhyme, but there is an obvious alliterating substitution for the scribes' *quod*.

518 The line probably modifies 'I' (Douglas) in the following one.

521–23 Cf. *Bruce* 20.448–50 'And quhen ye Saryzynys gan se | Yat ye chasseris turnyt agayn, | Yai relyit with mekill mayn'. With *ruschit in þe ... rowte*, cf. *MA* 2879, 2983.

525 *as fermes ynewe*: Translate 'as plenty (of people) affirm'.

526 *perell*: The line in A does not alliterate, and a noun has clearly dropped out after *in*, as B *pane* 'pain' shows. My reading assumes that Asloan's small slip has been palaeographically motivated, a fusion of two elements in the sequence *p.r ... þ.r.*

527 Cf. *Wallace* 7.1200: 'Derfly to dede [cf. *Howlat* 445] that chyftane was adew' (also rhyming, as here, with 'rescue').

529–33 See the Introduction, p. 39.

534 *and*: The word, over which B stumbles, does not seem entirely necessary; without it, one would translate, 'By this account, we understand (why), as our king granted (it to him)'. But Holland appears to argue that, although Robert made a grant, the full extent of Douglas heroism may only be assessed through the record he is providing. This shows Douglas, not simply following orders, but anticipating what his lord should have wished – which was in excess of his explicit grant.

536 For *breved in boke*, see *Cln* 197, *GGK* 2521, *WA* 4448.

537 *ful braid*: might modify either *battallis* or *baneris*.

538 *chevalrus chance*: The words appear together in alliterative rhyme at *AA* 269.

539 *worthy in weris*: Just as the off-verse of 541, the phrase presumably refers to Douglas.

541 *slang*: Riddy emends to BC *flang*, but her argument that this 'preserves the alliteration' is incorrect. A has a perfectly acceptable line in xa/aa, and its verb *slang* occurs (in nonalliterating position) in the first reference to this activity at 490. Riddy simply replicates the behaviour of the scribes, who may have been attracted by the alliteration. With the off-verse, cf. *GG* 675, 710.

542 Translate 'Then, (in the process of) retrieving it, he injures the infidels'; the line restates the preceding distych. This translation is predicated on normative alliterative usage; the cesura should fall after *agane*, indicating that it is an adverb associated with *reskewand* (not a preposition, as the scribes apparently thought). The line thus requires emendation, *men* instead of *mennis* (a reading which then must be seen as a routine bit of scribal inattentiveness, the noun attracted to the termination of the following word). The line alliterates aax/bb, with the cross-rhyme *syne:-skew-*.

547 *The sternis of anenothir strynd*: This describes the third quarter of the family blazon, 'Azure, three mullets argent', the arms of Murray of Bothwell, wife to Archibald 'the grim'.

550 *tressour*: A misread an abbreviated form or confused *r* with *n*, as Amours points out (followed by Riddy).

564 *gif he couth wyn it on weir*: Actually, Archibald conquered only west Galloway, and indeed obtained the the lordship of Wigtown ingloriously, by cash purchase in 1372. McAndrew (2006, 183–84, 267) describes these as 'arms of inferior dominion', signs of a lordship the product of territorial acquisition, rather than legitimate hereditary right. These do not represent, as Riddy suggests, 'a quartering of royal arms'; rather, the lion was the territorial 'sign' of Galloway and had been adopted as such a century before Archibald by the Balliols (cf. McAndrew 2006, 77, 332, 394).

573 *The forest of Ettrik*: From 1307, James Douglas had been active in the Borders, notably the Scots Middle March in 'The Forest of Selkirk', where he captured Roxburgh Castle in 1314. He received the lordship from the Bruce in the 1320s, and it always remained the centre of family power and influence – as well as its base for border aggression. James launched the great raids of the 1310s into northern England from this area. See *Bruce* 9.672–740; Brown 1998, 18–20, 24; and for the Douglas's Forest castle at Newark, McGladdery 2005, 172–74.

574 *landis of Lawder*: The fourth quarter of the shield is for Lauderdale, the valley of Leader Water, leading south from the Lammermuirs into the Tweed valley, just west of Roxburgh and Jedburgh. The dale, along with Ettrick Forest and the lordship of Jedburgh, formed the original lordship 'James the black' passed on to his descendants.

576 With the off-verse (along with the variant in 660), cf. *GG* 471, more distantly 784; 'out of weir' at *Rauf* 228, 'foroutin weir' 288, 'but weir' 499.

578 For the formula of the off-verse, see *GG* 213, 763, 901, 1344; *AA* 121, 190; *Rauf* 474.

579 *The barris of best gold*: Echoing 418. An allusion to the arms in the fourth quarter of the Douglas blazon, for Lauderdale, 'Azure, fretty or' (McAndrew 2006, 61). The heraldic 'fretty' describes a latticework of lines. For images and explanations of these various quartered forms, as well as the arms borne by the later Douglas generations, see McAndrew 2006, 204 [chart 10.4], 206–11.

The line has insufficient rhyme, and the culprit looks to be the word *hale*, possibly an echo of the rhyming use in 581. Derivatives of *clene* 'completely' or *clere* 'clearly' would, of course, repair the rhyme.

581 The line alliterates aba/xb, with stresses on *Re-*, *har-*, *-rald-*, *tell*, and *hale*.

586 *Secund syne*: Holland now passes to the second of the promised four Douglas blazons, that of his patron and eventual employer, Archibald, by marriage earl of Moray. These quarter the arms of Moray, from Archibald's wife Elizabeth, and of Douglas, 'Quarterly, 1st and 4th, Argent, three cushions lozengewise within a double tressure flory counterflory gules; 2nd and 3rd, Douglas' (McAndrew 2006, 211). There is also an image in the oldest Scots roll, Campbell 1995, 18–19. Thus, the on-verse in 587 and the off-verse in 590 should be read as complementary.

592 Insofar as this line alliterates at all, it does so on /th/, with rhymes on *th'armes*, *þe*, and *þar-*.

599 *erll of Ormond*: Hugh Douglas, fourth son of James 'the gross'. His title represented a new creation, a lordship of lands accrued by James in the Black Island. The title has no connection with the better-known Anglo-Irish earls of Ormonde, but was coined for Hugh as a Scotticised version of the name of 'the old council hill of Ardmeanach on the Black Isle' (Brown 1998, 270). His arms are recorded as 'Quarterly, 1st and 4th, Douglas; 2nd and 3rd, three mullets argent', i.e. Murray of Bothwell again. The differenced arms (cf. *with a differens* 600) were borne by *þe ferd*, James 'the gross''s youngest son, John, lord of Balvenie (Banffshire), whose field was ermine, not argent (McAndrew 2006, 211; although cf. Fraser 1885, 1:450, also with an image of the shield just mentioned). This 'differencing', a mechanism by which a younger son may retain some connection with the family coat whilst not compromising the rights of an elder heir, had occurred earlier in Douglas heraldry; Archibald 'the grim' bore the same ground 1364–88, and before he managed to seize the earldom, James 'the gross' did likewise (McAndrew 267 and 207, respectively). Both Hugh and John's blazons appear in the oldest Scots roll of arms, Campbell 1995, 20–21. These last Douglas shields, as Holland says in 604, bring the total described to four.

600 Perhaps the line rhymes as aba/bx, with slant-alliteration *-s'armes*. But possibly *armes* has replaced a word like *devyse* in the transmission.

604 The line apparently rhymes ab/ba, with stresses on *scheld-*, *pryce*, *pre-*, and *-sence*, and cross-rhyme of /š/ and /s/.

605 *so chevalrus*: Because *so* is linked with the subsequent *þat*, the

following word must be construed adverbially, rather than as a rather distant adjectival complement of *scheldis* 604. The 'knightly/ noble manner' Holland implies expresses the bands of family loyalty. *Of lokis nor lynis mycht lous* 606 sounds suspiciously as if Holland knows the more famous description of loyalty (*trawþe*), expressed as an inter-locked heraldic device, *GGK* 625–30 etc. On the rhyme here, see 408n.

608–11 Holland imagines the remaining, lower boughs of the tree as bearing arms of the Douglas affinity. *And* 609 functionally introduces a statement like 'As did (each shield), which was of their subordinates ... who were subservient to their wills'. As Riddy points out, with refer-ence to Stevenson 1914, 2:273–75, *Thar tennend or man* refers to 'arms of vassalage'. Feudal overlords might grant to members of their reti-nues the right to bear an overlord's arms 'with a difference'; Stevenson mentions, in particular, families from former Douglas properties, espe-cially Teviotdale, who bear the Douglas 'mullet'. This wheel contrasts such heraldry with that of the Douglases' *allyas*. Whilst this word certainly means 'allies', in context it may allude to the heraldic 'arms of alliance'. These are arms carried by the husbands of Douglas daughters, entitled to impale Douglas with their own coat (just as Archibald 'the grim' impaled his arms with Murray on his marriage). Cf. Stevenson 2:272–73.

612 *Alltherhieast*: The description now passes on to the 'full achievement' of the mid-fifteenth-century Douglas arms. Such a display includes the family's crests, helmets, and 'supporters'. The former indeed appear *Alltherhieast*, above the blazon, whilst 'supporters' are those figures represented on each side of the blazon and 'offering' that image to the viewer. Both the peacock (*povne* 614) and the green- or wild-men supporters appear on James 'the gross''s tomb. See 380n above, and cf. the later full achievement of James, the exiled ninth earl (with altered blazon), at McAndrew 2006, plate 9, following 271. Cf. McAndrew 2006, 206, describing the seal of Archibald, fourth earl Douglas, in 1413: 'a hairy savage holding in his right hand an erect club from which hangs the shield ... In his left hand he holds a helm afronté with a crest of ostrich feathers against his thigh'. Paired wild-men also appear on his father Archibald 'the grim''s seal, illustrated Brown 1998. *Alltherhieast* bears two stave-stresses to rhyme with *helmes* in the off-verse; the line is an example of aax|bab.

614 *in apart*: Translate the form reported by Asloan 'openly visible'; Amours prefers to adopt the B reading, *in aport* '(proud) in appearance'. In the context Holland has created, the peacock recalls the papal bird and alludes to the family's fidelity to Church, as well as king.

to repair: *DOST* s.v. Repar v., sense 1 cites the sense here (the halfline recurs at 901) as exemplifying a unique sense like 'ornamented'. But the verb appears frequently in ME, as well as Scots, in the modern sense 'restore, renew', surely relevant to the usage at 901 and the owl's claim to be peacock-like. Holland's usage relies upon the fairly well, although later attested, Scots sense 'furnish (with ornament)'.

615 Like 618, the on-verse here has vocalic rhymes; minimally, they fall on two of *als*, *ilk*, and *armes*.

617 *growe*: The word is cancelled in B, and Amours considers it is otiose.

620 *terrible*: The word does not alliterate and certainly sounds like scribal rewriting (but, in an alliterative context, cf. Dunbar *TWM* 266 'with a terrebill tail'). This might represent either an elegant dissimilating intrusion for *fell*, scribally suppressed as if repetitive dittography; or a substitution for a word rhyming /sp/, for example *(di)spitous* ('cruel, pitiless'; the parallel adverb at *Rauf* 901). For a metrical off-verse, *spreit* must be understood as disyllabic 'English' *spirit* or requires emendation to *spreitis* plural (cf. the emendation in 327).

622 *kyth to copy*: The sense – 'copy so as to make known' – inverts the overt grammatical relations. Translate the final pair of lines in the stanza: 'all the arms of other warriors (that were) displayed next to it (the *wodwys*)'.

632 The line has an implicit verb of motion, e.g. 'pass'. I correct the *frist* reported in A (B omits the word) to the synonymous rhyming form *erast*; Asloan has dissimilated the form from the *eir* of the off-verse.

633 Holland's alliterative rhyme here depends on placing two staves on '*lor'dinges*. The word then offers a pair of off-verse rhymes, with a tenuous connection to the on-verse, and rhymes xa/abb.

636 *rigour*: Although *DOST* rigour n. cites only three uses for the relevant sense 2b, the word is fairly common in ME, particularly in Lydgate. Cf. Mackay's comments (1981, 201–2) on Holland's recourse to Lydgatian 'aureate doction'.

637 *reir*: Although presented in *DOST* as a *hapax legomenon*, the usage represents a rhyme-driven truncation of *re(i)rd* 'outcry'. The word occurs elsewhere in the poem at 794; and cf. 13n.

638 *rerit*: The word carries two rhymes on /r/, and the line scans aab/bx.

639 *bacheleris*: Particularly in the context of *as it mycht be* 'as if they were' in the next line, one should understand an implicit 'as' here, another example of Holland drawing attention to the whimsy of his identifications of birds and social states. The hierarchical alignment of

birds of prey, paralleling the descending branches of the Douglas tree of arms, evokes an order, social and biological, the owl seeks to overturn.

642 *The pitill and þe pype-gled*: Although both nouns appear in *DOST* as unique usages, neither is particularly problematic. The first, as Amours sees, is a direct derivative of OE pyttel (cf. *OED* pittel n., which cites this passage, as well as the common *MED* puttoke 'kite', with different suffix). The first element of *pype-gled* is either echoic, given the end of the line (a fairly accurate rendition of the red-kite cries I hear outside), or implies a bird notorious for its cry. The ultimate etymon, Latin pipāre, after all, describes the sounds produced by birds.

646 Amours compares *Rauf* 415.

648–49 See *DOST* Wran n., where two other citations juxtapose the robin and the wren. Cf. *O&N* 563–64: 'Wat dostu godes among monne? | Na mo þe deþ a wrecche wranne'!

650 *dorche*: The word appears in *DOST* as a unique usage. But it simply represents a rhyme-constrained nonce-form, blending the vocalism of *droich* with the unmetathesised form *dwerch* (OE dweorg).

651 *was*: Perhaps an error for *wan* 'passed'; 'and' is implicit at the opening of the following line, also governed by the verb here.

þe harounis fa: There is no good reason why heralds should be antipathetic to the bird. After all, many less distinguished species, Cornish choughs, for example, appear as armorial devices. The scribes apparently fail to see that Holland recalls, and perhaps transposes, another pair of locutions from Chaucer's *PF*: 'the hardy sperhauk eke, | The quayles foo' and 'the eles foo, heroune' (338–39 and 346, respectively). Cf. the extensive description of hawking for waterbirds, *PTA* 208–45 (herons at 223). With the line's end, cf. *GG* 16.

hobby: *DOST* offers but a single parallel appearance of the word, but it is likely another 'anglicism'; cf. *MED* hobi n.1.

652 *steropis strecht*: This is literally an equestrian term, the bracing of a warrior in his saddle for a hard ride or a joust (as at *AA* 533–34). Here translate the rather jocular usage 'with their wings spread out, and flying quickly'.

653 With the off-verse, cf. *AA* 302, *GG* 1197, *Susan* 30.

655 *syris senȝourable*: For the singular, *senyourable sire*, see *Rauf* 714.

659–63 *iwist:blist*: The rhyme is actually *iwis:bliss*; Asloan has assimilated the verb of 663 to the earlier past tense *welcummit*, perhaps under the influence of stanza-linking *blissit* 664. However, alternation between present and past tenses is endemic in alliterative narrative. Compare *cliftis* 11 (for *cliffis*).

129

667 *wortheliche wane*: Cf. *Rauf* 7, 190, as well as *AA* 159 'worthi in won' (similarly *Susan* 54, 134).

668 *plesand all ane*: *all ane* 'all in a single group' is grammatically ambiguous. It probably modifies *þai* 667, the implicit subject of *Past* (and carried over from the independent clause in the preceding line). But it may equally well be associated, as the grammar of the line would imply, with the preceding adjective, 'pleasing to all of them, without exception'.

670 For similar locutions describing decoration, see *GG* 314, *AA* 353, *Rauf* 5 and 234.

673 *clathis*: The rhyme requires the variant *clais*; cf. *Rauf* 432, where the rhyme, however, is disyllabic *cla-īs*.

681 *pontificale*: For a metrical off-verse, one syllable needs to be suppressed. This may be one of the two medial syllables of this noun, but it is more likely that the off-verse *his* is otiose, a scribal echo of the use in the on-verse.

683 The construction is *hale ... with*, i.e. 'the complete group (of well-known figures) ... along with'. The off-verse in the following line is parallel to *cardinalis* here.

685–89 The rhyme may well be *mycht:knycht*, the transmitted forms attracted to the host of neighbouring plurals. Even if that is the case, *knycht* would remain nominally plural, another example of the grammatical adjustments in rhyme discussed at Introduction, pp. 49–50.

693 *myth*: Once again, the word is presented as a *hapax legomenon* in *DOST*. Again, it represents one of Holland's nonce-forms for rhyme, with both revocalisation and revision of the part of speech in a clearly parallel construction (see the Introduction, pp. 49–50). Here Holland's model is *MED* methe adj. 'gentle, modest, unassuming', which invariably appears with either 'mild' or 'meek'.

695–96 Translate 'With all the costly dishes that cooks could show off, when there were no dietary restrictions (lit. 'when fish were banished [from the table]')'. *Syne* 698 introduces an alternative steward for those seasons of dietary (or starvation) obligation; that the gannet, steward for those occasions, hunts by diving *fro þe firmament* (as opposed to foraging whilst wading, like the stork) probably gestures toward the religious obligation the deprivation is to serve.

698 *þe lang reid*: Riddy identifies the phrase as an Orkneyism, 'the period of poverty ... when most of the winter stocks were consumed', thus corresponding to customary Lent. *DOST* associates *reid* with ON hríð 'snowstorm, turbulent period'.

706 *þat phisik furth furis*: Just as the plants described in 29–30,

foods, which share with herbs physical properties like 'heat' and 'mois-
ture', have specifically medicinal uses.

furis: Although Amours cites *Wallace* 3.222 as unique, see the
well-attested *DOST* Fure v., from a continental cognate of OE feran
(cf. German führen). The sense is apparently 'impels or carries/brings
forth', but associations of the root with health may rely on *MED* feren
v.[4] and fere adj. 'healthy, well, strong, cured, healed' (most uses are
northern, in *WA* and *MA*, for example).

707 *maner*: AB agree in writing *man*, but have missed a suspension.

710 Cf. *AA* 341 'With al worshipp and wele', similarly *GG* 73.

714 *The blyth lark þat begynnis*: Because it is the nearly proverbial
harbinger of daybreak; cf. the appearance of the bird on Aurora's wrist
at Dunbar's 'The Thrissill and the rois' (Bawcutt's poem 52) 8–14, and
her note at 2:396. At Dunbar, 'Hale, sterne superne' (Bawcutt's poem
16) 41, the Virgin is addressed as 'gentill nychttingale'.

718–53 Both Amours and Riddy offer impressive materials, with
abundant references, on the genre of Marian lyric; see also McDiarmid
1969, 290 n.41. To these, add the important discussion, Woolf 1968,
274–308 passim. Of course, *PF* concludes with a set lyric produced
as birdsong ('But fyrst were chosen foules for to synge' 673), but a
greeting of the spring, not the religious lyric here; more nearly compa-
rable is Dunbar's poem 58/33–40, where birds are directed to produce
a nativity lyric. Here, as *þe menar* 748 promises, the birds' devotional
entertainment offers important mediation between the opening and
conclusion of *The Howlat*; see further 722–23n.

718 *Hal*: This bit of anaphora, the English equivalent to the angelic
salutation 'Ave' (cf. 736n), forms almost a defining *topos* of Marian
lyric; cf. Dunbar, 'Hale', with both the anaphora and a refrain incorpo-
rating the Latin source, 'Ave Maria, gracia plena'. See Woolf 285, 290.

temple of þe Trinite: Cf. Wenzel 1984, 9.615–18 (310–11), where
Mary is associated with the beams of the temple, for she 'strength-
ened the Church on Holy Saturday [when all others lost hope] ... [I]n
her constancy and devotion our faith is strengthened'; *Quat* 238, in a
description of Holy Saturday, states that 'All þe trewth of þis werlde
was in a trewe may'. The text Wenzel presents, a source for Chaucer's
'Parson's Tale', provides a collection of preaching materials, generally
a series of exegetical observations long commonplace in Latin tradi-
tion. But the phrase might also allude to the God-child sheltered in the
Virgin's womb, a paradox Holland again invokes at 749.

tronit in hevin: A very simple adjustment to transmitted *crovnit* will
create a metrical line. Marian lyrics frequently are structured about 'The

Five Joys' of the Virgin (cf. *GGK* 644–50); see Woolf 134–43, 297–300. Although this lyric is much more engaged with Mary as *menar*, mediator for man's sin, it alludes on a number of occasions to this devotional set, conventionally including Annunciation, Nativity, Resurrection, Ascension, and Assumption. For the first four, see, respectively, 729 (and the note), 728, and implicitly 744. Here, the invocation of the enthroned Virgin alludes to a widely dispersed extension of the 'fifth joy', her Coronation as 'queen of heaven'. Cf. EETS OS 98, 135/22 'Heil trone of þe Trinite' ('Cristes trone' at 137/97).

721 *bute ... and beld*: Cf. *GG* 938. Cf. Dunbar's formulation, 'Hale' 65–66 'Our wys pavys froenemys | Agayne the feyndis trayne', a somewhat more pointed echo of lines 384 and 515 here.

722–23 *Grane full of grace ... Ferme our seid*: Nature is also a 'noble mastres' (32) who distributes both 'granes of grace' and 'sauorus seides' (28, 31), sufficient for birds, but only for man's 'natural body'. As the further echo, that '[N]oght ... seidis of [man's] self' (977), implies, although ostensibly nobler, humans require the greater aid that the birds invoke here. Cf. Dunbar, 'Hale' 71–72 'flour de lice of paradys | That bair the gloryus grayne'.

726 Cf. Lindsay, 'The Testament of the papyngo' 25: 'As of rubeis the charbunckle bene chose'; and, more distantly, Dunbar, 'Hale' 62 'Bricht polyst precious stane'; EETS os 98, 136/26 'Heil perle, of al perey þe pris'; 137/105–6 'Charbokel neuer so cler schone | As ʒe schyne in Cristes see'.

729 *Blist throw þe bodword of blyth angellis*: Probably alludes to the Annunciation, and particularly Gabriel's 'benedicta tu in mulieribus' (Luke 1:28). In that case, the rhyme has plural for the singular of the biblical account. Alternatively, the plural in rhyme may refer more generally to angelic announcements, e.g. that to the shepherds (Luke 2:8–14). Cf. Dunbar, 'Hale' 54 'Louit with angellis stevyne'.

730 *completis all prophecis pur*: Marian lyrics routinely invoke a range of 'types' for the Virgin, Old Testament events understood exegetically to prophesy her appearance and salvific role; see 751–53 and the notes there for a sequence of standard examples. The most ubiquitous of these types, probably invoked here, is the prophecy of Isa. 11:1–2: 'And there shall come forth a rod out of the root of Jesse, and a flower shall rise up out of his root. And the spirit of the Lord shall rest upon him'. For discussion of these verses, see Wenzel 1984, 9.748–63 (318–19). But see also the provocative discussion of Mary, Wenzel 1984, 9.823–30 (322–23), where the Virgin is identified with the dawn, and with spreading branches of trees with singing birds, derived from Sap.

17:17 ('whether it were a whistling wind, or the melodious voice of birds, among the spreading branches of trees'): 'The whistling wind is the Holy Spirit that impregnated Mary with its holy breath; the voice of the birds is the preaching of the prophets, and the spreading branches of the trees are their hidden meanings'. Cf. EETS os 98, 135/46 'Heil blosme of brere, brihtest of ble'; and 136/74 'Heil gentel ȝerde of Iesse roote'.

731 *þe*: For the biblical event, the Visitation, frequently evoked in augmented lists of the 'joys of the Virgin', see Luke 1:36. AB *þi* is certainly wrong, since John was in Elizabeth's, not Mary's, womb. Amours first offers the correction (followed by Riddy) and notes the line as common error of AB (xxi). Bawcutt points out (2000, 31–33) that Holland may augment the 'joys' here in a deliberate compliment to his dedicatee, Elizabeth Douglas; cf. 989n.

732 *þi ant*: Probably for *þi n'ant,* with slant-alliteration to rhyme /n/, although unless Holland has scanned *aganis* as x x C, with alliteration on the third syllable, the line still lacks adequate initial rhyme.

733 As transmitted, the off-verse has a double strong dip. As in 681, an overly specifying demonstrative, here generated as doublet of *-ith* (and perhaps influenced by the form of 731), is at fault and should be suppressed. Since *with* is the usual ME adjective for indicating the agent in a passive construction, translate 'most distinguished by spiritual persons', possibly, and more allusively, 'most distinguished by (your) spiritual virtues'.

736 *Alterar of Eua in Aue*: See Wenzel 1984, 9.563–68 (308–9): 'She also opened paradise for us ... Eve has her name from "*eu*", which means good, and "*a*", which means without, because she lost all good [along with closing paradise] when she gave her consent to sin. In contrast, Mary was addressed with "*Ave*", that is without the *væ* ['woe'] of pain and sin. For she was not troubled in childbirth as she was not violated in conception'. The York Augustinian friar John Waldeby's first sermon on the 'Ave Maria', devoted to the salutation 'Ave', plays ceaselessly and copiously upon *a væ* 'sinless, thus truly happy (and beyond mourning)'; see Morrin 1975, 84–99.

Alterar: Although presented in *DOST* as a unique usage (and no example cited in *MED*), Holland's term is transparent. The same cannot be said of *but vre*, again a *hapax legomenon* in *DOST*, and, in its derivation from Scots *ure* 'fate' requiring an unduly contrived explanation. The extensively recorded *MED* ure n. 'use, custom' is much more to the point. *but vre* 'without (or outwith) customary usage' would imply 'against custom' (in which all women are cursed daughters of Eve), thus 'uniquely'.

737 *nocht of*: The unusual word-order (rather than expected *of nocht*) indicates that one should translate '(know) nothing of any other (well-spring of welfare)'. Perhaps *wait* should be associated, not with the common verb 'to know', but the verb *waiten* 'to watch, look for'.

740 *þi frute*: Like the Douglases' green tree, Mary is another natural source of plenty.

744 *quhar þow sittis be þi sonnis syd*: Cf. Wenzel 1984, 3.308–9 (116–17): Mary, the 'sea of glass' of Apoc. 4:6, 'is "round about the throne", because she intercedes for sinners throughout the space of all the lands'.

747 *menar*: In the manuscripts, the third letter is represented by a pair of minims, to be interpreted variously as *u* or *n*. Amours (followed by Riddy) reads A as *menar* 'mean actor, i.e. intercessor', or more directly 'medium, intermediary (between God and man)', a unique usage in *DOST*. Mary is the unique human who fully achieved salvific divine presence, and thereby, the subsequent 'mediatrix peccatorum'. Cf. Dunbar, 'Hale' 46–48: 'Thow bair the prince of prys | Our teyne to meyne and ga betweyne, | As hvmile oratrice'; and 67 'Oratrice, mediatrice, saluatrice'.

751 *seker trone of Salamon*: The first of three conventional 'types' for the Virgin; on the prevalence of such materials, see Woolf 284–87. The first and third here appear together at 'Haill glaid and glorius', STS 3rd ser. 23, 296/71–72; and in another Marian lyric, EETS OS 98, 137/97–100. For this example, see 3 Reg. 10:18 'King Solomon also made a great throne of ivory and overlaid it with the finest gold'. Cf. Wenzel 1984, 9.582–85 (549–50): 'Ivory betokens chastity, gold humility. And note that the gold covered the ivory, because humility is greater than chastity'.

752 *worthy wand of Aaron*: In Num. 17, Aaron's rod flowers without moisture, a figure of Jesus's birth with his mother's virginity preserved, through the absence of any male contact; see Wenzel 1984, 9.746–48 (318–19).

753 *ioyus fleis of Gedion*: A similar type or figure from Judges 6:37–40, since the fleece was supernaturally suffused with divine dew while all else remained dry, or alternately, remained immaculately dry while all around it was suffused with moisture. Again, the figure presents Mary as both unblemished and a tool of divine creation; see the extensive explanation, Wenzel 1984, 9.763–79 (318–21).

757 *sytharist*: As Amours notes, the word, a *hapax legomenon* in

DOST, properly denotes a zither-player, not the instrument. It has been pressed into service for the rhyme; see the Introduction, pp. 27 and 50. Riddy offers an extensive note on later catalogues of musical instruments in Scots.

759 *rivupe*: Again, a unique usage in *DOST*, although the related *MED* ribibe n. is reasonably common. Riddy eliminates the unusual form recorded in A and follows *ribupe* B.

rist: Another *DOST* hapax legomenon. However, compare the separate *DOST* wre(i)st n., 'tuning implement, plectrum', perhaps (as Amours's note indicates), a metonymy for 'harp' (similarly *MED* wreste n., sense 2a; *OED* wrest n.¹, sense 5a). In this interpretation, the manuscripts report early modern spellings, the scribes perhaps attracted by the alliteration; the line must rhyme aa/ax, since the etymon of this word is OE wræstan with /w/, although it is possible that Holland knew a form derived from ON reista (< *vreista).

760 *talburn*: As Amours's note suggests, perhaps a small error for *tabburn*, i.e. tabour.

761 *lilt-pype*: Riddy adduces Dutch lullepijp 'bagpipe' to explain the word, another *hapax legomenon* in *DOST*. But this may, like 'heron's foe' 651, particularly in the context of the following line (see 762n *dulset*), be a slightly inexact Chaucerian reminiscence; cf. 'The House of fame' 1223–24 'Liltyng-horn | And pipes made of grene corn ...'

762 The line probably rhymes aa/xa on /s/, although it might be an example of aa/bb on /d/ and /s/ with cross-rhyme with /š/.

dulset: The word appears on only one other occasion in *DOST*; in Chaucer's use at 'The House of fame' 1221, it appears to mean 'pipe or flute'.

dulsacordis: The word appears in *DOST* as a *hapax legomenon* and appears to have no ME parallel. Plainly, it is analogous to such formations as Latham's dulciloquium 'sweet speech', dulciloquus 'eloquent', and, especially dulcisonus 'mellifluous'. As the spelling indicates, the compound joins Latin dulci- with the OF derivative accord 'harmony' (cf. *DOST* Accord n., sense 3; *MED* accord n., sense 6b). If Holland has specific instruments in mind, rather than just 'pleasantly melodic sounds', they are probably dulcimers, since that word is alleged to have a parallel ultimate etymology, derived from unrecorded Latin *dulce melos.

766 *cymbaclauis*: Yet another word presented as a *hapax legomenon* in *DOST*. However, cf. Latham's cymba 'chime (the modern form of the OF derivative), gong'. Latham's citations indicate that such an instrument was used to call monks to refectory (thus translate, '[and there

were] chimes that sound so softly[, once they penetrate] into the individual monastic cells'). The second element, -*clave*, as in the modern *clavier*, indicates that the instrument produced its tones by striking a keyboard, not the resonant metal bits directly. The illustration conventional in psalters at the head of Ps. 80 regularly depicts monks playing an instrument with a series of small bells held in a wooden frame, perhaps what Holland has in mind here.

768 *ane schour*: Amours (followed by Riddy) prefers B *a schour* 'a bit, a division, a score' to A *and schour*. Whilst the emendation seems to me sensible, I would offer a different interpretation of the spelling, as a reflex of OE scūr 'shower', as Riddy implicitly may suggest. The musicians provided a plethora of notes. *DOST* connects Asloan's version with Sure adj.adv. 'with certainty of accomplishment, efficaciously, effectively'.

769 *point of paradys*: Amours cites as parallel Henryson, *Moral Fables* 1337; both uses, which describe bird-song, probably pun on the senses of *poynt*, 'a single bit' and 'a single musical note'.

771 *caryar*: Jackdaws, like American magpies, are famed for decorating their nests with various scraps and odd bits they acquire in foraging. A concatenation of relevant detail appears at *PF* 345–46: 'The thef, the chough; and ek the janglynge pye; | The skornynge jay …'

772–80 Although certainly indebted to Chaucer's 'Franklin's Tale' (see the Introduction, n.48), one might also recall the Franklin's attack on 'illusions' at F 1261–96. Similarly, the closest Scots analogue, *Ratis Raving* 1130–36, associates such transformations with the playful (and frivolous) imagination of a small child, who is able 'To mak a wicht hors of a wand, | Of brokin breid a schip saland, | A bunwed tyll a burly spere, | And of a seg a swerd of were, | A cumly lady of a clout'. For an analogue to the Franklin's suggestion that such acts are demonic, see the sermon exemplum of a 'ioculator' who turns a pease-wisp into a horse, Hanna 2008a, 193–94.

773 With the on-verse, cf. *AA* 5, 435; and with the off-verse, *AA* 43, 711; *GG* 472, 572; *Rauf* 419.

774 *Sound*: 'As well as' is implicit, following from *þe samyn hour* 772.

schippis of towr: *DOST* tour n.¹, sense 5a cites Wyntoun's Chronicle 4.681, where the phrase translates 'rostratas naves', i.e. 'beaked (for ramming in naval engagements) ships' and identifies the usage as a calque on a Celtic phrase.

775 With the off-verse, cf. *Susan* 226.

782 *corncrake*: Although there is only a single other *DOST* citation,

this is the modern bird-name. The bird is so called from its habitat, since it lives in standing corn and hay, where it emits its harsh cry.

pundar: The line does not rhyme, and this official title may have been imported from following line, where the root appears twice. Just as in 230, the synonymous English term for this office, the *hayward*, would provide an unproblematically alliterating line here.

786 *gold*: Although the word alliterates, the off-verse stresses fall on the rhymeword *'gar-'land*.

789 *iangland*: Again, this is actually a metrical off-verse. *iangland* probably has a medial syllable unreflected in the spelling (as if *iangeland*); alternatively, in alliterative tradition, the participial suffix, a derivative of ON *-andí*, is disyllabic. For the epithet, Riddy cites Whiting J 21.

794 *þe ruke with a rerd and a rane roch*: On the particularly Scots resonances of this identification, see 808n.

795 *A bard owt of Irland*: Amours considers this stanza, although recognisably imitative Gaelic, gibberish and therefore offers little explanation. In contrast to his dismissiveness, there have been several helpful discussions: Murison 1974, 78–81; Parkinson 1986, 497–98; and a particularly extensive account in Riddy's notes. Much of Riddy's report depends upon information provided her by the Edinburgh Celticist William Gillies. (His discussion of the poem, mentioned in Riddy's notes as scheduled to appear in *Scottish Studies*, has never been published.)

The Scots term 'bard' alludes to a distinguished and honoured feature of Celtic cultures. In the broad sense, 'bards' comprised a rigorously trained intelligentsia, individuals deeply schooled over a long period in mythic and historical (especially genealogical) lore, and especially devoted to praise-poetry honouring their patrons. But from a Celtic perspective, 'bard' might be perceived as somewhat dismissive. In Gaelic, the accomplished upper ranks of poets are *file*, and a lord's official poet/genealogist, an *ollamh* or *seanchaidh* (see 803 below). In contrast, 'bards' proper were not composers, but performers only; the alternative term for this role was *reacaire* 'reciter', a Latin loan into Gaelic (cf. *crekery* 805?).

All critics have found the passage expressive of a broad, if fragmentarily recorded, Scots antipathy to Gaelic, and perhaps more narrowly to the Celtic (and Norse) culture of the Isles and adjacent northern Ireland. For the Douglas family's contact with the expansive designs of the Lords of the Isles in the northeast, see the Introduction, pp. 44–45 above. In this context, the word *bard* 'entertainer' in Scots becomes loaded with pejorative associations comparable to those of *MED disour* n. or harlot n. (sense 2a), both also terms describing performers, not learned composers. Indeed, the *DOST* entry for Bard n. is littered with legal citations, prohibitions against encouraging such individuals; these group 'bards' with wandering beggars and other idlers. See further 808n.

banachadee: A truly parody opening, for the phrase of greeting, Gaelic *beannachd Dhe* 'God's blessing' seems to be the standard identifier in early Scots of a (usually scorned) Gaelic speaker. For further examples, see *Wallace* 6.140; the Bower citation in 801n; and Craigie 1923–25, 1:223/17–19. This line alliterates abb/ax.

796 Riddy makes a major contribution to understanding the two fully Gaelic lines, arguing that some of the material is exact, although corrupted in transmission. Apparently following Gillies's lead, Riddy offers some tentative translations and indeed emendations; these I summarise in the notes to this line and 798. Rather than insert her forms into the text, I have retained those reported by Asloan throughout, and I have filled in some details from materials in Thomson 1983 passim (see further his various studies of bardic culture). For Alexander Montgomerie's citation of one or two of these lines, see the Introduction, p. 15.

Gluntow: For *A' gcluin tu* 'Do you hear'?

dach ... doch: In Riddy's account, for *do dh'ola(dh) mise deoch*, or, following B's reading 'dynydrach', *tra(th) dh'ola mise deoch*, 'I would quaff a drink', or 'when I quaff a drink', respectively.

797 *Raike hir*: Through 797–806, as Riddy sees, Holland provides a traditional mock of Gaelic speakers as they attempt to speak Scots. They are supposed (the behaviour is completely imaginary) to regularly substitute the third person feminine pronoun for the first person in English (cf. Parkinson 1986, 497 n.8). Thus, translate 797–99, 806 'Give me ... or I will ... Give me a seat and a drink; what the hell's the matter with you? ... I know each one of them'. Like all linguistic ethnocentrism, this rests on a biased presumption: Scots speakers apparently noticed that the Gaelic form for 'she' is 'i' (in Gaelic, the first person is 'mi') and assumed that because the form sounds just like English 'I', silly Celtic speakers would offer in English the Gaelic equivalent for the sound.

The preceding translation partially depends on correcting a mistranscription that has survived since Amours. At the end of 799, Asloan writes ȝhe, the first letter written over 't'. And the joke extends to 801, which should be emended; there *his* is surely an error for *hir*, and one should translate 'These are my Irish kings'. With the off-verse of 799,

138

cf. Dunbar *TMW* 222 'as ye sum harme alyt'; and *Rauf* 95 'Quhy devill makis thow na dule …?' (explicitly associated with angry and over-bearing demands at 99–101).

scho sall ryme the: One bardic power was the alleged ability to inflict harm through verbal aggression. On such 'rhyming' a person (see 815), cf. Simms 1989, 184, reporting an entry for 1414 in the Irish *Annals of Connacht* concerning the poet Niall Ó hUiginn. Niall 'was already credited with causing the death of some enemies by a "poetic miracle" …, and now he joined other members of the Ó hUiginn family in composing such poisonously powerful satires against Sir John Stanley that he died in five weeks'. John Stanley was the king's lieutenant, who had been persecuting Irish learned men – and the person most usually considered the likely patron of *GGK*. For the considerably less august Scots perceptions of such poetic skills, see 808n.

798 Riddy prefers the B readings *Misch* and *mountir*, and omits *mach* as dittography after *ach*. She then transliterates the line as *Mise Mac Muireadhaigh muinntir Muigh Loch(a)* 'I am Mac Muireadhaigh of the people of Magh Loch' (=Moylough, county Meath; probably one should translate *Mac* 'a descendent of').

As Riddy points out, the family MacVuirich, MacMhuirich, or MacMuirich were the bardic *ollamh*'s in hereditary service to the MacDhomnuill (McDonald) Lords of the Isles. The family derived its power and talent from an Irish poet who fled to Scotland early in the thirteenth century, the man named here, Muireadhach Albanach (see Thomson 1968, 73–74, 82). The most famous of the line, Lachlann Mór MacVuirich, composed a famous incitement to battle (*brosnachadh*) before the engagement at 'red Harlaw' (Aberdeenshire) in 1411. Although the battle was a sanguinary draw, by it Donald MacDonald, second Lord of the Isles, solidified his claim to the earldom of Ross, eventually recognised in a royal grant to his son, Alexander. A later Lachlann MacMhuirich is identified as 'archipoeta' (i.e. *ollamh*) in a witness list to a MacDonald charter of 1485 (Munro and Munro 1986, liv–v, 187–89, 270–71). On Harlaw, where Eoin Mór, the first Ulster MacDonald, fought alongside his elder brother Donald, see Kingston 2004, 36–37, 49–50.

For the subsequent names and references to Gaelic custom, see the glossary and index of proper names, in the main dependent on Riddy's explanations (although cf. 803n, 804n).

800 *droch*: Riddy finds the word ungrammatical in Gaelic, but notes the use of *droch* 'evil' in compound forms (thus perhaps 'the evil O'Doherty'?).

801 *þe Irischerye*: Riddy wishes to connect the phrase with 'the great Irishry/Magna Irecheria', the indigenous area west of the river Bann in Ulster. However, so far as I can tell, the term would appear a legalism of the thirteenth century, only applicable until the collapse of the English earldom of Ulster in 1322. A less specific sense is implied in a document of 1425, in which James I refers to his friendship with 'his liege ande the gude alde frende of Erschry of Yrlande' (Kingston 2004, 56). The individual so described was Eoin Mór MacDonald, a younger son who became lord, not in the west Ulster areas earlier identified as 'the Irishry', but in the Glynns of Antrim. One should probably translate 'These are my Celtic-speaking kings ruling the Irish'. In the line, *ar* apparently bears one stave.

Murison 1974, 79 describes this account as 'a kind of burlesque' of an important bardic duty. The office of *ollamh* or *seanchaidh* required catalogue lore of a sort analogous to that Holland assembles about the Douglases, materials for factually exact genealogical panegyric. But in contrast to Holland's mock-apologetic restraint (cf. 421–29, 577–81), the rook, with the owl and the raven, is one of three figures in the poem who cannot shut up and who are characterised by their *rude ranes* (perhaps not coincidentally, the noun is probably a Gaelic loan into Scots). Celtic genealogical presentations rely upon exact renditions of extensive accounts, and Murison cites Walter Bower's partly Gaelic description of one such, at the coronation of Alexander III in 1249 (5:294). For an even more extensive example of such a lineage, that of the Cambro-Viking king Gruffudd of Gwynedd, see Russell 2005, 52–59 [¶¶2–6]).

802 *O'Knewlyn*: Riddy reports Margaret Mackay's suggestion, in her unpublished thesis, that one should read *O'Kuewlyn*, i.e. Cúchulainn, the hero of the Old Irish *Tain* and of the Old Irish 'Ulster cycle' generally. The suggestion is attractive, because the following name *O'Conochor* could well refer, not to a family of O'Connors, but to Cúchulainn's lord, and king of Ulster in the 'cycle', Conchubar mac Nessa. (His consort, Medb [Maeve, Mab], is probably better known to English speakers.)

803 *claischach*: This is the form Asloan writes, and B *clarschach* is correct. On the clarsech (or cruid), the Irish harp, see Stewart 1972, 9.

804 *benschene*: Both Riddy and Parkinson interpret the form as representing either Gaelic *bean seinn* or an error for Gaelic *bean scheire* 'a keening woman'. But one might notice that the sequence *schene* has appeared in the preceding line and arguably may have been echoed in the spelling recorded here. Reading simply *bensche* might be somewhat

less problematic than Riddy's suggestion; one would associate the form
with *bean sidhe* 'faery woman', perhaps an equally screechy figure (cf.
modern 'banshee'). A passing reference at Murison 1974, 81 implies
that he understood the word so.

808 *sparit no thingis*: As *DOST* Bard n. amply exemplifies, bards
(not necessarily Irish) are persistently associated with abusive language,
scolding and insult. But in literary tradition, the behaviour has a strongly
anti-Celtic tinge. Dunbar, *Flyting* 16 would avoid flyting, for 'wondir
laith war I to be ane baird' (one could compare the equally sanctimo-
nious nightingale at *O&N* 176–86). A major strain of Dunbar's invective
against the 'Highland' Walter Kennedy tars this adversary with what are
explicitly 'Irish' bardic behaviours (including vagrancy); cf. 49, 62, 96,
145, 183, and especially:

> Quhat ferly is thocht thow reioys to flyte?
> Sic eloquence as thay in Erschry vse,
> In sic is sett thy thraward appetyte. (106–8)

Some of Dunbar's materials in this strain include probable reminiscences
of *The Howlat*, particularly *Flyting* 141–42; cf. the similar locution at
'The Seven sins' (Bawcutt's poem 47) 116–17, describing a degenerate
'heland pad3ane': 'Full lowd in Ersche begowth to clatter | And rowp
lyk revin and ruke' (and Bawcutt's note, 2:388).

809 For the raven's earlier appearance, see 216ff. Parkinson 1986,
498 observes that, while *Corby messinger* 'could be applied to any unre-
liable servant', that the epithet is particularly apt, given that the raven
is a *corbanus* 'a rural dean'. Riddy cites Whiting M 516 and notes the
reference to the biblical account of Noah at Gen. 8:7. In 813, *ischit*
is not absolutely necessary to the line's vocalic alliteration and might
be construed as a word in /š/ alluding to the OE past tense/participle
gesciten, a prolepsis of the bard's unfortunate fate at 824–27 (as well as
to *shut* 'exiled').

815 *guttis and gall*: The phrase is repeated at 840. When the Irish
rook says this, it is bardic curse, the intention to harm the raven in these
organs. Further, the bard seems to have a specific and just 'personal-
ised' curse in mind. Cf. *MED* gut n., senses 1b and 1c; and galle n.¹,
senses 1a and 3 (the latter paralleled in citations at *DOST* Gall n.¹).
Both nouns, the first associated with gluttony, the second with rancor
or malice, accord with the raven/rural dean's behaviour, as described
at 215–21. When the phrase *guttis and gall* reappears, following the
jesters' devastating mockery of the bard (now exiled to clean himself;
see the previous note), it is a realised statement of physical damage –

apparently available even to 'fools', but *not* to bards. In contrast, the raven is only shamed by the bard's accuracy of portrayal, but not physically injured, and the bard's 'rhyming' may have failed of its object.

820 *flyrand* (cf. *mowis* 831): See Fletcher 2000, 18 on professional 'contortionists', moue-makers.

823 *thevisnek*: Amours finds the only other Scots use, also in *DOST*; the tuchet can appropriately call the rook by the name, since in *The Complaint of Scotland*, this is identified as the lapwing's cry. Here, of course, it is transformed into a probably ethnic insult, for at least one traditional Anglophone characterisation of Celtic peoples is as thieves; for references, see Hanna 1995, 83–85 (here of the Welsh).

824 *fylit*: Amours and Riddy follow B *fylit him*. While the reading is attractive, it is not truly necessary, since the object is clear from *him* 823 (which may have attracted Bannatyne). Although moderns tend to find anal behaviours like this offensive, rather than amusing, they were once routine forms of entertainment; cf. Langland's Hawkin, who laments his failure at minstrel entertainment 'for I kan neiþer … | Farten ne fiþelen at festes' (*PPB* 13.230–31); or the amusement expressed by Dunbar's narrator at a similar event, 'The Seven sins' (Bawcutt's poem 47) 202–7, 217–22. See further Fletcher 2000, 19, 24–25, 33, 114, 246–48, 326 nn.67 and 69, 327 n.71, 373 n.223; and Allen 2007 passim. Of course, the flyting also occurs publicly and makes skill at envisioning potty behaviour into an art form; cf. the comments at Mapstone 1999.

825 *smaddit*: The form is presented in *DOST* as unique (and is one of only two *OED* citations). Similarly, *DOST* also presents 827 *ydy* as a *hapax legomenon*; in this vocalism (< ON iða), as Riddy argues, the word probably represents an Orkneyism (and appears later only in Orkney and Shetland dialect). Cf. the modern *eddy* 'a whirlpool in a stream', cited as English by *OED* from 1553.

828 Cf. *GG* 1068: 'The lordis … for liking thay leugh'.

833 *figonale*: The word has always been problematic, in *DOST* as an undefined *hapax legomenon* and the only use known to *OED*. Usually, discussions of this derivative of a medieval Latin adjective in -*nalis* have largely attended to the modifying phrase *of frut* and suggested a translation like '(wicker?) basket for figs (or fruit)'. However, that interpretation would seem to suggest derivation from a Latin word in *fic*-, and it would be preferable to associate the received spelling with a derivative of Latin fingere (pp. fictus/*figtus). Cf. Latham's entries for figulator and figulus, both meaning 'potter'; assuming an unrecorded *figunalis* 'earthenware (dish or jug)' might represent more nearly what Holland has in mind here.

834 *tuchet*: A may read *tuthet*.

gird to: A bit of traditional alliterative battle diction, here used parodically; cf. *GG* 105 and 539; *Rauf* 149, *AA* 582.

839 *reid*: The word, 'an animal's stomach', appears but once in both *DOST* and *MED* (rede n.[1], from the northern *Sir Tristrem*). But see the extensive discussion *OED* reed n.[2] (with suggested etymon OE reada) and further, rud n.[4], a Staffordshire dialect form.

843 *remelis raucht*: As Amours points out, this is a set collocation ('delivered heavy blows') in early heroic verse, e.g. *Bruce* 12.558–59; and see *DOST* Rummill n., sense 1.

848 *greably*: Although the single example cited in *DOST*, *MED* greable, greabli provides a fair conspectus of uses; the word may represent another Lydgatism.

849 Cf. *Rauf* 143, 726.

853 In contrast to the completely parenthetical address to the audience in the off-verse of the preceding line, here the off-verse, as the parallel construction indicates, modifies/expands upon *lordis* 852. Then, 854 follows directly from *sucour*, 'he asked their aid, namely that they would ...'

856 *At*: uniquely in the poem, not representing the preposition, but the northern conjunction 'that'.

860 Like line 420, with *me-'tal-*, here the suffix *-tuale* may provide an alliterative stave in rhyme with *temp-*. The off-verse is probably metrical, since *kend* here is simply a variant spelling for the full past tense form *kennit* (the form reported in B). While Asloan universally writes apparently monosyllabic *kend* forms, cf. his alternation between *callit* (universal in the past tense, as well as in about half the uses of the past participle) and *cald* (only as participial form).

862 The line does not alliterate; perhaps *Natur* is a substitution for *þe goddess*. But both 866 and 867, although equally susceptible to conjectural repair, fail to meet minimal rhyming requirements. In the first of these, one might replace the limp rhyme-word *was* with *pas*, whilst *netherit* for *discendit* would emphasise Nature's cooperative willingness to address the owl's nature (and rebut his charge in 105).

878 Translate 'Because I myself have travelled here on your account'.

896 *Fro Burone to Berwike*: This locution conveys a sense of universal extent, from extreme north to extreme south, analogous to Chaucer, 'General Prologue' 692, 'Fro Berwyk into Ware' (phrasing that Holland may wittily be revising). Amours points out that the first

placename refers to an Orkney locale, another sign of Holland's origins in the far north.

904 *counterpalace*: *DOST* cites the word only once elsewhere, at *Wallace* 10.524. The owl's absurdly flashy garb recalls the description of the peacock, at 84 presented as the logic for choosing this bird as pope – as well as the amalgam of colours in the papal arms of 339–47. Of course, the owl remains even more monstrous in his patchwork quilt of various plumage, particularly as opposed to the 'clear colours' of Douglas arms (cf. 434–35). Cf. further 911–14.

910 *quhruyne*: *DOST* implictly suggests an emendation. The editors associate the spelling *ruyne* with the word *quhryne*, a derivative of primitive ON **hvrina*, the recorded ON *hrina* 'to squeal'. All other examples cited in *DOST* have spellings in *quh-*; in transmission of *The Howlat*, this appears to have been assimilated to the much more common noun 'ruin'.

914 (and 944) Cf. *Quat* 416 'Full scharply to schawe'.

918 *wycit, walentyne*: Both words appear in *DOST* as unique examples. The first is rather readily explicable as a derivative of OF *vicier* or Latin *vitiare*. The second has one parallel, from *Sir Fierumbras*, at *OED volentine* n., but is certainly a close analogue to the fairly common *volatile* n. (OF *volatile*, Latin *volatilis*). Holland's use is most likely derived from this last, with exchange of suffixes, *-ilis* and *-inus*. But the usage may equally be inspired or re-enforced by *PF* 309–10 'For this was on Seynt Valantynes day | Whan euery foul cometh there to chese his make', capable of being construed as an etymological joke joining birds and 'their saint'.

919 *with assent*: The underlying sense and alliteration rely upon the noun cloaking a form like *ane mendes* for *amendes* 72, viz. *with ane (as)sent* 'unanimously'. The line thus rhymes aab/bx on vowels and /s/. *DOST* includes no entry for *sent*, the aphetic form of the common noun *assent* the scribes have written, but see *MED sent* n.[1] (including several citations from alliterative poems and northern romances).

932 *our-hie*: The participle 'being' may be implicit. Equally, this may be an example of technically ungrammatical forms forced into rhyming service, the word here conveying *our-hicht* 'excessive height', with adjective expressing analogous noun (see the Introduction, pp. 49–50). The noun is unrecorded, but would seem, given *hicht* 965 and the large number of Scots words with prefix *our-*, transparent enough.

933 *Lyke Lucifer*: As Mackay points out (1981, 204), the ghost of *AA*, who laments her luxurious life, appears, she says, 'In the lyknes of Lucyfere, layetheste [var. lauyst] in Helle' (84; cf. 164–65, 214, the

last with 'in a lake lo3 am I light'). See the discussion of stanzaic death poems in the Introduction, p. 34, and subsequent notes.

935–36 Alluding to Luke 14:11 'Everyone that exalteth himself shall be humbled(, and he that humbleth himself shall be exalted)'. One might note the universality of the statement, which sets the terms for the following moralisation (not pointed to any especial political situation, as Stewart 1975 argues).

937 Cf. (anticipating the coming moralisation here) *PTA* 634 'Ne there [in death] es reches ne rent may rawnsone 3our lyues'.

940 *catif of kynd*: There is a small grammatical quibble here, although given the moral's insistence upon recognising the general wretchedness of the human condition, perhaps a telling one. Is *catif of kynd* appositive to *þe*: 'And make you, a wretch by your nature, recognise who you are'? Or is the phrase the object of *knawin*: 'And make you recognise for yourself that you are a wretch by your nature'? Or, in contrast to the previous two possibilities, does *þe* represent 'the' (and not 'thee'): 'And make that person, a wretch by his nature, recognise this fact for himself'?

941 *thraly in thrang*: The verse echoes the depiction of the owl's overbearing mien, *thraly and thrawin* 918. The word *thrang*, of course, has been specifically chosen to indicate that the owl receives the universal opprobrium he had lamented at the opening (esp. 61–67), that he is 'mobbed'. See Parkinson 1986, 500; and with the phrase cf. *Rauf* 701.

950 Cf. *AA* 108 'nauthyr on hide ne on huwe', sim. *Quat* 303, *DL* 157.

953 *bannyt ... his birth*: 'cursed the day he was born', as 954–55 elaborates, a complaint considerably more general than the owl's earlier cursing his appearance. Cf. *AA* 89 'I ban þe body me bare'; see also *William of Palerne* 1644 (and cf. 2100); *PPB* 1.62. Similarly, *bailefull in beir* answers the ghost's 'grym bere' lamenting her damnation, at *AA* 125–26, 327. At the end of the poem, the owl is reduced to its unchanging nature as a similar mourner (or 'yowler', cf. 53n), although uttering sad home truths to a general audience, rather than complaining about perceived defects merely personal. Cf. further Job 3:3–13.

956 *crepillit, crengit*: According to *DOST*, these are the sole usages in Scots. But the second is OE cringan 'to fall' or crengan 'to cause to fall', and there are ample English examples. For the first, see *OED* cripple v.

957 The construction is, 'He was immersed in and lamented with sighs'. The line echoes the owl's first appearance, at 42.

145

961–62 See Prov. 16:18.

963 The off-verse of this line has been rendered a thorough mess in transmission; the manuscript renderings – *wreth wast* A, *wrech wayest* B – provide very nearly useless information, since, being at least two syllables short of any metrical off-verse, both have lost a considerable amount of material. Past editors have struggled to make something of what remains. Amours apparently reads A *wreth* as unproblematically *wre(t)ch* (Riddy emends in B's *wrech*, but offers no further comment). Amours construes *wast* as the contracted form *wa-ast* 'most woeful'. But no such form can licitly exist; *wa* is a noun, not an adjective, and one would expect a superlative like *wafullast*. Were one to follow Amours's account, there would still not be enough syllables to construct a metrical off-verse (although *wafullast* would probably be acceptable).

To extend Amours's suggestion, one could read *wrech allther-wast* 'most woeful wretch of all', but this does not address the grammatical problem and would repeat the rhyming phrase at 967. Perhaps the way forward is to see *welth* and *wast* as antonyms in some contrastive statement, and I reconstruct one possible, thoroughly conjectural way of accounting for what remains: *wrech vsit to wast* 'scoundrel accustomed to deprivation'. Whatever solution one chooses to adopt, the line appears intended to echo 43, the howlat's first utterance, 'Wa is me, wretche, in þis warld wilsome of wane'; and cf. 251–52 'netherit ane owle ... | Wre[c]he of all wretches, fra worschipe and wele'. (Cf. the triggering echo of 42 in 957.)

966 *for craft þat I can*: Translate 'in spite of (any) strength I know'.

968 *ressoun and richt*: The phrase conventionally refers to proper legal possession. (In medieval English common law, the *breve de recto* 'writ of right' is the normal way of initiating a suit for real property.) The legal implications of wrongful possession are elaborated in 971–74, and the only injunction the owl offers is an allusion to righteous self-regulation in 984. For other evocations of the phrase, cf. *AA* 350, 362; *GG* 189; 'be ressonabill richt' *Rauf* 758; *PPB* 18.278, 330, 349 (and the derived *DL* 238, 260); note the stanzaic alliterative poem *SJB* 115–16, where the phrase, as in the owl's account, is associated with proper instruction against worldliness (here John the Baptist sermoning to Herod and Herodias).

969 *lyme*: *DOST* Lyme n. recognises only senses like 'mortar' and 'bird-lime'. But cf. the citation from *Liber Pluscardensis* 384, 'Of lawest lyme of erd al maid ar we', like Holland's usage arguably derived from Latin limus. Cf. Odo's use of the word in his moral to this fable, p. 24.

970–84 As McDiarmid points out (1969, 283), this moralisation of

the fable is directly drawn from Odo of Cheriton's. But for the imbrica-
tion of the thirteen-line stanza in 'death poetry', see Turville-Petre 1974
and particularly 976n below.

970 *maik ȝour merour by me*: The most famous Scots example,
Henryson's Cresseid, offers similar advice at 'Testament' 347–50.
However, the injunction, spoken by either the dying or the dead, is a
staple of earlier medieval mortality poetry, e.g. *PTA* 290, *AA* 167–69,
GG 1232–35, *TDK* 120, Wakefield *Lazarus* 125–28. In contrast, at
EETS OS 98, 136/67, the Virgin is addressed as 'Heil schadewe in vcha
schour schene' (like Holland's examples at 751–53 above, an image
of the virgin birth, neither the passing light nor the glass affected by
the process of reflection); and at 136/83 'Heil mirour vche mon on to
tote'. For discussion of the traditions underlying these injunctions, see
Bradley 1954.

971–72 The relative clause of the second line directly follows from
3e princis, while the off-verse of the first develops *pullis ... ay*. Trans-
late 'You princes, who pillage the poor in order to win pennies (*for
penneis and prowe* is hendiadys) ...'

974 *All ȝour welth will away*: This line, or something like it, forms
the conventional trigger to the contemplation of death and the horrify-
ingly nauseating spectre of the bare corpse, a rebuke to pride in raiment.
The alliterative lyric Richard Rolle intercalates into his tract 'Ego
dormio' magnificently epitomises the tradition in very brief compass:

> It wanes into wrechednes, þe welth of þis worlde:
> Robes and ritches rotes in dike;
> Prowde payntyng slakes into sorow;
> Delites and drewryse stynk sal ful sone,
> Þair golde and þaire tresoure drawes þam til dede ...
> Þe wretchesse fra wele falles into helle.

Cf. among many other examples, *PTA* 637, *Quat* 462, *AA* 215, *DL* 9
(but 5–16 generally, in this poem wittily front-loaded), *SJE* 198. All
these loci answer and indicate the cogency of the appeal to the Virgin
at *Howlat* 748, 'For ws wappit in wo in þis warld wyde'.

976 *Think how bair þow ... ay will be*: Most alliterative mortality
texts narrate 'mirrors' of the sort the owl promises at 970. They typi-
cally bring proud worldlings face to face with the corpses that they will
become, glamorously clothed aristocrats into confrontations with bare
rotten cadavers. The still visible artistic analogue to such a presenta-
tion is the aristocratic *transi* tomb, like Alice Chaucer's in the church
at Ewelme (Oxon.) – a two-tiered construction with, above, a splendid

recumbent effigy decked in worldly finery, and beneath, a rotting, worm-riddled corpse. Cf., for example, *TDK* 110–12 'Þaȝ ȝe be neuer so fayre, þus [in rottenness] schul ȝe fare ... | Leuys lykyng of flesche and leue nat þat lare'; *Quat* 400–3: 'Þan es all our pryde gane, | Oure robis and our riche pane, | Alle bot a crysome onane | Þat we were crystened in'. In contrast to the rich array the owl here seeks, the trappings of pride, the poems particularly urge, as the owl implicitly does in 971–75, penitential almsgiving; see for example, the 'bare' ghost's repeated injunctions in *AA*, or the extensive discussion of *Quat* 430–81 (in another poem with protracted praise of the Virgin). *bair ... bair* ('bare') carefully echoes *bair ... bair* ('bore'), referring to natural bounty, at lines 16–17.

976–77, 983 Surely Odo, and probably Holland, had in mind Job 1:21, 'Naked came I out of my mother's womb, and naked shall I return thither. The Lord gave, and the Lord hath taken away ... Blessed be the name of the Lord'.

977 *sedis*: The verb appears in *DOST* as a hapax legomenon, but cf. *MED* seden v., sense 1c 'to flourish'. Cf. 722–23n.

979 The line alliterates on two rhymes, vowels and /f/. The stresses probably fall on *of, frute, erd*, and *fus-*, an aba/xb pattern.

980 *has þe awne*: Translate 'has only what it is its own (by right)'. With the following line, cf. *AA* 152.

982 *hawles*: Again, presented as a hapax legomenon in *DOST*, but there are profuse parallels, many of them northern uses, at *MED* havenles adj.

984 Cf. with this corrective echo of 968, God's injunction to Noah, 'For þou in reysoun hatz rengned and ryȝtwys ben euer, | Þou schal enter þis ark' (*Cln* 328–29).

989 *for ane dow of Dunbar*: The poem's actual dedicatee is not, biologically, a Douglas at all, but Archibald's wife, Elizabeth Dunbar. The fragmentary record could well imply that she was a person of considerable culture, perhaps better equipped than her husband to appreciate Holland's poetic achievements. Sanderson (2002, 149–51) reproduces and discusses her signature on an indenture with the earl of Huntly in 1454, 'believed to be the earliest signature of a Scotswoman so far discovered'. Her literacy may have extended further; I have not seen the discussion of a private prayerbook likely hers, now in a New Zealand collection, McKim 2002.

Elizabeth's epithet, *dow*, is engaged in an elaborate sequence of puns here. Most obviously, she is a 'dove' – and thus associable with two of Holland's most dedicated and competent fowls: the true and dutiful turtle-dove secretary (126–36, 287–90, conceivably an allusion to Elizabeth's writing ability) and the gracious and dutiful curate (231–34). And like proverbial 'true turtles', she and Archibald express mutual and lasting devotion.

Equally, in the following line, Holland puns on the verb 'dowen'. Although the grammar is reversed (she is 'assigned to' a Douglas), this forms a reminder of the prosperity Elizabeth's estates brought to the family, as well as of the proper use, alien to the owl's behaviour, to which this will be dedicated. Finally, *dow* alludes to the very family name she has now assumed, Douglas. Such a reading is suggested by Gavin Douglas's rebus at the end of his translation of Virgil (Coldwell 1957–64, 4:139), where he parses his surname as if the compound dove+glass, perhaps indeed a reminiscence of this stanza (cf. p. 49 above).

992 With the off-verse, cf. *GG* 293, 417, 755; more distantly *AA* 35, *Rauf* 547.

996 *þat*: 'to whom'.

Glossary

Although I have built in a number of cross-references, readers may find it easier to cross-check common Scots variant forms, for example *a/ai*. In the alphabetical arrangement, *i* and *y* are not distinguished and appear as *i*; *i* representing modern *j* follows *i*; consonantal *u/v*, when it represents *v*, follows vocalic usage as *u*; and *u/v* to represent *w* follows *v*. The letter thorn appears integrated with words spelled in *th*; the letter yogh follows *g*. In the case of common 'function-words' (conjunctions, prepositions, the verb 'to be', etc.), I cite only the first five examples and any further problematic uses. Readings discussed in the textual commentary are in bold-face, and emendations of the text have been starred.

General

a, see **ane**

abbotis *n.pl.* abbots, the heads of monastic houses 177, 687

able *adj.* capable 381, 653

able *adv.* capably 229

abone *adv.* above 892

about *adv.* on every side 4; around, surrounding (along the edges of a shield) 370, 477, 588

abuf *adv.* on top 16

ac(c)us *v.* to accuse, charge *71, 113

active *adj.* active, energetic 350

addit *v.pt.* added; **addit in** inserted 438

adewe *adj.* departed 527

adres *v. (refl.)* to address oneself, come, address a subject, turn oneself 280; **addres** 421; **addressit** *pt.* 684

affray *n.* fright 46

affray *v.* to frighten, terrify 597; **affrayd** *pp.* 620

agane *adv.* again, anew, once more 542, 836, 889, 919, 939

aganis *prep.* against, in opposition to 58, 732

ay(e) *adv.* ever, always, at all times, eternally, continually 102, 141, 152, 164, 187, etc.

air, see **eir**

air *n.* air/weather/climate 9; the sky 315, 353; aroma; **of air** sweet-smelling 5

air *n.* heir 376, 549

airly *adv.* early 200

ald *adj.* old (historical?) 544; **auld** 291; **ald men** ancient authoritative writers 268

alis *v.pres.3sg.* afflicts 735, 799

alkyn *adj.* every sort of, various 5, 189, 653, 892

all *adj.* all, every(thing) 9 (see **owr**), 16, 29, 33, 61, etc.; *as n.* all things, all of a class 111, 241, 266, 273, 340, 407, etc.; **all ane** every one, as a single group 668; **(þar) alleris/allaris** *pl.poss.* of them all 276, 856, 864; **all** *adv.* completely 5, 157, 253, 340, 356, etc.

allace *interj.* allas 480, 839, 958

allane *adj.* alone, only 513, 516, 948; *adv.* **him/hir/þe allane** all by him/ her/themself/-selves, to himself (etc.) alone 513, 516, 927

allaris, alleris, see **all**

allegiance *n.(pl.)* something alleged, point(s) raised in discussion 267

allyas *n.pl.* allies, associates, kinsmen (perhaps specifically through marriage) **609**

allow *v.* to praise 917, 994; **allowit** *pp.* 447

all-quhar *adv.* everywhere 375, 551

almous *n.* amice, clerical hood 210

als *adv.* also 615, 699

als *conj.* as (someone who was) 25

also *adv.* as well, in addition 599

alterar *n.* alterer, one who changes **736**

alterit *v.pt.* altered, changed 929

alltherhieast *adj.super.* most noble/lofty of all 967

alltherhieast *adv.* very highest, at the top 612

allthermaist *adv.* most of all 452

amang *prep.* among 490, 494 (postposited)

amend *v.* to improve, better (it) 591

amyable *adj.* lovely, pleasant 9, 763

ancestry *n.* ancient stock, lineage 282, 291, 392, 594

ancient *adj.* ancient 315

and *conj.* and 6, 9, 17, 18 (3x), 19 etc.

ane *art.num.* a(n), one, a single 12, 15, 41 (2x), 48 (2x), etc., including *768; **a** 2, 45, 53, 57, 59, etc.; **an** 57; **ane** *n.* a person 548; **all ane** as a single group 668; **in ane** as one, in a group, unanimously 151, 213, 861, 929 (cf. **in-ane**); cf. **tane**

anenothir *adj.* a second, a different 36, 547, 599

angellis *n.pl.* angels 729

anone *adv.* immediately 682, 716; cf. **in-ane**

ant *n.* aunt 732

apart *adj.* open, clear; **in apart** easily visible 614; cf. **pert**

apon *prep.* on 111, 208, 209, 515, 828; about or concerning 119

apparale *n.* clothing, habit, uniform of office 125, 230

apparalit v.*pp.* equipped, furnished 670

appeir, apper *v.* to appear, enter, have a (noble) appearance 60, 341; **apperd** *pt.* 316; **apperit** made a formal appearance 152, 241; **till apper** in his bearing 334

appele *n.* appeal, complaint, formal charge 248, 850

appele *v.* to appeal, complain 41, 74; **appelit** *pp.* 109

apperans *n.(pl.)* conception(s), idea(s), opinion(s) 269

appering *n.* appearance, the act of (first) appearing (as the 'patriarchis' do) 159

approche v.*pres.pl.* approach 306; **approchis** *pres.3sg.* 932

approvit v.*pp.* approved, confirmed (as a right or property properly belonging to a person) 365

archedene *n.* archdeacon, assistant to a bishop, responsible for supervision and discipline of the clergy of a diocese (and officiating in an ecclesiastical court) 211

ardent *adj.* eager (for), desirous (of) 353

argewe *v.* to argue (about) 266; *pres.pl.* 273, 274

ark *n.* Noah's ark 813

armes *n.(pl.)* arms or weaponry, heraldic arms 347, 351, 358, 362, 380, 392, 422, 435, 438, 535, 546, 578, 592, 594, 600, 615, 623, 627

array *n.* display, furnishings or ornament, appearance 368, 416, 669

ar(r)ayd v.*pt.* displayed, arranged 624; *pp.* dressed, clothed 172

arras *n.* (perhaps a proper name, the French city, where the material was made) tapestry 675

arrest *v.* draw the attention of, detain 857

as *conj.* as (if) 1, 28, 57, 59, 133, etc.; **as now** for this occasion 33; **sic ... as** 93

ascendit v.*pp.* ascended, passed upward 943

askis v.*pres.1sg.* ask 110; **askit** *pt.* 929

assay *n.* trial, test, battle 372, 394; demonstrated ability: **of assay** of proven quality 596, 762

assay *v.* to attempt 565

assemblit v.*pt.* assembled, gathered 655, 919

assent *n.* accord; **with assent** (= **with ane sent**) unanimously **919**

assent v.*pres.pl.* assent, agree 275

assure v.*pres.1sg.* assure 603

asure *n.* blue (the heraldic tincture azure) 346, 361, 409, 413, 431, 570

at *conj.* that 856

at *prep.* at (the hands of) 1, 52, 66, 67, 110, etc.; cf. **feid, hand, hicht, poynt**

athile *adj.* noble 279; **athill** 314, 682

atyr *n.* dress, ornament 420

attend *v.* to heed, pay attention to 589

auld, see **ald**

aue *v.imper.* (Latin) hail 94, 736 (cf. **haile**)

away *adv.* away, afar 629, 696, 974

awant *adv.* at the front (of an army), speedily 349

awenant *adj.* appropriate, courteous, noble 350, 653

awfull *adj.* awe-inspiring, terrifying 314, 618

awys *n.* judgement, (capacity to provide) counsel 280

awys *n.* manner, style 198

awysit *v.pt.* advised 264

awn(e) *adj.* own 50, 477, 611, 903, 938, 939, 951; *as n.* þe **awne** its own (property) 980

awowit *v.pt.* vowed 443

bachel(l)eris *n.pl.* the lowest rank of knights 639, 691

bad(e), see **bid, bydand**

bay *v.* (lit. 'bark') shriek 66

baile *n.* distress 959

bailefull *adj.* miserable, wretched 953

bair *adj.* bare, open to view 17; naked, thoroughly bereft 976 (2x)

bair *n.* boar 775

bair, see **bere**

baith *num. adv.* both 272, 384, 461, 619, 815, 822, 840, 860, 983; **bath** 299; **boith** 324, 793, 990

bakwart *adv.* backward, to the rear 498

bald *adj.* bold 293, 394, 639, 787

baldly *adv.* eagerly, vigorously 98

ballach *n.* (Gaelic ballach) warrior or (Gaelic bathlach) servant 804

ban *v.* to curse 811; **bannit** *pp.* 953

banachadee *phrs.* (Gaelic) God bless (you) **795**

bancouris *n.pl.* cloth coverings for a bench or seat 672

bane *adj.* (= **bayn**) well-arranged 588

baneris *n.pl.* war-standards 537

bar *n.* barricade or barrier 384; **barris** *pl.* a barlike pattern, the heraldic 'fretty' 418, 579

bard(e) *n.* specific class of Celtic entertainer, specialising in historical and genealogical lore, usually presented in panegyric verse, as well as in poetic invective 795, 811, 818, 822, 825, 829

bare, see **bere**

baret *n.* strife, combat 332, 721

barmekyn *n.* battlement, defensive wall 384

barne *n.* child 996

barneteme *n.* offspring 728

bastounis *n.pl.* clubs, staves 616

batall, battell *n.* battle, battalion 492, 508; **bat(t)allis** *pl.* troops, batal-lions 488, 498, 537

batalland *v.pres.p.* engaging in battle 775

batall-wricht *n.* warrior 916

be *prep.* by (in its various senses, incl. by means of, with, beside) 21 (2x), 32, 68, 94, 105, etc.; at, around 40; **by** 19, 197 (postposited), 214, 381

be *v.* to be 123, 374, 441, 485, 495, etc.; *v.pres.subj.* if I be 62; *pres.1sg.* 69; **am** 57, 94, 101, 105, 250, etc.; **art** *pres.2sg.* 481, 482, 496, 743, 934, 982 ; **is** *pres.3sg.* 37, 43, 55, 57, 70, etc.; **nis** *neg.* 113; **ar** *pres.pl.* 165, 177, 225, 239, 801, etc.; **was** *pt.* 7, 9, 15, 18, 27, etc., including *445 (pl. in 176); **war** *pt.pl.* (had, as auxiliary for intransitive verbs) 5, 32, 162, 173, 175, etc.; **war** *subj.* would be 34, 78, 312, 421, 579

becaus *conj.* because 20

bedene *adv.* altogether, fully 380

befor *adv.* previously 522

befor *prep.* in front of, ahead of 92, 335, 643, 810

beft *v.pp.* beaten 959

begyn *v.* to begin 633; **begynnis** *pres.3sg.* leads (singing) 714, 848

behald *v.* to watch, look upon, see 87, 95, 543, 646, 781; **behold** 325, 342; **beheld** *pt.* 408

behest *n.* promise 470, request 855

behufis *v.pres.3sg.* (*impers.*) it is necessary (that) 754

beik *n.* beak 66; **beke** 357

beir *n.* outcry, noise 953

beir, see **bere**

beld *n.* camp (i.e., place where the enemy sheltered) 508; building, protection 721

beld *adj.* (well)-shaped **332**, 406

beld *v.pt.* emboldened 428

beldit *v.pp.* covered 892

beld-kytis *n.pl.* bald-headed buzzards 640

belyf *adv.* promptly, immediately 137, 145; **belyve** 295

bellis *n.pl.* bells 765

bemes *n.pl.* beams or shafts of light 3

bene *adj.* excellent **384**

benesoun *n.* blessing 98, 243

benyng *adj.* gracious 160

benkis *n.pl.* benches 672

benschene *n.* (perhaps Gaelic bean seinn, or an error for bean scheire) singing or keening woman; or (for **bensche,** Gaelic bean sidhe) faery woman **804**

beryit v.*pp.* buried 530

bere *v.pres.pl.* (**beir** *v.* 347) bear (in its various senses, incl. comport oneself, bear as an heraldic device, have as a bearing, drive) ***426**, 436, 613 (possibly *pt.*); **beris** *pres.3sg.* 352, 535; **bair** *pt.* 16, 903; **bur(e)** 26, 27, 196, 339, 363, 366, 399, 409, 498, 555, 568, 591, 595, 599, 629, 922; **bare** 616; **body bure** had physical form 107; **bur office** had appointments (with specific titles) to perform specific duties 129, 196; **borne** *pp.* either carried (by winds) or (well)born 639, born 976

berne *n.* warrior 787; *as pl.* 996; **bernis** *pl.* 293, 775; **birnis** 680

beseike *v.* to beseech, plead for 862; **besocht** *pt.* 853, 926

best *adj.adv.super.* best, finest 249, 418, 579

bet *v.pp.* beaten 829

betid *v.pt.* befell, came to pass 506

betill *n.* mallet 787

beugh *n.* bough 400, 607; **bewes** *pl.* 897

bewte *n.* beauty 319, 903

bewschiris *n.pl.* noble men 148

by, see **be**

bid *v.pres.1sg.* ask, wish, desire 70; **bad** *pt.* commanded 98, 126, 680, 810, 909

bydand *v.pres.p.* remaining 197; **bade** *pt.* remained, waited 87

bill *n.* scroll, document, written account 401, 536

bypartit *v.pp.* in two parts, split, open 357

bird *n.* bird 67, 112, 895; **birdis** *pl.* 17, 107, 915, 925

birnis, see **berne**

birth *n.* things born or generated, growth 25, 27, 406, 626; birth 953

bischop(p)is *n.pl.* bishops 173, 197, 685

bysyn *n.* monster 69, 107, 959

byte *v.* (lit. 'to bite, deal a wound') to peck 66

bitterly *adv.* angrily, spitefully 811, 953

blak *n. adj.* black 178, 778

blame *v.* to blame 69

blason *v.* to blazon, describe a coat of arms/blazon 347; **blasonde** *v.pp.* 631

blawin *v.pp.* inflated, puffed up 916

ble *n.* colour, heraldic tincture (or the colour of a charge) 3, 17, 357, 409

bled *v.pt.* bled 536

blent *v.pt.* (lit. 'glanced') gleamed 3; **blenkit** *364

blyn *n.* delay 148

blis *n.* bliss, happiness 721

blissit *v.pt.* blessed, showed favour to 243, 394; **blist** (probably representing **blis**) *pres.pl.* **663**; **blist** *pp. a.* blessed, consecrated 173, 727, 729, 996; **blissit** 664

blyth *adj.* pleasant, happy, joyous, delighted 25, 87, 160, 556, 680, 691, 714, 729; **blythar** *comp.* 173; **blythest** *super.* 3, 17, 399, 409

blyth *v.pres.subj.* make happy 996; **blythit** *pt.* gave joy to, encouraged 393

blythar *n.* one bringing joy (to) 731

blyth-bodyit *v.pp. adj.* pleasantly formed 332

blythly *adv.* happily, with delight 663

blomit *v.pt.* bloomed, grew 626; **blomand** *v.pres.p. adj.* flourishing 556

blossomes *n.pl.* blossoms, blooms 17

blud *n.* blood, source of vitality, lin(eag)e 384, 394, 536

bludy *adj.* (lit. 'bloody') red, the heraldic gules 436, 535, 545

bodword *n.* message 729

body *n.* body 107

boist *n.* boasting, exaggeration 332; **bost** 916

boith, see **baith**

boytour *n.* bittern 703

bold *adv.* proudly 364

bordouris *n.pl.* (flowery) borders 4; borders, marchlands 639

borne, see **bere**

bot *adv.* only 57, 778, 981

bot, but *conj.* but (rather) 33, 72, 121, 145, 188, etc.; unless, except that 59, 70, 119, 484, 697, 984; see also **but**

bourd *n.* sport, jest 87

bowallis *n.pl.* belly, womb 731

bowe *v.* bow down to, bend before, honour or revere 915; **bowis** *pres. pl.* 996 **bowit** *pt.* 607

bownis *v.pres.pl.* move, hasten, depart, pass 302; **bovnis** 685; **bownyt** *pt.* 508

bowr *n.* bower, the domestic rooms of a great house 324

bowsome *adj.* obedient 869

braid *adj.* wide or spacious, hence complete or full 98, 375, 672; extended (the front of an army) or displayed (banners) 537

brayd *adv.* widely 626

braid *v.* to raise 680; *pt.* moved, swung 498

brays *n.pl.* banks, slopes (by a stream) 16

branche *n.* branch, bough 406; **braunche** 607; **branchis** *pl.* (first use synecdoche for 'trees') 16, 399, 626

brane-wod *adj.* furious or insane (in a vatic frenzy?) 811

brathly *adj.* fierce, violent 488

breid *n.* breadth; **on breid** spread out, fully displayed 4, 399; **on breidis** 27

breme *adv.* boldly 357

breth *n.* (fit of) anger, rage 69, 916

brevit *v.pt.* communicated (in writing) 536

bricht *adj.* splendid 488, 556

brichtnyt *v.pt.* became bright or colourful 4

brym *adj.* bold, fierce, warlike 488, 775

brym *n.* body of water, stream 16

bring *v.* to bring 678; **brocht** *pt.* 814

brynt *v.pt.* burned, shone 418

bront *n.* vanguard 160, 492, 498

browdin *v.pp.* (lit. 'embroidered') adorned 27

brusit *v.pp.* embroidered **398**

bunwede *n.* stalk (of ragwort) 778

burd(e) *n.* board, shield, table, (ship)board 341, 685, 775; **burdis** *n.pl.* tables 672, 680

bur(e), see **bere**

burly *adj.* sturdy, strong 406; **burely** 588

busardis *n.pl.* buzzards 640

busk *v.pres.pl.* prepare (themselves) 148

but *prep.* without 14, 56, 130, 131, 148, etc.

bute *n.* remedy 721

cace *n.* casing, capsule 469

cairful *adj.* full of care 966

cais *n.pl.* jackdaws 191

cais(e), cas(e) *n.* circumstance, situation, condition, legal proceeding 71 (2x), 108, 235, 262, 300, 860, 877; **in case þat** in the circumstance that 71

caytif *adj.* miserable 966

caytouris *n.pl.* purchasing agents, provisioners 645

call *v.* to call, name 121, 257; **callit** *pt.* 124, 823, 931; *pp.* 548, 703; **cald** *pp.* 91, 545

can *v.* to have the power (to do something), be able, know how 120, 235, 966; **couth** *pres.subj.* 564; *pt.* 93, 206, 266, 277, 359, 644, 695, 701, 776, 779, 785, 963; cause (or have something done) 469

can *v.* 'do' 510; see also **couth**

cape *n.* cap **82**, 202

capitanis *n.pl.* leaders, military officers 566

capone *n.* capon (a gelding) 222

caralyngis *n.* ring-dances 792

cardinal(l)is *n.pl.* cardinals 121, 161, 683

carfully *adv.* full of care 956

cary *v.* to carry (away) 776

caryar *n.* carrier, someone who removes things, thief 771

carioun *n.* carrion, putrid and rotting 981

cassyn *v.pp.* drawn out, arranged or formed 417; **cast** assigned, consigned 454

castis *n.pl.* contrivances 771

catif *n.* wretch 940

caus *n.* cause, reason, legal case 108, 245, 438, 561, 861; **causs** *pl.* 225; **for caus** because 784

cawtelis *n.pl.* tricks, deceptions 771

celestiale *adj.* heavenly, associated with the sky **333**

cellis *n.pl.* monastic cells 766

celsitud *n.* heavenliness, exalted state 316

cerkill *n.* orbit, sphere 31

certane *adv.* certainly 586

ces *v.* to put an end to 926

chace *n.* pursuit 510

chalmer *n.* chamber 725

chance *n.* fortune 538

chancillar *n.* chancellor, the cathedral official responsible for official records 205

channonry *n.* collection of canons, cathedral chapter **203**

chantour *n.* cantor, chorister; **chantour full cheif** precentor, leader of the choir 203

charbunkle *n.* (lit. 'ruby or a similar red stone') gem or paragon 726

chargis *n.* duties, responsibilities ***327**

chargit *v.pp.* given a duty or responsibility 205

chast *adj.* chaste 223

chastite *n.* chastity 725

cheif *adj.* principal, leader 203; **as cheif** the heraldic 'dexter chief' **408**

cheir *n.* demeanour, manner 54, 680

chenʒeit v.*pp.* chained, linked or joined 605

chennonis *n.pl.* canons, members of religious orders serving churches or cathedrals (rather than a monastic house), e.g. Augustinian [black] or Premonstratensian [white] canons 189

cherite *n.* charity, love 223, 726

chevalrus *adj.* chivalrous, knightly 327, 538; *adv.* in a noble manner 605

cheuerand v.*pres.p.* trembling (for rage) 54

chevit v.*pt.* achieved, gained, won 538; see **chewis**

chewalry *n.* chivalry 479

chewis *v.* to acquire, obtain 644

chydand v.*pres.p.* complaining 54

chiftanis *n.pl.* chieftains, captains 327

chikinnis *n.pl.* . young fowl 644

chosyn v.*pp.* appointed 203; *pp. adj.* excellent 327

churliche *adj.* churlish, impolite 54

cymbaclauis *n.pl.* chimes or bells **766**

circulit v.*pp.* encircled, surrounded 333, 343, 514

circumstance *n.(pl.)* circumstance(s), factual situation 266

clay *n.* (mortal) clay, earth 981

claik *n.* barnacle goose 212

claischach *n.* (for **clarschach**) harp **803**

cla(i)this *n.pl.* cloth(e)s 673, 978

claryonis *n.poss.pl.* trumpets' (the long ones) 764

cled v.*pp.* clad, covered 673

cleir, cler *adj.* bright, shining, resplendent, transparent, distinct or manifest 10, 82, 201, 222, 338, 339, 340, 345, 435, 469, 479, 678, 892; **cleir** *adv.* clearly, fully 235

cleke *v.* to clutch or seize 645

clene *adj.* virtuous, chaste, pure or purified, spotless, precise 185, 201, 331, 673, 894

clepit v.*pp.* named, called, appointed 212

clergy(e) *n.* religious men or order 201, 257

clerk *n.* clerk, record-keeper, cleric 204, 222

clething *n.* clothing 187; cf. **hair**

cliftis *n.pl.* cliffs, steep banks 10

clos *v.* to enclose 469; **closit** *pt.* completed 463; *pp.* (lit. 'shut up in') consigned, committed 454

coddis *n.pl.* cushions 587

cok *n.* cockerel 202

college *n.* corporate body, esp. a religious institution 161, 201

colour *n.* colour, armorial tincture 337, 431, 587, 892; **colouris** *pl.* 420

colourlyke *adj.* colourful 894

come *n.* coming 245

come *v.pres.1sg.* come 100; *pt.* 158, 161, 196, 204, 471, 502, 635, 711, 770, 794, 820; **cum** *v.* 194; *pres.pl.* 983; **cummis** *pres.3sg.* 978; **cummyn** *pp.* 912

command *n.* command(s), orders 455

committis *v.pres.pl.* pledge, commit 738

com(m)oun *adj.* common 462; *adj. as n.* the common people 983; **commonis** *pl.* the commons, the common people 645

companys *n.pl.* companies, groups 236

compas *v.* to encompass, fly around 330

completely *adv.* fully 850

completis *v.pres.2sg.* fulfills 730

compt *v.* to account, recount **162**

conclaif *n.* council-chamber 124

concludit *v.pt.* agreed 861

confectionis *n.pl.* elaborate dishes 706

confess *v.* to confess, explain 235

confessionis *n.pl.* confessions 234

confide *v.pres.pl.* trust 746

connand *n.* covenant, vow or promise *487

connysaunce *n.* cognisance, heraldic sign 339; **conysance** 381; **cognoscence** the science of heraldry? 417

conquer *v.* to conquer 566

consait *n.* opinion 284

consauit *v.pp.* understood 300

consent *v.pres.1sg.* consent 877

considerand *v.pres.p.* considering 861

consistoriale *adj.* consistorial, reserved for a church court 225

constance *n.* constancy **430**

constant *adj.* constant, steadfast 82

contemplatif *adj.* given to contemplation **185**

content *v.pp.* contented, fulfilled 23

contra *adv.* (Latin) against (the proposal) 271

copy *n.* accurate reproduction 622

corach *n.* (for Gaelic coránach?) ritual mourner, keener 805

corage *n.* courage 435

corate *n.* curate, someone with responsibility ('cure') for souls, perhaps specifically a paid substitute for a non-resident incumbent of a parish 233

corby *n. adj.* raven; **corby messinger** unfaithful messanger 812

corne *n.* grain 191, 784

cornecrake *n.* (lit. 'grain-crow') the land rail **782**

corne-ʒard *n.* cornfield 194

correker *n.* corrector, disciplinarian 212

cors *n.* corpse, body 981

cosingage *n.* kinship 912

cost *n.* side, hence territory 330

cost *n.* price, expense or expenditure 978; **of cost** of great price, expensive 695

costlye *adv.* at great cost 469

costlyk *adj.* expensive 704

cot-armour *n.* coloured cloth surcoat with arms (worn over mail) or the arms on it themselves 336; **cot-armouris** *pl.* 426

counsall *n.* council, body of counsellors, counsel or advice 121, 262, 849, 877

counsall *v.pres.pl.* counsel, advise 278

counterpalace *n.* equal, peer 904

cours *n.* course 462

coursable *adj.* subject to anthema or excommunication 225

court *n.* court 634

courtassy *n.* courtesy, proper behaviour 93

couth *v.pt.* 'did' (an empty auxiliary usually deployed for metrical purposes) 20, 42, 51, 468, 476, 562, 566, 811; see also **can**

cowerit *v.pt.* regained 502

cowpe *n.* cup, goblet 776

cowschotis *n.pl.* wood-pigeons, ring-doves **230**

craft *n.* strength, skill 966; **craftis** *pl.* 704

crannis *n.pl.* cranes 162

cravis *v.pres.pl.* desire, ask for 191

crawis *n.pl.* crows 191

crawis *v.pres.3sg.* crows 202

creature *n.* created being 605

credence *n.* evidence (of a commission), credentials 300

crekery *n.* (Gaelic [c]reacaire) a professional reciter 805; cf. **O'Gregre**

crengit *v.pt.* cowered, shrunk down **956**

crepillit *v.pt.* walked lamely, stumbled **956**

cry *v.* cry out, beseech or plead, lament 111, 478; **cryis** *pres.3sg.* 202; **cry(i)d** *pt.* 839, 956; **cryand** *pres.p.* 191, 221, 642

cryme *n.* crime 108

croce *n.* cross 345

crope *n.* top (of a tree) 408, 612

crovde *n.* a fiddlelike instrument 758

crovnd, crovnit *v.pp.* crowned 315, 414, 571; **crovnit** *pp. adj. as n.* crowned one, king 464

crovne *n.* crown 294, 562; **crovnis** *n.pl.* 340

crovs *adj.* high-spirited, confident, jaunty 222

crows *adv.* confidently, in a self-satisfied manner 221

crucifix *n.* crucifix 340

cruell *adj.* brave 294

cubicular *n.* groom of the chamber 124

cude *n.* chrisom-cloth 978

cuke *n.* cook 703; **cukis** *pl.* 695

cumly *adj.* attractive 338, 339

cummyng *n.* coming 236

cunnand *adj.* knowledgeable 204

cur(e) *n.* care, keeping, (spiritual) responsibility 257; **curis** *pl.* 704; **in cur** under his control or guidance 111; **costlyk of curis** expensive to produce 704

curis *n.pl.* cooked dishes ('curries') 695

curlewe *n.* curlew 204

day *n.* day, daylight 40, 59, 170, 580; **dayis** *pl.* 551

dayly *adv.* daily, continually 710

daylicht *n.* daylight 63

dait *n.* (space of) time 425, 445

dale *n.* portion; **in dale** among those associated with him 281

dame *n.* lady (also as title) 32, 70, 857, 867, 887, 942

dansis *v.pres.pl.* dance 792

dar *v.* (for *pres.p.*) to lie hidden 188

dar *v.pres.1sg.* dare 59

darrest, see **deir**

de *v.* to die 516, 520; *pres.subj.* 71; *pres.1sg.* 116; **deit** *pt.* 549

defence *n.* defence 486, 525

defend *v.* to fend off, stop 383

deformed *v.pp.* deformed, misshaped 250

defoulit *v.pt.* treated with scorn, disparaged 906

degradit *v.pp.* demoted 952

degre *n.* status, order, manner 154

deid *adj.* dead 481, 527, 702

deid *n.* death 65, 169, 445, 459, 482

deidis *n.pl.* deeds 226, 505

deir *adj.* dear, beloved, precious 164, 320, 342, 422, 439 (for 'dearest' *super.*), 549, 633, 684; *as n.* dear one 136, 170, 482; **darrest** *super.* 281

deir *v.* to harm, injure, discomfit 562; **deris** *pres.3sg.* 329

de(i)s *n.* dais 684, 776

dele *n.* devil; **what dele** 'what in the hell ...'? 799

deme *v.* to judge (fitting), offer (an opinion), appoint, describe 280; *pres. pl.* 876; **demyt** *pt.* 136, 199, 690, 941; **to deme as efferd** were one to judge properly 320

dene *n.* dean or deacon, either (a) [the plural uses here] the administrative head of a cathedral chapter; or (b) (cf. **rurale**) the direct supervisor of clergy within a division of a diocese (with powers of visitation) 216, 809, 816; **denys** *pl.* 199, 690

derf *adj.* violent, destructive 575

derfly *adv.* violently 445

des *n.* dais 776

desyre *n.* desire 422

det *n.* what is owing (i.e. death) 519; **(has ...) done ... his det** has done his duty 136

devoid *v.* to deliver or rescue 519

dewe *adj.* dutiful 575

dewly(e) *adv.* properly, appropriately 136, 888*; adj.* (duly) appropriate (to) 422

dyademe *n.* crown 342

dicht *v.* to construct or arrange, handle, treat, give over or consign 64; *pp.* 342, 482

dyet *n.* meeting, council 280

differens *n.* difference; in heraldry, an added feature designed to distinguish arms (usually of younger sons) from those of the main family line 600

digne *adj.* worthy 168, 281, 320, 342

dignite *n.* dignity, honorable position or office 164, 168, 329; **digniteis** *pl.* dignitaries 690

dyng *v.* to strike, give a blow 65

dynt *n.* blow(s), stroke(s) 575

discend *v.* to descend, come down (from heaven) 863; **discendit** *v.pt.* 867

displait *v.pp.* wide spread, spread out (the heraldic term) 354

distres *n.* adversity 393

dyte *n.* poem 989

dyte *v.* to compose 391, 421

do *v.* to do, perform, act 59; **did** *pt.* 505, 601; **done** *pp.* 136, 876, 888, 941

dorche *n.* dwarf **650**

douchter *n.* daughter 549

douchty *adj.* vigorous, daring, courageous 199, 380, 391, 527, 551

dovle *adj. as n.* dull one, dullard, dolt **59**

dovn(e) *adv.* down(ward) 7, 14, 566, 745, 799, 845

dow *n.* dove 231, 989; **dowis** *pl.* 990

dowble *adj.* double 370, 588

dowit *v.pt.* endowed, assigned **445**, 990

dowt *n.* fear; **but dowt** certainly, truly 199

drak *n.* drake 210

drawin *v.pp.* drawn, passed 942; **drew(e)** *pt.* drew, approached 170; composed 989

dredles *adv.* without doubt 116

dreid *n.* fear 329; **but dreid** fearless 294

dreid *v.imper.* fear 876

dres *v.pres.1sg. (reflex.)* address, turn 391

drew(e), see **drawin**

drink *n.* a drink, alcohol 799

droupe *v.* to lay hidden 59; **droupand** *pres.p.* **188**

duke *n.* duke 299 (for the plural); **dukis** *pl.* 281, 294, 320, 329, 684

dulfully *adv.* grievously 64

dulsacordis *n.(pl.)* (?) dulcimers **762**

dulset *n.* a kind of flute **762**

dure *n.* door 826

dure *v.pres.pl.* endure, last 169

durst *v.pt.* dared 622

e *n.* eye 67; **eyne** *pl.* 333

effect *n.* value; **of effect** of worth 165

effeir *n.* behaviour; **in effeir** in manner or bearing 560, 617

efferis *v.pres.3sg. (impers.?)* befits, is appropriate 146, 354; **efferd** *pt.* 320

egill *n.* eagle 313, 353

eik(e) *adv.* also 189, 236

eild *n.* eld, ancient times, (of) long standing, antiquity 426, **eld** 594

eyne, see **e**

eir *adv.* previously 287, 615, 632, 690; **air** 618; **erast** *adj. super.* first, previous(ly discussed) *632

elate *pp. adj.* raised or puffed up 934

elles *adv.* otherwise 116; **ellis** 610; **nocht ellis** not … at all 301

ellis *n.* (an)other 737

eloquence *n.* eloquence, ability at composition 37

embrace *v.* to embrace or surround 400; **till embrace** encircling, surrounding

empriour *n.* (the Holy Roman) emperor 279, 291, 296, 314, 323, 335, 358, 634, 682, 781

end *n.* end, death 436, 464, 708

end *v.pres.1sg.* conclude 580

end-day *n.* death-day (understood as that naturally appointed) 117

endurand *v.pres.p.* lasting, drawing on 170

entent *n.* intent, purport, opinion 143, 277, 873

enteris *v.pres.pl.* comes in, arrives 304; **enterit** *pt.* 130, 196

entre *n.* free leave to pass 142

erast, see **eir**

erd *n.* earth 5, 9, 314, 813, 979; **in erd** prob. pleonastic 653; **in herde** 898

erekit *v.pp.* built 669

erll *n.* earl, noble 322, 595, 599; **erlles** *pl.* 282, 686

ernes *n.pl.* sea-eagles, ospreys 315

ernistly *adv.* seriously, with vigour 274

esiast *adj.super.* most readily attainable, most common 675

estait(e) *n.* high estate 933; **sternes of estait** noble stars 555; **estatis** *n.pl.* social ranks, the community of the realm 437; cf. **stait**

ete *v.pt.* ate 784

ettill *v.* to intend to go, direct one's way 291; **etlis** *pres.3sg.* 353

euer *adv.* ever, always 107, 379, 386

euerlestand *v.pres.p. adj.* eternal, everlasting 997

evinsang *n.* the service compline or vespers, concluding the day of monastic observance 188

evirmor *adv.* evermore 528

ewyn *adv.* in a straight or direct fashion (i.e., from Adam to the line of David, as in Matt. 1) 722

ewyn *n.* evening 195, 196

exces *n.* excess; **in exces** excessively 925

expremit *v.pp.* expressed, stated, named 138, 692

fa *n.* foe, enemy 593, 651, 746; **fais** *poss.* foe's/foes' 383; **fays** *pl.* 494, 597

fable *n.* fable, tale; **but fable** truly, in truth 651

face *n.* face 77, 106; **fax** 55

fader *n.* father, metaphorically lord or leader, the pope's title 80, 261

fay *n.* faith, allegiance 566; **in fay** in good faith, truly 370

faile *n.* lack; **but fa(i)le** continually 679; in truth, completely 851

faynd *v.* to attempt, venture 602; **fandit** *v.pt.* 593

fayne, fane *adj.* joyous, happy 78, 592, *adv.* eagerly 79

fair *adj.* beautiful 15, 23, 114, 158, 260, 308, 410, 589, 598 ('level'), 612, 679, 790, 899, 913; **farest** *super.* 321, 893; **fair** *adv.* beautifully 206, 547

fair *n.* manner 820

fair-farrand *adj.* handsome 153

fairhed *n.* beauty 6

fairlie *adv.* pleasantly, graciously 261

faith *n.* (the Christian) faith 486, 518, 525; **in faith** truly (and faith-fully) 495

faithfull *adj.* faithful 128

falcone *n.* falcon 321; **falcoune** 679

fale, see **faile**

fall *n.* downfall 962; **gaif ... a fall** knocked down 834

fal(l)owe *n.* fellow, companion, equal 11, 913

fals *adj.* pagan, heathen 501, 522

falt *n.* lack, defect 851; **faltis** *pl.* 250, 875

fand *v.pt.* found 293, 308, 451

fand, see **faynd**

fane, see **fayne**

fang *v.* to seize, take 702, 939

fantasy *n.* imagination; **of fantasy** in my imaginings 621

farest, see **fair**

farly *adv.* wondrously 15; **ferly** 511

fasandis *n.pl.* pheasants 158

fassonit *v.pp.* formed, crafted 55

fast *adj.* firm, unmoving 128

fast *adv.* firmly, vigorously 510; quickly 826

faucht *v.pt.* fought 842

fax, see **face**

febilly *adv.* feebly, only with difficulty 228

fecht *n.* battle 486

fecht *v.* to fight 518

fedder *n.* feather 880, 885, 939; **fedderis** *pl.* 899; **fetheris** for 'clothes' 838

federem, see **fetherem**

feid *n.* feud, violence or hatred 165; **has me at feid** show enmity toward me 61

feidis *v.pres.3sg.* feeds 228

feye *adj.* doomed (to death) 495

feild *n.* meadow, plain, battle(field), heraldic field (the 'background' colour of a shield) 346, 352, 570; **feld** 361, 410, 511, 541, 586, 598; **fe(i)ldis** *n.pl.* 6, 503

feile *adj.* many 250, 503, 511, 522; **quhat fele** how many 627

feir *n.* companion 11, 232, 962

feir *n.* fear, dread; **but feir** without doubt, 'there's no denying it' 56

feldefer *n.* fieldfare 228

fell *adj.* fierce, destructive 597, 741, 875

fell *v.pt.* fell 46; threw himself down 93

fellis *n.pl.* wasteland, desert **303**

fellit *v.pp.* felled, cut down 495; **feld** *pp.* 511

fellony *n.* crime 165

felloun *adj.* fierce, criminal 541, 746; *as n.* 620

fende *n.* enemy, devil 746; **fendis** *pl.* 741

ferd *ord.num.* fourth (shieldbearer) 601

ferdfull *adj.* terrified 621

feris *n.pl.* behaviours 541

feris *v.pres.3sg.* befits 348

ferly *n.* marvel 46; cf. **farly**

ferme *adj.* firm, unmoving, steadfast 128, 567

ferme *adv.* firmly 355

ferme *v.* to (con)firm, make strong 888; *imper.* 723, 888; **fermes** *pres. pl.* affirm 525

fete *v.pp.* fetched, brought, drawn 518

fetherem *n.* (i.e. 'feather-hame') plumage 56, 913; **federem** 888

fetheris, see **fedder**

fewe *adj.* few 175

fydill *n.* fiddle 761

figonale *n.* earthenware pot or dish (?) **833**

figur, figour *n.* shape, likeness 106, 259

fyle *n.* wretch 55, 79, 250

fylit *v.pt.* defiled, dirtied (with shit) 824

filth *n.* filth, foulness 61

fynd *v.pres.pl.* to find 567

fyne *adj.* refined, purified 360

fyr(e) *n.* fire 418, 838

firmament *n.* the heavens, the sky 317, 701

first *adj.* first, original 928; *adv.* 951; **first front** forefront, vanguard 158

firth *n.* woodland 23, 880, 893, 906

fische *n.pl.* fish 696, 702

fische-fanger *n.* fish-catcher (a necessity for a monastic house, with fishponds, given the number of days of obligation celebrated) 181

fist *n.* fist, hand 761

flammit *v.pt.* flared forth, shone 346

flang *v.pt.* flung, threw 838

flat *adj.* down flat 838

fle *v.* to fly 140, 355

fle *v.* to flee 510; **fled** *pt.* 522

fleis *n.* fleece 753

flemyt *v.pp.* banished, driven away (into exile) 696

flesche-tyme *n.* those portions of the ecclesiastical year without dietary restrictions 696

flet *n.* hall floor 830

flicht *n.* flight 317, 321, 511, 944; flying equipment, wing-feathers 885

flyrand *v.pres.p.* grimacing, mocking 820

flour *n.* paragon, exemplar 479, 899

flour de lycis *n.pl.* fleurs-de-lis 360, 371, 589

flowrit *v.pp.* ornamented with flowers or fleurs-de-lis 370

flure *n.* (hall-)floor 832

flurist *v.pp.* filled with blooms, adorned 6, 407

fold *n.* the earth, the ground 15, 46, 321; **on fold** usually pleonasm, but 'on the ground/field of the shield' 346, 355

folk *n.* people 501, 522

followe *v.* to follow, pursue 495; **followit** *pt.* 510

fonde *v.pt.* (= **fonned**) behaved foolishly 830; *pp.adj.* foolish 820

for *conj.* because 75, 140, 206, 644, 701, etc.; cf. **caus**

for *prep.* for (in its various senses, including because or on account of, against) 29, 60, 61, 126, 133, etc.; **for to** to (marking the infinitive) 20, 86, 95, 149, 238, etc.

forest *n.* forest (a legal designation of territory, as well as trees) 15, 228, 308, 573, 991

formast *adj.* first 493

forme *n.* shape, appearance 56, 851

formed *v.pp.* shaped, created 101, 321; **formyt** *pp.* 355

fors *n.* force, strength 317; **force** 383, 593; **on force** in plenty, many 706

forsaid *pp.a.* previously mentioned 307, 991

forsicht *n.* providence 558

forsuth *adv.* in truth, truly 275, 316, 419, 603, 694

forther *adv.* further, any more 873

forþi *adv.* therefore 432

forthocht *v.pt.* regretted 843

forthward *adj.* enterprising, precocious, skillful 192; **forthwart** 140

fortope *n.* (lit. 'forelock') crest (on a bird's head) 824

foule *adj.* ugly, deformed, disgusting 77, 851, 981

foule *adv.* foully, in such an ugly way 55; **fowle** 101

foundis *v.pres.pl.* go, pass 317

four *num.* four 158, 407, 604, 612

fowle, foule, foull *n.* bird 106, 114, 354, 880, 885, 893, 939, 944; **fowlis** *pl.* 61, 165, 261, 636, 656, 899, 906, 919; **foule** *pl.* 80

fra *prep.* from (in its various senses) 252, 433, 539, 577, 645, etc.; **fro** 3, 303, 701, 741, 742, etc.

fra *adv.* away, i.e. opposed the proposal 270

frayis *v.pres.3sg.* terrifies 501

franit *v.pt.* asked 261

fre *adj.* free, generous, noble, at liberty 153, 740; *adv.* freely, nobly 304

frely *adj.* noble, excellent 308, 679; *adv.* nobly 991

freres *n.pl.* friars, orders of unclaustrated religious, dedicated to poverty and living by begging 192

fret *v.pp.* adorned 6

fro, see **fra**

front *n.* the front, vanguard 158, 493; cf. **first**

frut(e) *n.* fruit, produce or offspring 740, 833, 979

fule *n.* court fool 106; **fulis** *pl.* 820, 830

fulfill *v.* to fulfill 462

full *adj.* full, filled with 6, 223, 264, 674, 722, 916; *adv.* very (largely expletive) 123, 158, 175, 203, 204, 221, 229, 250, 366, 412, 460 (2x), 477, 511, 537, 538, 590, 612, 763, 875; **ful** 171

fure *v.pt.* travelled 486, 601; *pt.subj.* 79

furis *v.pres.3sg.* brings or carries forth **706**

furth *adv.* forth, further, forward 79, 396, 601, 639, 706

fusoun *n.* plenty 979

fut *n.* foot 824

ga *v.* to go 449; **go** 86; *v.pres.1sg.* 884; **gane** *pp.* 947; see also **gang, ȝeid, went**

gay(e) *adj.* pleasant, beautiful, shining 28, 366, 398, 630, 758; *adv.* pleasantly 412

gaif, see **gif**

gayly *adv.* beautifully, in profusion 889

gaist *n.* spirit 463

gait *n.* road, way 149, 285

galiard *adj.* gallant, spirited 540

gall *n.* gall-bladder 815, 840

gane *adj.* fit or suitable 590

gane *v.* to gain, achieve, avail 149, 666; **ganit** *pt.* 848

ganeris *n.pl.* ganders 198

gang *v.* to go 285; *pres.pl.* 983

gar *v.* to cause to 883; **gart** *pt.* 476, 678, 772, 781, 889

garland *n.* garland, wreath 786

garment *n.* garment 630

gat *v.pt.* got 836

geirfalcounis *n.pl.* gerfalcons 319

gem *n.* gem; **in gem** richly, beautifully 344

generale *adj.* common, widely held 269

gentilly *adv.* nobly 319

ges *v.pres.1sg.* think 397, 419, 561

gevar *n.* giver, donor 743

gyde *n.* garment, gown 397

gyde *n.* guide 871

gif *conj.* if 162, 263, 312, 459, 564, etc.; **gif þat** 258

gif *v.imper.* give 799; **gaif** *pt.* gave, emitted 53, 98, 448, 463, 563, 826, 834; **gaf 243**, 295

gift *n.* gift 8; **giftis** *pl.* 451

gird (to) *v.pt.* made a sally at, attacked 834

girs *n.* grass 28

gittyrnis *n.pl.* citherns 758

glad *adj.* pleasant 638

glemyt *v.pt.* gleamed 412

glyde *v.* to glide, pass 742

glos *v.* to expound, explain 35

go, see **ga**

goddes *n.* goddess 871

godhed *n.* divinity 8

goishalkis *n.pl.* goshawks 326

gold *n.adj.* gold (the metal, its colour, or the heraldic metal 'or') 28, 340, 360, 369, 414, 418, 571, 579, 672, 786

GLOSSARY

golk *n.* (= **gowk**) cuckoo 821, 834, 836

gome *n.* warrior 540

gorrit *v.pp.* pierced 840

goule *n.* gull 179

governouris *n.pl.* directors, generals 326

gowlis *n.* red (the heraldic tincture) 366, 372, 412, 590

gowlyne *n.* yowling, howling 52

grace *n.* grace (incl. the theological concept), favour, prayer 86, 465, 471, 722, 742, 848, 862; bliss or happiness 952; **of grace** benificent 28

gracious *adj.* gracious, stately 412, 451

gray *n.* grey 786

grane *n.* grain, seed, source 722; **granes** *pl.* 28

grant *n.* grants of land and privileges 451

grantar *n.* granter, bestower 743

grantit *v.pt.* assented (to) 666

grap *v.* (lit. 'grope') seek, examine 86

grat *v.pt.* wept 53

grathis (þam) *v.pres.pl.* prepare (themselves), decorate or adorn 149; **grathit** *pp.* 397

gre *n.* degree, rank 407; the highest degree or rank, the prize 448, 743

greable *adj.* pleasant, pleasing 8

greably *adv.* appropriately, in accord with degree **848**

grene *a.* green, growing 2, 210, 398, 584

gret *adj.* great 53, 198, 326, 451, 465, 471, 521, 637, 818, 826, 836, 862, 952, 986; **gretest** *super.* 313, 407

grym *adj.* fierce, angry 53, 313, 369, 617

gryntar *n.* monastic official responsible for granaries 179

grysly *adv.* terrifyingly 53, 617

ground *n.* earth 26, 27, 742; the field of a shield 369; **on ground** pleonasm 198, dead 540; **on groundis** anywhere, alive 313

ground *v.* to find a foundation or root, establish a place 889

growe *adj.* horrifying 617

growe *v.* to feel horror, shudder, shrink 51; **growit** *pt.* 449

growe *v.* to grow 884, 889; **growis** *pres.2sg.* 722

gruching *n.* murmuring, complaint; **but gruching** politely *149, *666

gud *adj.* good 292, 463, 561; *as n.* 86, 666

gudly *adj.* distinguished, noble 154, 198, 398, 628; *as n.pl.* 947

gukkit *adj.* foolish, silly 821

gus *n.* goose 786

guttis *n.pl.* guts 815, 840

ȝa *adv.* yes, in favour of the proposal 271

ȝaipe *adj.* vigorous, active 602

ȝald *v.pt.* gave 289

ȝe *pron.* you (the polite or deferential form) 111, 114, 247, 310, 382, etc.; **ȝhe** 799; **ȝour** *poss.* 95, 96, 109, 110, 114, etc.; **ȝow** *obj.* you, for you 151, 441, 456, 581, 930, etc.; **ȝou** 459

ȝeid *v.pt.* went 821

ȝemyt *v.pt.* looked after, kept, preserved 132

ȝit *adv.* still, yet, nonetheless 170, 196, 209, 386, 841, 930, 961

ȝong *adj.* young 602

ȝowle *n.* howl, screech 53, 102

ȝowt *v.* howl, screech 102

habitacions *n.pl.* dwelling places, castles 552

habitis *n.pl.* habits, gowns appropriate to a specific (monastic) status 184

haboundis *v.pres.pl.* have in profusion 319

haid *n.* order, kind, colour 630

haile *adj.* whole, entire, complete or unanimous, healthy 163, 245, 867; **hale** 234, 470, 581, 683

haile *adv.* completely 275, 855; **hale** 579

ha(i)le *v.imper.* hail 718–22, etc.; cf. **aue**

hair *adj.* hoar, grey 773

hair *n.* hair 822 (i.e. plumage), 950; **clething of hair** hair-shirts, worn for penitential self-abuse 187; **of hair and of hyde** in external appearance 950

haist *n.* haste 38, 110, 931; **hast** 886; **in(till) haist** immediately, quite suddenly 48, 965

haist *v.* to hasten 424

half *n.* side (of a coat of arms), here 'quartering' 434

haly *adj.* holy, sacred 661

halynace, -nas, -nes *n.* holiness (papal title) 75, 95, 110, 114, 309

hall *n.* (noble) hall, the public space in a great house 142, 324, 819, 836; **in hall** perhaps only pleonasm 'in attendance' 301, 846

hallow *v.* to bless, sanctify 476

hals *n.* neck 477

halsit *v.pt.* greeted 309

haltane *adj.* haughty 923, 931

hame *n.* home 532, 945

hand *n.* hand; **tuke ... vpon hand** took in their care 529; **at hand** nearby, local 782

hant *n.* customary dwelling-place 945

happin (þat) *adv.* (lit. 'it may befall') perhaps 75

happinit *v.pt.* befell, happened to 1001

hard *adv.* harshly, severely 263

hard, see **heir**

hardely *adv.* vigorously, violently 490

hardy *adj.* bold, brave 529

harme *n.* harm, injury 735

harmes *v.pres.3sg.* injures 543; **harmit** *pp.* 965

harounis, see **herounis**

harrald *n.* messenger, herald 139, 290, 301; **harraldis** *pl.* 147, 581, 631

harrald *v.* to perform as an herald, to describe arms **427**

hart *n.* heart, spirit or strength 388, 436, 444, 449, 453, 476, 477, 502, 529, 535, 545; **hert** 30, 411, 469, 490, 538, 543

hartes *n.pl.* harts 20

hartlie *adj.* eagerly, from the heart 424, 886

hast, see **haist**

hathillis *n.pl.* warriors 846

hatit *v.pp.* despised 982

hattis *n.pl.* hats 163

haue *v.* to have, possess, preserve 142; *pres.1sg.* 35, 109; **haf** 913; **haife** 118; **has** *pres.3sg.pl.* 61, 68, 73, 111, 135, etc.; **haue** *pres.pl.* 882; **haf** 941; **had** *pt.* 92, 300, 407, 444, 530, etc.

hawles *adj.* (= **haveles**) destitute, without possessions **982**

he *pron.* he 51, 53, 93 (2x), 99, 124, etc.; **his** *poss.* his 8, 50, 75, 82, 84 (2x), etc.; **him** *obj.* him(self) 74, 92, 98, 227, 293, etc.

hecht *v.pt.* commanded *131; promised 470

hed *n.* head(-feathers) 163, 187, 210, 779, 837; **in hed** chief 290

heilfull *adj.* promoting healing or health 30

heir *adv.* here 441, 580

heir *n.* heir 969

heir *v.* to hear 233, 247, 310, 390; **herd, hard** *pt.* 41, 692; **herd (= her it)** *v.* to hear it 318

heirdis *n.pl.* herds, groups 20; **herdis** 773

heirly *adj.adv.* stately, splendid(ly) **411**, 846; **herely** 898

held *v.pt.* kept or preserved, haunted (a place), restrained (oneself), held or bent (their way) 217, 470, 945; **held ... a greit pleid** tried a serious legal case 818

held *v.pr.1sg.* bend or turn aside (from) 427

helmes *n.pl.* helmets, warhelms 612

helpe *n.* help, aid 30, 110, 735

help(e) *v.* to help 263, 754

hende *adj.* courteous, noble 325, 631; **hendest** *super.* 893

hende *adv.* devotedly 477

hennis *n.poss.* hen's 779

hens *adv.* hence, from this place 38

hensman *n.* henchman, retainer 648

herbery *n.* a place for resting or stopping over (as an inn) 646, 945

herbes *n.pl.* plants 5

herd (= **her it**), see **heir**

herde, see **erd**

her-eft *adv.* hereafter 960

herely, see **heirly**

heretable *adj.* inheritable, included in the estate (without need of a further grant) 563

herounis *n.pl.* herons 185; **harounis** *poss.* *651

hert, see **hart**

hethin *adj.* pagan, non-Christian 490, 542

hevin *n.* heaven 718, 942

hevinliche *adj.* heavenly, sky-like (blue) 431

hewe *n.* hue, colour, heraldic tincture 399, 431; **hewes** *pl.* 893

hewe *v.* to trick out or blazon 424; **hewit** *pp.* coloured, adorned (with pun on **hevit** 'elevated') 967

hicht *n.* height, loftiness, lofty behaviour 965; **at hicht** on high, aloft 898; **on hicht** aloud 985

hiddy-giddy *adv.* whirling, helter-skelter 821

hiddir *adv.* hither 878

hyde *n.* hide, skin, exterior 950; cf. **hair**

hidowis *adj.* hideous, ugly 950

hie, hiegh *adj. adv.* high (up), proud or splendid, intense 142, 353, 408, 411, 630, 638, 819, 923, 982

hiely *adv.* proudly, grandly 905

hyit *v.pt. reflex.* exalted himself 905

himself *pron.* himself 940

hyng *v.* to hang 476

hyre *n.* hire, pay; **but hyre** for no pay, voluntarily 424

hobby *n.* a kind of hawk **651**

holyne *n.* holly-bush 48

holtis *n.pl.* woods 773

hone *n.* delay 130, 131, 886

honest *adj.* virtuous (or quasi-adverbial virtuously) 129

honorable *adj.* virtuous, honourable 177, 385, 392, 438, 552, 594

honour *n.* honour 298, 322, 635; **honouris** *pl.* positions of distinction *686; **in honour** in order of distinction 362

hope *n.* hope 735

horrible *adj.* terrifying 103

hors *n.pl.* horses 783

hospitular *n.* keeper of a hospital or hospice (a religious institution devoted to charity, e.g. the support of the poor and of travellers, not necessarily care of the sick) **229**

hour *n.* hour, space of time 772, 863; **in þe hour** immediately 297; **houris** *pl.* the conventional sequence of services comprising the daily rota of monastic prayer 188

hous *n.* house (as a type of common dwelling) 142, 217

hove *v.pres.pl.* to stand about, remain stationary 301; **hovit** *pt.* 369; **huf(e)** *v.* 20, 646

hover *v.* pause, hesitate 646

how *adv.* how 152, 265, 635, 922, 976

how *interj.* a call like 'hey' 812

howlat, howlet, howlot *n.* owl 48, 88, 263, 875, 881, 886, 890, 898, 922, 931, 949, 950, 985; **howlatis** *poss.* 850

hudis *n.pl.* hoods, cowls 187

huf(e), see **hove**

huntyng *n.* hunting 773

hurt *n.* injury, sickness 30

hurt *v.pp.* injured, wounded 965

I *pron.* I 1, 12, 22, 35, 38, etc.; **my** *poss.* my 37, 55, 56 (2x), 57, 60, etc.; **myn** 67, 254; **me** *obj.* me, to myself 19, 61, 64, 65, 66, etc.

i', see **in**

ydy *n.* eddy, stream **827**

(þat) ilk *demon.* the same, that very 241, 357, 864

ilk *adj.* each 343, 400, 406, 607, 608, 615, 885, 939, 944, 980

ilkane *adj.* each (one) 147, 664, 806, 865, 925, 931; **ilka** 880

ill *adv.* evilly 460

importinat *adj.* offensive 924

in *prep.* in(to) 1, 5, 20, 22, 46, etc.; **i'** 904

in-ane *adv.* immediately, directly, suddenly **47**, 887; cf. **ane, anone**

indur *v.* to last 734; **induris** *pres.pl.* 710

ynewe *adj.* plenty 176, 282, 437, 573; *as n.(pl)* (people) aplenty 525

iniur *n.* injury, crime 921

inrold *v.pp.* adorned, ornamented **344**; cf. **railit**

instance *n.* request 864, 868

into *prep.* in 58, 100, 137, 139, 246; **intill** 110, 409

intollerable *adj.* insufferable, unbearable 921

inwart *adv.* within 389

ischit *v.pt.* issued, exited or left 813

it *pron.* it 30, 33, 34, 119, 134, etc.

iwis *adv.* truly, certainly 97, 512, 717; **iwist 659**

ia *n.* jay 770, 789

iangland *v.pres.p.* chattering 789

iapand *v.pres.p.* jesting 770

iaspis *n.pl.* jaspers, precious stones 344

ioynit, ioyned *v.pp.* joined, linked, locked in combat 344, 489

ioyus *adj.* joyous, joyful 753

iowkit *v.pt.* (lit. 'moved evasively') practiced sleight of hand 789

iuglour *n.* entertainer, illusionist 770

iuperdys *n.pl.* (conjuring) tricks 789

keyis *n.pl.* keys (the symbol of St Peter and the papacy) 345

kelit *v.pt.* struck 566

kene *adj.* brave, fierce 331, 689

kennis *v.pres.3sg.* knows 806; **kend** *pt.* taught (himself) 703; **kend** *pt.* recognised 587, knew 860; *pp.* displayed, demonstrated, made known, revealed 108, 430, *adj.* well-known 683

kepe *v.* to attend to, guard, preserve 201, 487; **kepit** *pt.* 615

ketchyne *n.* kitchen 704

kid *v.pp. adj.* well-known, renowned 504

kyn *n.* lineage 912

kynd *n.* nature, type, manner or variety 162, 236, 337, 462; **of kynd** by their inherent nature 331, 940

kynde *adj.* natural(ly appropriate) 587

king *n.* king 463, 470, 562, 983; **kingis** *pl.* kings 294, 315, 322, 683, 801; *poss.* 449, 502, 776; *poss.pl.* 645

kirk *n.* the church 133, 150

kirkland *n.* church glebe 784

kirklyk *adj.* clerical, appropriate for a cleric 82

kirkmen *n.* clerics, persons in clerical orders 212

kis *v.* to kiss 478; **kissit** *pt.* 843

kyth *v.* to make known, reveal, explain, demonstrate, show 235, 622, 695

knawe *v.* to know, recognise, reveal 339, 373; **knewe** *pres.subj.* 579; *pt.* 172, 262, 435; **knawin** *pp.* 381, 912, 940

kneis *n.pl.* knees 93

knellis *n.pl.* bursts of sound 764

knycht *n.* knight 515, 521, 526; **knychtis** *pl.* 331, 487, 689, 791

lady(e) *n.* lady 724, 739, 740, 927; **ladyis** *pl.* 461, 724, 790

laid *v.pp.* laid out, i.e. filled up 217

laif *n.* the remainder, the surviving (remaining, all other) examples of a type, in the second example perhaps 'commons'? 122, 446

laike *n.* body of water 19, 49, 214

layne *v.* to hide, conceal 267, 852

lair *n.* wisdom, teaching, lore 905

laith *adj.* hostile, hateful 227; **lathest** *super.* 958; **lathast** 969

lak *v.pres.1sg.* am lacking, fail 994

lamentable *adj.* sorrowful, plaintive 249

land *n.* land, property 457; **landis** *pl.* 131, 137, 574, 628

land *n.* glade 18

lang *adj.* long, (over)extended 34, 425, 787

þe lang reid *phrs.* the low provisioned period of late winter and early spring (an Orkneyism) 698

langage *n.* language, speech 249

lansand *v.pres.p.* (lit. 'moving') the heraldic 'rampant' 560

lap *v.pt.* lept 841

lard, see **lord**

lardner *n.* larder, storeroom 217

lark *n.* skylark 714

lat *v.imper.* allow 742

latis *n.pl.* behaviours 917

lauch *v.* to laugh 188; **leuch** *pt.* 828, 927

law *n.* law 224

lawe *adj.* low, abased 936

law(e) *adv.* low, down 214, 460

le *adj.* sheltered 18

ledar *n.* leader 374

legeman *n.* liege, vassal 496

leid *n.* man, person, people 188, 371, 750; **in leid** among men, publicly 267, 852

leid *n.* language 288, 994

leid *v.pres.subj.* lead, control, direct; **leidis** *pres.3sg.* 224

leif *n.* leave, permission 193

leif *v.pres.1sg.* live 480

leif, leve *v.* to leave off or behind, stop, abandon or remain, relinquish 777, 810; *pres.1sg.* 631; **left** *pt.* 633; **levit** 540, 948; *pp.* 961

leil(e) *adj.* faithful, just, compelling (i.e. in accord with truth) 167, 267, 496; **lelest** *super.* 288, most trustworthy 433

leile *adv.* loyally, truly 750

leis, les *n.* lying; **but le(i)s** in truth 224, 698

leit *v.pt.* considered 907

leme *n.* light 724

lemyt *v.pt.* shone 900

len *v.* to give, grant 881; *pres.subj.* 997; **lent** *pp.* 886

lence *n.* linch-pin; **(nor…)worth a lence** not worth a pin, valueless 606

lend(e) *v.* to linger (over) 19, 627

lent *v.pp.* passed down (into) [with auxiliary **war**, a pluperfect] 5

lent, see **len**

lenth *n.* length; **at lenth** fully 288

lenthing *n.* lengthening, extension 34

leris *v.pres.3sg.* learns 356; **lerit** *pp. a.* learned 214, 365; *as n.* learned ones, implicitly the clergy 122, 446

les *adj.comp.* lesser, less distinguished 190

lesinges *n.pl.* vain, frivolous, or untrue statements 807, 810

lestis *v.pres.pl.* lasts, endures 528

let *v.* to stop, leave off 807

letteris *n.pl.* written documents 137, 145, 288, 295

leuch, see **lauch**

levar *adj.comp.* more pleasant (perhaps 'more preferable', implicitly 'than removing from the place') 19

lev-, see **leif**

levit *v.pt.* granted 534

leving *n.* manner of life 167

ly *v.pres.1sg.* lie (low) 969; **lyand** *pres.p.* 227

lichory *n.* lechery 227

licht *adv.* brightly 900

lichtest *adj.super.* brightest 724

lichtit *v.pt.* alighted 214

lyf *n.* life 739, 997

lykame *n.* body 900

lyke *adj.* like, resembling 895, 933; **lykar** *comp.* resembling more closely 106

lyking *n.* pleasure, delight, happiness 18, 385, 496, 755, 828, 997; (?) heavenly joy 528

lykis *v.pres.3sg. (impers.)* is pleasing to (thee) 249; **lykit** *pt.* 460

lilt-pype *n.* some variety of musical instrument **761**
lyme *n.* slime, muck **969**
lympit *v.pp.* (lit. 'befallen') having become 969
lyng *n.* line; **lyne** genetic line, lineage 385; **in a lyng/lyne** directly, straightway 161, 365, 841; **lynis** *pl.* links, ties 606
lynkit *v.pp.* joined 365
lyo(u)n *n.* lion 366, 414, 560, 568
lippyn *v.pres.pl.* place trust or faith in 456
lyst *n.* delight, pleasure 755
lyte *adj. n.* little (bit) 927
littill *adj.* little 649
loft *n.* the sky; **on loft** on high, up above 560, 627; on the outer or upper side (of the shield's 'tressure') 371; **apon loft** loudly 828
lois *n.* praise, fame, honour 385, 425, 456, 568; **los** 528
lokis *n.pl.* locks 606
lord *n.* lord, the Lord, nobleman 366, 374, 448, 457, 530, 548, 560; **lard** 193; **lordis** *pl.* 145, 281, 295, 311, 446, 461, 652, 828, 852
lordingis *n.pl.* lords 628, 633, 810
lordschipe *n.* lordship 425, 457; **lordschipis** *pl.* lands associated with a lordly estate 574
lost *v.pp.* lost, destitute 958
love *v.pres.1sg.* love 456; **lufis** *v.pres.3sg.* 750; **lovit** *pt.* 371
louely *adj.* beautiful 627
loving *n.* praise 568
lovit *v.pt.* praised 755
lous *v.* loosen, untie 606
lowde *adv.* loudly 764
lowe *n.* fire 841
lowne *adj.* calm, quiet, still 18
lowtit *v.pt.* bowed 460
luf *n.* pleasure 18
luke *v.* to look, examine, inspect, venture 63, 295; *imper.* 750; **lukand** *pres.p.* 49; **lukit** *pt.* 900
lute *n.* lute 761

may *v.pres.* may, have the power to 44, 76, 96, 114, 396, etc.; **mycht** *subj.* 259, 263, 285, 591, 606, etc.; *pt.* 500
maid, see **mak(e)**
maikles *adj.* matchless, without compare 367
mair *adj.adv.* more, greater or more exalted 24, 44, 144, 190, 456, 618; **mayr** 879

mak(e) *v.* to make, construct, cause to be or bring about, compose 72, 115, 707, 780, 786, 940; *pres.pl.* 200; *imper.* 740, 749; **maik** 970; **maid** *pt.* 52, 73, 255, 532, 567, 633, 807, 832; *pp.* 367, 591, 902

maker *n.* creator 719, 749

making *n.* creation 928

makles *adj.* matchless, unique 902

malice *n.* malice, threatening behaviour 240

man(e) *n.* a man, one's man, one's dependent or feudal inferior 609, 780, 807, 907, 970; **men** *pl.* 214, 268, 365, 490, 497, 514 ('many a man'), 529, *542; **mennis** *pl.poss.* 29, 938

mane *n.* moan, lament, appeal 41, 531, 749, 859

maner *n.* usual custom, behaviour, a kind or type (group singular) 83, 190, 237, 265, *707, 717, 970; **maneris** *pl.* 331

manerit *pp. adj.* well-mannered, courteous 240

manifest *adj.* manifest, open and clear 255

manly *adj.* humane, courageous, virtuous 497; **manlyke** 155

manswet, mansweit *adj.* mild 83, 240

mapamond *n.* world 328

markit *pt.* betook myself, made my way 2

marschalit *v.pp.* placed or seated (at table) 693

marschell *n.* an official in an aristocratic household, originally responsible for horses but more usually in charge of the hall 323; **marschale** 677

marschionis *n.pl.* marqueses, great nobles 685; **marchionis** 328

martoune *n.* (?) some variety of upland game bird **213**

mast, see **most**

mastres *n.* mistress, director 32

mater *n.* (literary) material, event, affair, facts of the case 35, 265, 396, 632; **materis** *pl.* 144

mavis *n.* thrush 712

medicyne *n.* healing, antidote, cure 29, 719

meid *n.* meadow 2

meike *adj.* humble 240

meikly *adv.* humbly, deferentially 693

me(y)ne *v.* to speak, express 44, 583, 756; **menit** *pp.* conveyed, indicated 255

meit *n.* food, meal 665, 677, 693, 711; **mete** 831; **metis** *pl.* foods 707

mekle *adj.adv.* much, great 24, 35, 531, 654

mell *v.* to speak *144

mellit *v.pt.* participated in a melee, attacked 497

memberis *n,pl.* limbs (i.e. wings) 354

men, see **man**

menar *n.* intermediary, 'mediatrix (peccatorum)' **747**

mendis *n.pl.* amelioratives, cures, recompense 29, 72 (**ane mendis =
amendis** *sg.*)

mene, see **meyne**

menstralis *n.pl.* minstrels 711, 756

ment *v.pt.* intended (to go), directed (my) steps 1, 157

mercy *n.* mercy 747

merle *n.* blackbird 712

merlӡeonis *n.pl.* merlins, sparrow-hawks 638

merour *n.* mirror, prominent example or paragon 970

mes *n.* mess, a meal 780

messinger *n.* messanger 231, 812

metallis *n.pl.* metals, the heraldic designation for such field-colours as
gold and silver 420

meter *n.* verse 35

mycht *n.* power, strength 367, 484, 509, 557, 902, 986; **mychtis** *pl.*
328, 685

mydday *n.* midday 665

myddis *n.* midst, middle 1, 156, 711, 999

myld *adj.* merciful 717

mynd(e) *n.* memory, mind 44, 255, 654

myresnype *n.* common snipe 213

myrth *n.* pleasure, merriment 2, 24

mirthfull *adj.* happy, pleasant 998

mys *n.* sin 719

myself *pron.n.* myself, I 878

mistar, misteir *n.* craft, trade; **for mistar** as (his craftsman's) tool 207;
need 440

myte *n.* mite, particle 72

miterit *v.pp.* wearing the papal mitre *83

myth *adv.* gently, graciously **693**

mo *adj.* more (in number) 756

moder *n.* mother 719, 747

mold *n.* the earth, the 'ground' (properly field, of a shield) 2, 73, **413**;
on mold 'on the ground' but frequently pleonastic 2, 367, 902

moneth *n.* month 998

mony *adj.* many 148, 237, 267, 371, 404, 489, 514, 540, 689, 705, 707,
807, 831

monycordis *n.pl.* a musical instrument, although not, as etymology
suggests, with a single string, ? zithers 758

monkis *n.pl.* monks 178; **monkis … blak** Benedictines; **monkis …**
  quyte Cistercians
monstour *n.* monster, freak of nature 73
morn(e) *n.* morning 1, 195
mornyng *n.* morning 157
most *adj.super.* most, greatest 314, 328; *adv.super.* 892; **mast** 433
mot *v.pres.* may 727
mountis *v.pres.pl.* mount, ascend, fly 638
movis, see **mufe**
mowis *n.pl.* moues, facial grimaces; **mowis … maid** pulled faces 831
mufe *v.pres.1sg.* move, advance, pass, affect 396; **movis** *pres.3sg.* 452;
  mufe *pres.pl.* 677; **movit** *pt.* 367
multitud(e) *n.* multitude 237, 654
murcoke *n.* moorcock, the male red grouse 213
mure *adj.* grave, serious 83
murn *v.pres.1sg.* mourn 524
murnyng *n.* mourning, sorrow 44
muse *v.* to think, consider 396
musicianis *n.pl.* musicians 756

na(y), see **no**
nay *n.* denial; **þis nis no nay** this cannot be denied 113
nakit *adj.* naked 981
names *n.pl.* names 33, 151
nane *num.* none, no one 70, 500, 591; cf. **ane**
natur(e) *n.* (the course of) nature 58, 462, 732; **naturis** *pl.* 708; cf.
  Natur
neb *n.* nose, beak 57, 207
nech *v.* to approach, to near 908; **nechit** *pt.* neared, approached 47, 682,
  887; touched, concerned 276
neidis *n.pl.* needs 29
neidis *v.pres.3sg. (impers.)* there is need (to) 33, 253, 709; **nedis** 872
neir *adv.* near 908 (postposited); **nerar** *comp.* nearer 47
neir *prep.* near (to) 682
nest *n.* nest 251; **in nest** birdlike, associated with a bird 47
netherit *v.pp.* abased, humiliated 105, 251; bent down 57
neuerþeles *adv.* nevertheless 423
nevyn *v.* to name, enumerate 33; **newyne** *pres.subj.* 716
neuir *adv.* never 189; **never** 485, 618, 961
nicht *n.* night 58
nychtgalis *n.pl.* nightingales 715

nyte *v.* to deny 70

nixt *adv.super.* next (to), nearest (to) 316, 329; **next** 378

no *adv. adj.* no 113, 458, 605, 654, 807, etc.; **na** 217, 239, 329, 814; **nay** never (in opposition to a proposal) 271

noble *adj.* noble 32; **nobillis** *adj. as n.pl.* noblemen 437; **nobillest** *super.* 453, 887

nobillis *n.pl.* gold coins 788

nocht *adv.* not (at all) 33, 60, 70, 96, 99, etc.

nocht *n.* nothing 59, 737, 938

noys *n.* noise **47**

noyus *adj.* disturbing, vexing 251

nok *n.* hook 57

nor *conj.* nor 235, 237, 239, 606, 978

not *v.* to note, list, put down in writing 151

notis *n.pl.* musical notes 716

now *adv.* now, at this time 33, 151, 452, 465, 484, etc.

nuris *n.* nurse, person who offers nourishment, fostering force *276

nurist *v.pp.* nourished, fostered 32

nutschellis *n.pl.* nutshells 788

obedience *n.* obedience 160; **obediens** those obedient to one, one's retinue 302

obeyand *v.pres.p.* obeying 197

obeysance *n.* submission, reverence, respect 869

occupy *v.* to fill up (a space) 580

of *adv.* off, away 522

of *prep.* of (in its various senses, including out of, from) 1, 3, 5, 6, 8, etc.; with 23, 24, 25

offend *v.* to attack 593

offens *n.* violence, attack, battle 304, 602

offerandis *n.pl.* religious offerings 472

office *n.* duty, position, rank 129, 196

officeris *n.pl.* officers, those with assigned duties in a household 653

officiale *n.* official, the judge in an ecclesiastical court (with powers over cases of sexual misconduct) 224

oft *adv.* often 393, 478, 593, 763

oft-sys *adv.* often, continuously 274

oist *n.* host, troop 326

on *prep.* on, in 2, 4, 15, 59, 63, etc.

ony *adj.* any 144, 457, 908, 977

or *conj.* or 11, 14, 95, 108, 165, etc.

or *conj.* before 79, 117, 196, 734, 879, 884

ordanit *v.pp.* appointed, established, predestined 229, 734

ordour *n.* religious order, generally one bound by a(n ordaining) rule (in 177, specifically monastic ones) 229; **order** order, (full) arrangement 578; **ordouris** *pl.* 177, 189, 687

orere *adv.* (pass) backwards or away 984; (with implicit verb of motion) back away!, get back! 909

organis *n.pl.* church-organs 763

orient *adj.* the east; **orient perle** a pearl from the east (considered of higher quality) 341

osillis *n.pl.* blackbirds, merles 713

ostend *v.* to display 709

othir, see **vþir**

oucht *n.* anything 872, 977

our *prep.adv.* over 303, 345, 375, 385, 407, 673, 904; see also **owr**

our-all *adv.* everywhere 104, 314

our-arrogant *adj.* unduly proud 924

ourbeld *v.pp.* covered over 672

ourgrowin *v.pp. adj.* huge, grown beyond normal size 617

our-hie *adj.* excessively proud 932

our-man *n.* 'over-man', superior or director 211

ourset *v.pt.* overwhelmed 509, 517, 524

ourtirvit *v.pt.* threw over or down, threw head over heels 837

out, owt *adv.prep.* out (of) 63, 150, 302, 795, 813

owle *n.* owl 57, 103, 248, 251; **owll** 105

owr *adv.* everywhere **9**

pacok(e) *n.* peacock 81, 90

paynit *v.pp.* tormented 263

pair *n.* pair; **be pair and be pair** in pairs 21 (2x)

palace *n.* palace 668

pane *n.* rich cloth; **in pane** richly, with rich adornment 670

pantit *v.pp.* stained, coloured 670

pape *n.* pope 74, 80, 91, 92, 97, 118, 131, 152, 241, 243, 248, 256, 278, 306, 659, 664, 681, 848, 865, 904, 911; **papis** *poss.* 139, 289, 347

papeiaye *n.* parrot 125

paradys *n.* paradise, heaven 769

pardoun *n.* pardon 662

parfyte *adj.* perfect **182**, 991

parfytelye *adv.* perfectly 183

part *n.* part, portion 387 *(sg. for pl.)*, 423, 583; **part of** of the same substance as (a larger entity), sharing with **410**

party *adj.* particoloured 184

partrikis *n.pl.* partridges 176

pas *v.* go, travel 74; **past** *pt.* 643, 668; **passit** 681

pastour *n.* pastor (director or guide of souls), religious leader 80

patriarkis *n.pl.* patriarchs, possibly officers of the eastern church? 122, 159, 659, 683, 865, 911

peir *n.* peer, equal 907; **per** 951

penitentis *n.pl.* penitents 866

penneis *n.pl.* pennies 971

perces *v.pres.pl.* penetrate, pierce 318

perell *n.* danger, peril 119, **526

perle *n.* pearl 341; cf. **orient**

persounis *n.pl.* parsons, incumbents in their churches (or their patrons) 219, 230

pert *adj.* expert 643

(in) pert *adv.phrs.* openly 60; cf. **apart**

pete *n.* pity 882

petuos *adj.* pitiful 256; *as n.* pitiful (one) 41

pewewe *interject.* an imitation of a kite's cry 642

physik *n.* medicine 706

pik-mawis *n.pl.* black-headed gulls **183**

pyndit *v.pp.* impounded 783

pyotis *n.pl.* magpies 176

pype-gled *n.* some variety of kite **642**

pite *n.* pity 118, 526

pitill *n.* hawk or buzzard **642**

place *n.* place or location, seat 40, 473, 520, 608, 646, 681; **in þe place** in public, in full view of all 241, 664, 864

playit *v.pp.* played (an instrument) 769

plane *adv.* directly, promptly, straight on 74

plane *n.* an open space; **in plane** openly, outdoors (to laymen, as opposed to a clerical group) 211

planyt *v.pp.* complained, pleaded 850

planly *adv.* openly or directly 289

plantit *v.pp.* set throughout (the surface of), strewn (for the heraldic 'semy') 341

pleid *n.* plea, complaint, legal plea; verbal dispute or debate (lit. 'charge against someone') 818; outcry, squawk 835

pleyne *v.* to complain, lodge a formal complaint 119; **plenȝeit** *v.pt.* 920

pleis *v.* to please 930; **plesand** *pres.p.* 668

plesand *adj.* pleasant, pleasing, able to please 614, 901; **pleasant** 81

plicht *n.* situation, danger or peril *118; state or condition 904

pluwaris *n.pl.* plovers 176

poynt *n.* the smallest portion of a thing (incl. a single musical note), a single feature, the gist 256, **769**; **at poynt** proper in every detail 139, 347

pompos *adj.* magnificent, ostentatious, haughty 924

pontificale *n.* papal robe *681

portatiuis *n.pl.* portable organs 765

possible *adj.* possible 930

povne *n.* peacock 614

poverte *n.* destitution 951

pray *v.* to ask, beseech, entreat, appeal to 854; *v.pres.pl.* 866; **prayit** *pt.* 256, 664

prayer *n.* prayer(s) 76, 662

pransand *v.pres.p.* prancing 21

precept *n.* command 289

prechand *v.pres.p.* preaching 211

precious *adj.* priceless, of great value 81, 109

preif *v.* to attempt 930

prelatis *n.pl.* churchmen (not necessarily bishops) 269, 659, 865

prent *n.* imprint, thus image, likeness 854, 901; **prentis** *pl.* 971

pres *v.pres.1sg.* strive, attempt 692

presence *n.* presence, attendance (at a court) 306; **to ȝour presence** in your hearing or audience 109; **into presence** before a person of status 604

present *n.* presence: **into present** (to appear) before a person of status 139

present (þaim) *v.pt.* presented themselves 152, 159, 184; *pp.* 92

pryce *n.* value, nobility 951; **of pryce** noble 90, 604, 668

pryde *n.* pride 932, 952, 961, 971

prime *n.* the hour for the liturgical service 'Prime', 9 a.m. 40

princes *n.* princess 730, 932

principale *n.* main or most important (portion) 423

princis *n.pl.* princes 299, 643, 904, 911, 971; **princes** *pl.poss.* 951

priouris *n.pl.* priors, (in an abbey) the leaders of the monks 183, 688

prys *adj.* of value, excellent 526, 783

pro *prep. adv.* (Latin) for, in favour (of the proposition) 272

procuracions *n.pl.* fees exacted by church officials for their expenses whilst on visitation 220

prolixt *adj.* protracted (and thus tedious) 34

proper *adj.* excellent 125; **propir** *adv.* thoroughly (?) 901

prophecis *n.* prophecies 730

prophetis *n.pl.* prophets 122

propone *v.imper.* propose, put forward 248; **proponit** *pt.* 269

provd(e) *adj.* ostentatious, showy 125, 334, 614, 901

proudly *adv.* splendidly 670

prow(e) *n.* profit, benefit 971; prowess or skill 911

prowestis *n.pl.* heads of religious chapters, i.e. what are elsewhere called either priors or deans 688

prunʒeand *v.pres.p.* preening or grooming, (?) hence strutting **21**

psaltery *n.* psaltery, harp 757

pullis *v.pres.pl.* pillage, pluck 972

pultre *n.* poultry 644

pundar *n.* person responsible for impounding wandering livestock (and thus keeping them out of fields of growing grain) **782**

pundfald *n.* stockyard 783

purchace (-ches) *v.* to attain, acquire 76, 644

pur(e) *adj.* poor, miserable 41, 192, 850, 983 (2x); *as n.* 92; *as n.pl.* 972

pur(e) *adj.* pure, purified 81, 109, 369, 571, 730

purpos *n.* purport, point 39, 40; **to the purpos** as an indication (of the point) 572

pursevant, -want *n.* pursuivant (a rank of herald) 334, 348, 363, 629; **pursevantis** *poss.* 397

purviouris *n.pl.* purveyors, foregoers (who arrange food and board for a travelling lordly retinue) 643

put *v.pp.* impelled, obtruded 951

quaynt *adj.* clever, ingenious 771

quarterly *adv.* in 'quarters' (of a shield) 417, 591

quha *pron.* who(ever) 72, 80, 356, 435, 656, 697; **quhom** *obj.* whom 69, 329, 869

quhar *adv.* where 307, 367, 369, 475, 499, etc.

quharof *adv.* for what reason 982

quharthorow *adv.* through which 867

quhat *adj.* which, whatever 144, 311, 627, 785, 799, 874; **what** 468

quhen *conj.* when 92, 244, 300, 445, 488, etc.

quhy *conj.* why 55, 101, 480 (2x)

(þe) quhilk *rel.* which 51, 296, 317, 374, 393, etc.

quhill *adv. conj.* so long as 217; until 306, 502, 808

quhyte *n. adj.* white 172, 177

quhoso *pron.* whoever 992
quhruyne *n.* (lit. 'squeal') cry *910
quod *v.pt.* said 55, 79, 100, 118, 250, etc.

Raby *n.* (Aramaic) teacher, lord 94
rad *adj.* terrified 94
raid *v.pt.* rode 335, 648
raif *v.pt.* tore 835; **revyn** *pp.* 839
raike *n.* rake(-handle) 216
rayke *n.* journey 443
raike *v.imper.* reach, hand over 797
raykit *v.pt.* journeyed, passed 12, 89
railit *v.pp.* adorned, ornamented 674; cf. **inrold**
rair *n.* roar 826, 839
rais *v.pt.* rose 474
raith *adj.* (= **reth**) severe, strict **200**
raith *adv.* immediately 475; cf. **rath**
ramp *v.* to rear up (the heraldic 'rampant') 416; **rampand** *pres.p.* 368
ran *v.pt.* ran (went on foot), flowed abundantly, wandered 14, 647, 826, 968
ran(e) *n.* a long string of (meaningless) words 45, 215, 794
rang , see **ring**
rangit *v.pp.* arranged, disposed 244
rank *adj.* firm, unbending, headstrong **216**
rath *adj.* angry, violent 835, 859; cf. **raith**
raught *v.pp.* (lit. 'reached one another') exchanged (blows) 842
ravyn(e) *n.* raven 215, 809, 815
rawis *n.pl.* rows 244
rebaldis *n.pl.* rascals, scum 909
rebalkit *v.pt.* abused 915
rebellit *v.pt.* opposed 562
recordis *v.pres.3sg.* records 656
recourdour *n.* recorder 759
red *n. adj.* red 163, 543; **reid** 816
redbrest *adj.* with a red breast; the robin 647
redles *adj.* lacking good counsel 968
referris *v.refl.imper. pres.3sg.* (I) appeal (to evidence provided by) 581
reforme *v.* to recreate, construct anew, improve 77, 259, 875
reid *n.* (an animal's) stomach **839**
reid, see **lang reid**
reid *v.* to read, understand, direct 146, 216, 395, 463; *pres.pl.* 474, 534

reif *n.* robbery or seizure; **fowlis of reif** raptors, birds of prey 239, 656

reir, see **rerd**

reird *v.pt.* resounded *13

reiosand *v.pres.p.* making (us) glad 389

relevit *v.pt.* rallied, advanced or returned to battle 512, 523

religioun *n.* religion, the state of being committed to the religious life 190

relykis *n.pl.* relics 475

remayne *v.* to remain, stay 665; **remane** 946; **remanyt** *pt.* 846; remained (unresolved, or yet to be considered) 265

remelis *n.pl.* (severe) blows 842

remord *v.* to remember (grievously) 531; **remordis** *pres.3sg.* 654

rencwe *v.* to renew, reform 854, 872; repeat, reiterate 253, 708

renkis *n.pl.* warriors 624

renovnis *n.pl.* (for *sg.*) renown 548

rent *n.* income from property 554, 937

repa(i)r *v.* to adorn, ornament; **to repar** in his ornament, ornamented **614**, 901

report *v.* to report, repeat 692

reprovable *adj.* worthy of rebuke 924

reprovit *v.pt.* scolded, admonished 809

request *n.* request 856

rerd *n.* clamour, outcry 794; **reir 637**

rerit *v.pt.* rose up 638

residence *n.* residence; **mak residence** maintain continuous residence (unlike their canons) 200

reskewe *v.* to rescue, retrieve 433, 521; **reskewand** *pres.p.* 542

ressaif *v.pres.pl.* receive 868; **resauit** *v.pt.* 146; **ressauit** 298

ressoun *n.* statement, account, (good) reason 534, legally appropriate behaviour 968; **ressonis** *pl.* 544, 554

resting *n.* rest, stopping 14

restord *v.pp.* restored, returned, preserved 532, 658

rethnas *n.* ferocity, cruelty *239

reule *v.reflex.* govern (oneself) 984

reuthfully *adv.* piteously 45

reveir, rever *n.* flowing stream, or its bank 12, 14

reuerence *n.* reverence, sobriety 146, 868

revyn, see **raif**

rewardit *v.pt.* rewarded 147

rewe *v.* to take pity (on) 858; **rewit** *v.pt.* 859

ryally *adv.* nobly 13, 669

riallis *adj. as n.pl.* royal ones 859

riche *adj.* 'rich', noble, powerful, abundant(ly flowing) 14, 296, 548

richely *adv.* bountifully 147

riches *n.* 'richesse', wealth 554; **richas** 674; **ritches** 937

richt *adv.* correctly, thoroughly, completely, immediately or directly 94, 151, 162, 172, 716, 841, 876; upright *368; **richt so** just as, similarly 601

richt *n.* what is correct or proper, just or correct interpretation, legally appropriate behaviour 262, 435, 656, 968

richtuis *adj. as adv.* just(ly), righteous(ly) 474, 984

rig *n.* back 835

rigour *n.* severity, harshness, violence **636**

ryke *adj.* powerful, rich 368, 669

ryme *v.* to abuse or satirise (in verse), curse through an incantation 797, 815

ryng *v.* to reign, rule 474; **rang** *pt.* 937

ryngis *n.pl.* rings formed by dancers 791

rys *n.* branches 89

rys *v.* to arise 200

rist *n.* plectrum, pick; hence harp **759**

rivupe *n.* a stringed instrument **759**

rocatis *n.pl.* clerical vestments, surplices 172

roch(e) *adj.* rough, rude, savage, hoarse *45, 215, 794; **rouch** 616

roy(e) *n.* king 368, 443, 534

rolpit *v.pt.* shouted, roared, cried out 45; **rolpand** *pres.p.* 215

rost *n.* roast meat 797

rote *n.* a stringed instrument 759

rouch, see **roch(e)**

rovme *n.* room, place (perhaps specifically 'shrine'), authority 475, 984

rownand *v.pres.p.* whispering 232

rowte *n.* troop 521

rubyis *n.pl.* rubies 344

rude *adj.* harsh, unmannered, crude 45

rude *n.* (Jesus's) cross 94

rudly *adv.* crudely, hoarsely 215

ruf *n.* rest, stint; **but resting or ruf** continuously 14

rug *n.* chunk, torn-away bit 797

ruggit *v.pt.* tugged (at), tore away 822

ruke *n.* rook 794

rule *n.* regulation 968

rurale *adj.* pertaining to the countryside; **dene rurale** an ecclesiastical official, responsible for supervision of the clergy within a district (cf. **dene**) 216, 809, 816

ruschit *v.pt.* rushed 521, 822

sa *adv.* so 425, 558, 793, 794; **so** 7, 10, 55, 101, 120, etc.

sable *n.* the heraldic tincture black 356

sad *adj.* sober or solemn, serious, stable, sad 85, 96, 188, 514, 596; **said** 132

sadly *adv.* sadly 42

say *v.* to say, speak, tell 42, 120, 671; *pres.1sg.* 973; **said** *pt.* 94, 248, 270, 450, 491, ***516**, 615, 958; *pp.* 246, 411, 768; *pp. adj.* foresaid, already mentioned 363, 397, 600, 625, 629

saif *v.pres.subj.* save 120, 450

saik(e) *n.* behalf 565, 878

saile *n.* hall 279, 694, 853

saland *v.pres.p.* sailing 774

salf *n.* salve, medicinal potion 720

sall *v.pres.* shall 69, 72, 121, 123, 151, etc.; **sal** (in sequence **sal be**) 123, 441; **suld** *pres.subj. pt.* 99, 144, 580, 707, 993; **shold** 415, 676

sals *n.* sauce 705

salt *n. adj.* salty 303

salust *v.pt.* saluted, greeted, did homage to 242

saluatouris *n.poss.* saviour's 473

samyn *adj.* same, identical 354, 434, 473, 772, 863, 890

samyn *adv.* all/both together, (with) one another, (with) each other 275, 524, 844, 883

sampill *n.* example, paragon 960

sanctis *n.pl.* the holy dead 988

sanctitude *n.* holiness, his holiness, a papal title 85, 96, 242

sand *n.* sand, beach 209, 788

sang *n.* song 943

sapheir *n.* sapphire, the precious stone or its blue colour 343: **sapheris** *pl.* 333

sat, see **sittis**

saught *v.pt.* were reconciled 844

saull *n.* soul 466, 484, 739; **sawlis** *n.pl.* 987

sauorus *adj.* tasty, appealing to taste or smell 31; **sawouris** 705

saw(e), see **se**

sawis *n.pl.* speeches, statements 246, 442

scaith *n.* injury 433

scarth *n.* cormorant 181

schadowe *n.* reflection 50, 68

schalme *n.* shawm, a woodwind instrument 762

schame *n.* shame 60, 817

schand *adj.* handsome **84**, 112, 891

schane *v.pt.* shone 891

schap(e) *n.* shape, (created) form or appearance 60, 68, 84, 891; **schaipe** 260

schape *v.* to shape, form, create 112; **schapyn** *pp.* 404

scharplie *adv.* intelligently, cleverly (but also contentiously) 268

schawe *v.* to show, to look or gaze at, display, state or say 372, 377, 404; **schawin** 944; *pp.* shown, gazed at 914; cf. **schewe**

scheld *n.* shield 404, 608; **scheldis** *pl.* 582, 604

schenachy *n.* (Gaelic seanchaidh) historian, genealogist 803 (and **795**)

schene *adj.* beautiful, bright 84, 404, 582, 914

schewe *v.pres.pl.* show, demonstrate, display 268, 577; cf. **schawe**

schippis *n.pl.* ships; **schippis of towr** beaked warships 774

schir *adv.* shining, bright 404, 914

schir *n.* sir, the title for a priest 210

scho *pron.* she, used in all forms as a (fictive) Gaelic pidgin for 'I' 797, 806, 928, 931, 941; **hir** *poss.obj.* 72, 797, 799 (2x), **801, 862, 927

schort *adj.* brief 112, 246, 310, 442

schortly *adv.* briefly 944

schour *n.* (lit. 'shower, downpour') a full complement or supply (of notes) 768

schroude *n.* covering, plumage 891, 914

schroude *v.pp.* (lit. 'wrapped') clothed 84

scorn *n.* scorn 67

scutiferis *n.pl.* shield-bearers 691

se *n.* sea 303, 774

se *v.* to see, observe, look at 96, 123, 258, 333, 415, 676, 772; *pres.1sg.* 68, 359, 517; *pres.pl.* 980; **saw(e)** *pt.* 48, 50, 188, 209, 618; **seyne** *pp.* 61; **sene** 378, 485

secoundlie *adv.* in second place or position 316, 352

secretar *n.* secretary 126, 132

secular *adj.* secular, worldly (not religious) 283

secund *ord.num. adv.* secondly 586

sedis *v.pres.3sg.* springs or grows, originates **977**

se-fowle *n.* marine or water-birds 238

segis *n.pl.* warriors 655

seid *n.* seed, race 723; **seidis** *pl.* seeds or grains, the plants that are their product 31

seid-fowle *n.* birds surviving on seeds 238

seike *v.* to seek, travel; **socht** *pt.* 827, 878; **was nocht for to seik** (lit. 'did not need to be sought') were present 238; **seikes** *pres.pl.* passes 303

seyne, see **se**

seir *adj.* various, diverse 137, 661, 957; **sere** 574, 628, 988

seker *adj.* sure, secure 751

sekerly *adv.* securely, stably, worth trust 22, 85, 378

selcouth *n.* a wonder or marvel 318

sele *n.* seal (for authenticating documents) 126, 132

self *n.* said being/person, selfsame 356, 903 (with **him** detached); cf. **myself**

sellarar *n.* ccllarer, the monastic official responsible for provisions 180

se-mawis *n.pl.* mews, gulls 178

semble *v.* to assemble, gather, join (in battle) 134; *pres.1sg.* 484; **semblit** *pp.* 123

semely *adj.* beautiful 569, 671; *adv.* 694, 890

semyt *v.pt.* seemed or appeared, beseemed, was befitting 134, 603, 694, 772, 793

sen *conj.* since, because 255, 262, 276, 428, 517, etc.

send *v.* to send 126; *imper.* 745; **sent** *pt.* 7; **send** 137, 705; **sent** *pp.* 700; **send** 432

senȝeourable *adj.* worthy of lordship 655

senȝeouris *n.pl.* great lords 641

sentence *n.* meaning, purport 36

sepultur *n.* sepulchre, grave 473

sere, see **seir**

serenite *n.* (his) highness (royal title) 379

sermonis *n.pl.* speeches, words 661

seruabile *adj.* eager to serve 379

seruit *v.pt.* served 379, 694

se-sand *n.* beach 208

sessoun *n.* season or time, 'weather' 7, 977

set *n.* seat, court 723

set *v.imper.* give a place to 799; *v.pres.subj.* may set or place 466, 987; *pt.* set out, attempted 565; *pp.* prepared 355; fixed 372, 411

sevyne *num.* seven 720

sewaris *n.pl.* attendants preparing for and serving at a banquet 705

sib *adj.* closely related, akin 603

sic *adj.* such 93 (here **sic ... as**), 709, 882

sicht *n.* sight 62, 318, 943, 987

syd(e) *n.* side, party 509, 744; **on ilk syde** around the edges 343
sighingis *n.pl.* sighs 957
signe *n.* insignia, emblem 377, 378, 596; **senȝe** 432; **signes** *pl.* ***373**, 418
sygnit *v.pp.* marked (with a heraldic device) 372
signifer *n.* standard-bearer 359
sylit *v.pp.* equipped with 'silours', hangings covering the ceilings 671
silk *n.* silk 405, 671
siluer *n.* silver, the metal or its colour (the heraldic 'metal') 345, 359, 410, 411, 415, 434, 569, 586, 788
syndry *adj.* various 419
syne *adv.* afterwards, then, next 137, 161, 275, 289, 345, etc.
syng *v.* to sing 973; **syngis** *imper.* 812; *pres.pl.* 712, 792; **songyn** *pp.* 768
singulir *adj.* unique, sole 483
synkis *pres.3sg.* falls (and penetrates) 387
synner *n.* sinner 745
synnis *n.pl.* sins 720; **synnis sevyne** the seven deadly sins
syris *n.pl.* lords 655
sytharist *n.* zither or harp **757**
sytholis *n.pl.* citoles 757
sittis *v.pres.2sg.* sit 744; **sat** *pt.* sat 22, 845
skrym *v.pres.pl.* dart, attack 67
skripe *v.pres.pl.* mock, deride 67
slane *v.pp.* slain 511
slang *v.pt.* threw 490, **541**
smaddit *v.pt.* was begrimed **825**
smaik *n.* low fellow 825
smedy *n.* smithy 825
smorit *v.pp.* smothered, hidden 825
so, see **sa, þat**
soft *adj.* soft, pleasant 7, 757; as *adv.* 767
softly *adv.* quietly, pleasantly 768
solace *n.* delight, joy, heaven 22, 466, 943
soland *n.* gannet 700
solar *adj.* solar, of the sun 31
soldiouris *n.pl.* foot-soldiers 641
solpit *v.pt.* (was) immersed 957; *pp.* 42
son *n.* son, one dedicated to the behaviour of the parent ***226**, 723, 749; **sonnis** *poss.* 744; *pl.* 577
sone *adv.* immediately 122, 126, 387, 745, 890, 943

son(e) *n.* sun 3, 318

songyn, see **sing**

sore *adv.* grievously, in pain 524

sorowe *n.* sorrow 42, 812

sorowfull *adj.* sorrowful 188

sorowit *v.pt.* lamented 957

sound *adv.* freely 774

soundis *v.pres.pl.* sound 767

south *n. adj.* south 303

souerane *adj.* outstanding, leading, lordly 359, 378, 903; *as n.pl.* powerful or lordly ones 853

souerane *n.* lord (in the first use God) 7, 279, 373, 450, 483, 744 (the Blessed Virgin), 863; *poss.* 565

space *n.* space, esp. a 'space' of time 34, 112, 310

spair *v.* to spare, stint, leave off, be niggardly 99, 292; **sparit** *pt.* 808

sparhalkis *n.pl.* sparrowhawks 330

sparrowe *n.* sparrow (traditionally associated with lechery) 226

specht *n.* woodpecker 334

speciall *adj.* special; **in(to) speciall** particularly 100, 138

specialy *adv.* in particular 879

specifyet *v.pp.* distinguished, singled out 733

speciose *adj. as n.* beautiful one 733

sped *v.pp.* brought to a prosperous or desirable state 879

spedely *adv.* quickly, immediately 99, 330

speid *n.* speed 292

speike *n.* speech 242

speike *v.* to speak 99, 467, 808; **spokin** *pp.* 808

speir *v.* to inquire 100

spell *v.* to speak 99; *pres.pl.* 879

sper *n.* spear 787

spirituale *adj.* given to things of the spirit, religious 166, 242, 283, 860; **spiritualis** *adj. as n.pl.* spiritual virtues 733

spreit *n.* spirit, person 100, 620

spring *v.* to leap forth (fly off) 292

sqwyeris *n.pl.* squires or esquires, the second rank of knighthood 691

stable *adj.* constant 174

stait(e) *n.* state of things (regarding the owl's case) 266; estate, class, rank (here those represented in a church council), high estate 283; **sta(i)tis** *pl.* 133, 150, 709; cf. **estait**

staitly *adv.* in a stately or proper fashion 658

stallwart *adj.* firm, bold 697

stanchalis *n.pl.* kestrels 652

stand *v.* to stand, hold a position, resist or withstand 500; **standis** *v.pres. pl.* 133; **stude** *pt.* 461

start *n.* moment, brief space of time 500

stawe (= **stale**) *v.pt.* stole (away) 817

steid *n.* (the usual or proper) place, battlefield 150, 437, 461, 500, 817, 833; **sted** 778

steidfast *adj.* firm and stable 174

steir *v.* move about, exert themselves 709; **steris** *pres.pl.* move 150; twinkle (?) 547

stele-weidis *n.pl.* iron clothes, armour 555

stern *adj.* fierce, brave 652, 658

sternis *n.pl.* heraldic 'mullets' (stars) 410, 547, 555

steropis *n.pl.* stirrups **652**

stewart *n.* the king's deputy, high-ranking official 697, 700

style *n.* state, condition, title 658; **stylis** *pl.* 709

stirlingis *n.pl.* starlings 713

styth *adj.* firm, steadfast 697

stork *n.* stork 697

straif *v.pt.* contended, struggled 833

strecht *v.pt.* fully extended, straight **652**

strynd *n.* strain, lineage 547

stur *adj.* bold, violent 500

succedis *v.pres.3sg.* inherits 559

suc(c)our *n.* help, aid 720, 745, 853

sudanelye *adv.* immediately 120

suffys *v.* to be sufficient or of power 96

suld, see **sall**

sum *adj.pron.* some, a certain (selected number), certain one(s) 64, 65, 66 (2x), 67 (2x), 270 (2x), etc.; **sum ... sum** certain ones ... other ones 66, 67, 270, 271

summondis *n.* summons 134

sumptermen *n.pl.* packhorse-drivers 641

sure *adj.* secure, certain 22, 569; *adv.* securely, dependably 55

suth *n.* truth 356

suthly *adv.* truly 671, 980

suerthbak *n.* black-backed gull 180

suowchand *v.pres.p.* making a rushing or rustling sound 171

swallowe *n.* swallow or swift 138, 290

swannis *n.pl.* swans 171

swar *n.* neck 171

swerd *n.* sword 575
swetest *adj.super.* sweetest 171
swyft *adj.* swift, fast 138, 290
swith *adj.* quickly 171

ta *v.* to take, receive 880; **tuke** *pt.* 529, 944; **tane** *pp.* 145, 885; **tane with** given (his) attention to **135**; given or committed (an office) 209
table *n.* table; **in table** at the meeting 657
taile *n.* tail 835
takynnyng *n.* token, sign, symbol 163, 430
talburn *n.* small drum or tabor 760
tale *n.* tale, account 95
(þe) tane *num. n.* the first 590; cf. **ane**
tane, see **ta**
taryit *v.pt.* delayed, lingered 814
teynd *num.ord.* tenth (part) 625
teir *adj.* difficult, tedious 578
tell *v.* to tell 95, 143, 421, 501, 523, 578, 581, 873; *pres.1sg.* 625; **tellis** *pres.3sg.* 307, 507; **tauld** *pt.* 287; **tald** *pp.* 253
temple *n.* shrine 718
temporale *adj. as n.* those not in religious orders, the worldly estate 277, 860
temporalite *n.* the temporal estate, those representing secular lordship 657
tend *v.* attend, give heed or attention 434
tender *adj.* caring, attentive 174, 286, 403, 992; **tenderest** *super.* 439
tennend *n.* tenant 609
tentfull *adj.* careful, meticulous, requiring attention **420**
termes *n.pl.* terms; **be termes** precisely 253
terrible *adj.* terrifying 620
test *n.* (a statement of the) evidence 253
thai, þai *pron.* they (th-forms mainly at line-openings) 123, 148, 152, 169, 173, etc., including *448; **þar** *poss.* their 33, 62, 151, 159, 167, etc.; **þair** 863; **þaim, þam** *obj.* them 146, 149, 152, 159, 184, etc.
þai *demon.pl.* those 551, 554, 641, 652, 810
than *adv.* then 78, 106, 148, 261, 512, etc.; than 44, 457
thar *adv.* there 176, 184, 204, 237, 311, etc.; **þore** 526
þarby *adv.* next to them 623
tharfor *adv.* therefore 38, 168, 278, 394, 568, 580, 625, 969; **þarfor** 524
tharin *adv.* in them 427

þarof *adv.* of it 592, 743

þarout *adv.* outside (the door) 827

tharwith *adv.* with it 365, 449, 460, 497, 927, 942

þat *demon.rel. conj.* that (in its various senses) 4, 5, 9, 13, 15, etc.; (of) that type 182, 204; so that 4, 62, etc.; (against those) who 225; that (one) 371

thesaurer *n.* treasurer 209

thevis-nek *n.* thieves' neck **823**

thing *n.* thing 980; *pl.* things, matters or affairs 166, 472, 618; **thingis** 808

think *v.imper.* think, consider 976

þis *demon.adj.* this 14, 43, 69, 71, 108, etc.; **þir** *pl.* these 10, 20, 31, 61, 144, etc.

þiself *n.* yourself 977

þocht *conj.* although 579, 602, 929

thocht (me) *v.pt.3sg. (impers.)* it seemed (to me) 19, 155; considered (himself) 902

þore, see **thar**

þow *pron.* you (the familiar form) 123, 481, 482, 491, 496; **þi(n)** *poss.* 118, 248, 496, 723, 728, 733, etc.; **þe** *obj.* 249, 495

thousand *n.pl.* thousands 489

thraly *adv.* fiercely, violently 489, 918, 941

thrang *n.* throng, troop; **in thrang** in hosts, in a single troop or all at once 489, 941

thraw *v.* to twist; **to thrawe in a widdy** to hang 823

thrawin *adv.* perversely, with ill-temper 918

thre *num.* three 340, 360, 587

thrid *num.ord.* third 362

thrys *adv.* thrice 823

throw(e), throu *prep.* through (in its various senses, incl. by means of, in accord with) 2, 8, 10, 14, 49, etc.

thus, þus *adv.* thus 10, 22, 61, 73, 105, etc.

tichit *v.pp.* tied 405

tyde *n.* time 867, 873, 954

till *prep.* to (in its various senses, the variant used before vowels and h-, esp. as marker of the infinitive) 2, 12, 60, 71, 74, etc.; postposited at 456, 607

tyme *n.* time, occasion 506, 1000

tymeralis *n.pl.* crests 613

tympane *n.* drum or tambourine 760

tyrefull *adj.* tedious, wearying 421

tit *v.pt.* seized, pulled 837

tythandis *n.pl.* message, news 135; **tythingis** 814

to *prep. adv.* to (in its various senses) 19, 30 (2x), 33, 35, 39, etc., including *482, *963; **to**, i.e. supported the proposition 270

top *n.* top (of his head), crest 837

toppit *v.pp. adj.* pointed, peaked 186

(þe) toþer *num.ord. n.* the second 590; see **vþir**

townis *n.pl.* settlements 218, 550

towr *n.* tower, centre of a castle 293, 774 (see **schippis**); **towris** *pl.* 550

tray *n.* treason, betrayal; **but tray** in truth 760

trayne *n.* strategem (but perhaps 'retinue') 515

traist *adj.* trust(worth)y, firm or strong 287; **trast** 405, 867; *as adv.* certainly, firmly 992

tranoyntit *v.pt.* marched, travelled swiftly 515

tratour *n.* traitor, unfaithful person 814

tre *n.* tree 398, 405, 584, 625

tressour *n.* cord, fillet (the heraldic term) 370; **tressur** 588

tressour *n.* treasure *550

trete *n.* treatise, i.e. the letters 307

trete *v.* to discuss, negotiate 277; **tretit** *pp.* 657

trety *n.* entreaty, request 253

treuth *n.* fidelity, integrity 430

trewe *adj.* faithful 135, 174, 286, 287, 388, 403, 515; *adv.* 523, 589; **trewest** *super.* 127

trewly *adv.* truly, in truth 434, 501, 613, 781

tryid *v.pp. adj.* tested (for quality), excellent 613; **tryde** 992

trist *n.* meeting place or point of assembly 307

trone *n.* throne 751

tronit *v.pp.* enthroned *718

trowe *v.* to believe 781; **trowis** *pres.3sg.* 992

trumpe *n.* trumpet 760

tuchet *n.* lapwing 821, 834, 837

tuke, see **ta**

turtour *n.* turtle-dove 127, 135, 287

tuscheis *n.pl.* bands or tassels of fine cloth **405** (cf. **398**)

twa *num.* two 345, 523, 820

vnamendable *adj.* incapable of improvement 928

vnchangeable *adj.* unchanging, consistent or persistent in a behaviour 223

vnder *prep.* under, beneath 31, 48, 82, 89, 222, etc.; **wnder** 133, 897

vnfalȝeable *adj.* incapable of lack or error 383
vnfrely *adj.* ugly, unpleasant 56, 851
vngraciously *adv.* disastrously 840
vnhele *n.* misfortune 253
vnloveable *adj.* unpraiseworthy, dishonourable 227, 917
vnsufferable *adj. as n.* insufferable person 926
vntald *v.pp. adj.* beyond count 550
vre *n.* use, custom; **but vre** against custom, uniquely **736**
vrisounis *n.pl.* prayers 472
vsit *v.pt.* made use of, performed on 763; accustomed (to) ***963**
vþer, vthir *adj.* other 189, 297, 419, 472, 573 (implicitly pl. 'lands');
other 582, 938; *poss.pl.* 623; **vþeris** *pl.* 282

v-, see also **w-**; **vale**, see **waile**
vicaris *n.pl.* persons who serve in a church (often as substitute for the
nominal pastor) 219
vyle *adj.* low or shameful 226

wa *n.* woe, distress 43, 499; **wo** 748
way *sb.* way, path 468, 667, 874; **wayis** *pl.* 305; **quhat way** (in) what-
ever way 785
wayage *v.* travel, journey 349
waike *adj.* weak, feeble 37
waile *v.* to choose 447; **vale** 585; **walis** *pres.pl.* 305; **walit** *pp. adj.*
chosen, selected, thus excellent 539; **worthy to vale** deserving to be
selected as superior 847
waynd *v.* to turn aside 458
wait, see **wyte**
wald, see **will**
walentyne *adj. as n.* birds **918**
walk *v.* to wake, keep a vigil 619; *pres.1sg.* 58
wan *adj.* miserable 964
wan, see **win**
wand *n.* rod or staff, scourge, instrument of correction 483, 752
wane *n.* dwelling, shelter 43, 667
wantoun *adj.* frivolous 964
wappit *v.pp.* wrapped, enveloped 748
war *adj.* aware 512
war, see **be**
ward *v.* to guard 619
ware *n.* possessions 553

waryit *v.pt.* cursed 954

warld *n.* world 43, 748, 955

warme *adj.* hearty, heart-felt 386

warn *v.pres.1sg.* warn, threaten 975

was, see **be**

wast *adj. as n.* desolation, destitution 963

watchis *n.pl.* watchmen, sentries 619

watter *n.* water 678, 827

we *adj.* wee, little 649

we *pron.* we 467, 474, 534, 567, 737, etc.; **our** *poss.* 7, 373, 383, 385 (2x), 457; **ws** *obj.* 389, 580, 740, 748, 754, etc.

weddit *v.pt.* wedded 553

weid *n.* garment, clothing 84, 914; **weidis** *pl.* 222

weile, see **wele**

weilfair *n.* welfare, health 737

weir *n.* doubt, a doubtful situation or confused state 955; **into weir** fearfully 58; **but weir** without doubt, certainly 576, 650

weir *n.* war 564, 576, 619; **weris** *pl.* 327, 539

weir *v.* to wear (clothing) 351; **weris** *pres.3sg.* 358

welcummit *v.pt.* welcomed, greeted 660

wele *adv.* well 993; **weile** 703; **wele** properly 134

wele *n.* happiness, prosperity 252

well *n.* fountain or spring, source 97, 678, 737; **wellis** *n.pl.* 305

wellit *v.pp.* (lit. 'boiled') submerged, plunged **499**

welterit *v.pt.* rolled about, writhed 954

welth *n.* wealth, prosperity 710, 963, 974; **welthis** *pl.* joys 847

wend *v.* go, travel, pass 468; *imper.* 491; *pt.* 629; **went** 499, 667, 849

wene *n.* doubt 382

weraly *adv.* truly 264

werd *n.* (one's personal) fate or destiny 459; **werdis** *pl.* 964

werk *n.* (noble) deeds 395

wertewe *n.* virtue 264

wer-wall *n.* bulwark 382

wesche *v.* to wash 678, 827; **wosche** *pt.* 849

wesit *v.pt.* visited, i.e. subjected to ecclesiastical examination or inspection (with subsequent punishment for misconduct) 226

wgsum *adj.* horrifying 104

what, see **quhat**

wyce *n.* visage, face **88**

wicht *adj.* vigorous 513, 539; *as n.* 499

wicht *n.* being, person 553

wichtly *adv.* vigorously 576

wycit *v.pp.* treated badly or arrogantly **918**

widdy *n.* (lit. 'twisted [willow] rope') noose 823

wyde *adj.* wide 748

wy(e) *n.* warrior 458, 513; **wyis** *pl.* 499, 539

wyld *adj.* wild, savage 616

wylest *adj.super.* vilest, most loathsome 88

will *n.* desire, pleasure, ability to command 611, 874, 964, 993; **willis** *pl.* desire(s), pleasure(s); **gif ӡour willis war** if it would be pleasing to you 312

will *v.pres.1sg.pl.* to want or wish, desire, mark of the future tense 38, 64, 66 (2x), 74, 86, etc.; **wald** *pres.subj.* would wish 79, 111, 459, 807, 854, etc.; *pt.* 290, 478, 785, 807, 908, 915

wilsome *adj.* wandering, astray 43

wyn *v.* to win, conquer 564; **wan** *pt.* 503, 508, 576; travelled 813

wynly *adv.* joyfully 650

wirk *v.* to work, perform, create 458, 785; **wrocht** *pt.* 874, 955

wys *n.* manner, fashion, condition 278, 564

wis *n.* wish, desire **459**, 847

wys(e) *adj.* wise 175; *as n.pl.* 995; **wysest** *super.* 447

wyslie *adv.* wisely 97

wit *n.* intellect 993

wyte *n.* blame 995; **has þe wyte** is to blame, is at fault 68

wyte *v.* to know, understand 79; **wit** *imper.* 382, 576; **wait** *v.pres.* know 429, 710, **737**, 874

with *prep.* with (in its various senses, including by means of, against) 5, 18, 28, 41, 44, etc.

within *prep.* within 124, 731

withoutin *prep.* without 11, 108

witnes *n.* witness, testimony; **to ӡour witnes** as your evidence 395

wlonk *adj.* beautiful 553

wnder *prep.* under 133, 897

woddis *n.pl.* woods 305

wodwys *n.(pl.?)* woodwose, wild or green man 616

wofull *adj. as n.* woeful one 955

won *v.* accustom oneself to 963

wont *adj.* familiar, accustomed 164, 491, 946

word *n.* word, statement, sentiment 386; **wordis** *pl.* 175

worschipand *v.pres.p.* honouring 503

worschip(e) *n.* honour 97, 164, 252, 447, 710, 995; honourable things 847

worth *adj.* having (the) value (of) 72, 606

worth *v.pt.* became 811; **worthit** 816

wortheliche *adj.* noble 667

worthy *adj.* honourable 175, 311, 513, 539, 553, 585, 752; *as n.* honourable man 447; **worthyis** *pl.* 849

wounder *adv.* wondrously (but generally only 'very') 206, 274; **wonder** 386

wounderis *n.pl.* prodigies, wonders 785

wpe *adv.* up 836

wplandis *adj.* rural 218

wrait, see **wryte**

wran *n.* wren 649

wretche *n.* miserable person 43; **wrech** *963; **wretches** *pl.* 252; **wreche** outcast, exile *252

wretchit *adj.* miserable 650

writ *n.* document, written material 395, 507

wryt(e) *v.* to write, send messages 131, 206, 278, 993; *pres.1sg.* 429; **wrait** *pt.* 288, 935; **writtin** *pp.* 401

wrythe *v.imper.* display or show, uncover 995

wrythit *v.pt.* twisted (in anguish) 954

wrocht, see **wirk**

ws, see **we**

Proper Names

Aaron Aaron the first high priest and Moses's brother 752

Adam Adam 734

Adwent Advent 699

Almane Germany, the Holy Roman empire 358

Archebald Archibald 'the grim' Douglas (1320s-1400) 552

Arestotill Aristotle the philosopher 268

Babulone Babylon (with strong overtone of Babel) 302; **Babilonis** *poss.* 293

þe Baptist St John the Baptist 731

Berwike Berwick-upon-Tweed 896

Brettane Great Britain 375

þe Brus(e) Robert Bruce, king Robert I 393, 428, 436, 443; see also **Robert**

Burone Burian, a place in North Ronaldsay, Orkney 896; **fro Burone to Berwike** anywhere in Scotland

Cardros Cardross (Dunbartonshire), site of king Robert I's death 464

Charterouris *n,pl.* Carthusian monk-hermits 185

Crist Christ, more generally God 111, 120, 133

Cristindome Christendom 381, 487, 504

(þe) Dowglas 'The Douglas', principally James 'the black' Douglas, but also his continuing lineage (Archibald 'the grim' at 563) 380, 390, 432, 448, 516, 527, 535, 546, 551, 575, 591, 990; **Douglas** 402 (2x), 482, 559, 563; **Dowglace** 467; **Dowglas** *poss.* 600; *pl.* 391; see also **Archebald, Iames**

Dunbar the earls of Dunbar, the line of Elizabeth Dunbar, Archibald Douglas, earl of Moray's wife 989

Elizebeth Elizabeth, Mary's aunt and mother of St John the Baptist 732

Ettrik Ettrick forest, in the Scottish 'Middle March', estate of James Douglas 573

Eua (Latin) Eve 736

Ewangelist gospel-writer (here Luke) 935

Ewrope Europe 304

Fraunce France 360

Galloway Galloway, southwestern Scotland 561

Gawane Gawain, Gavin, a name here assigned to the duck **210**

Gedion Gideon the judge 753

God 450, 463, 465, 986; **Go(d)dis** *poss.* 471, 558, 979

þe Haly Graif/Graf the church of the Holy Sepulchre in Jerusalem, burial place of Jesus 444, 471

Holland Richard Holland the poet 1001

Iames, lord Dowglas 'Sir James the good' (1288–1330), companion of the Bruce and founder of the Douglas line 448

Irischerye Ireland, particularly Ulster **801**

Irland Ireland (or the Celtic west more generally) 795; *adj.* 801

Lawder Lauderdale 574

Lentryne Lent 698

Lucifer Lucifer, the proud angel who fell 933; **Luciferis** *poss.* 905

Mahownis *poss.* Mohammed's (perhaps **Mahownis men** = idolatrers) 497

May the month of May 1, 156, 157, 998

Makgrane the McGrains (a Galloway family) 802

(sanct) Margaretis *poss.* St Margaret's **376**

Mary the Blessed Virgin 717

Murray (1) the Murray family of Bothwell, the line of Archibald 'the grim''s wife 548, **Murrayis** *poss.* 557

Murray(e) (2) Moray 595, 999

Natur the goddess Nature 32, 105, 113, 119, 251, 258, 276, 854, 857, 862, 867, 872, 887, 920, 926, 942; cf. **natur**

Noyis *poss.* Noah's 231, 813

O'Conochor Gaelic equivalent of O'Conchobhair [O'Connor] **802**

O'Deremyn the Dermonds of Inishowen (county Donegal) 800

O'Dochardy the O'Dohertys, the clan/lords of Inishowen 800

O'Donnall the O'Donnells of Tyrconnell (county Donegal), the most powerful clan/lords in Ulster after the O'Neills of Tyrone; or the Uí Dhomhnaill/MacDonalds, the family of the Lords of the Isles, with a cadet-branch in the Glynns of Antrim 800

O'Gregre Ó Creacaire 'descendant of the reciter'? (so Riddy) 802; cf. **crekery**

O'Knewlyn the O'Connellans **802**

Ormond the earldom constructed in the Black Isle (Ross-shire) for Hugh Douglas 599

Our Lady the Blessed Virgin 755

Robert þe Brus 443; see also **þe Bruse**

Robyn the name of the robin ('redbreast') 647

Salamon Solomon 751

Sarazenis *pl.poss.* 'Saracens', Muslims ruling Palestine 484, 509, 514

Sathanas *poss.* Satan's 509

Saxonis the English 483, 577

Scotland Scotland 373, 382, 433, 446, 485, 533

Scottis *adj.* Scottish 384, 388, 567

Tern(e)way Darnaway Castle, Morayshire 992, 1000

Trinite the Trinity 718

Wenus *poss.* Venus's 226

Bibliography

Aitken, A. J. 1971. 'Variation and variety in written Middle Scots', *Edinburgh Studies in English and Scots*, ed. Aitken et al. (Edinburgh), 177–209.

—— 1983. 'The Language of Older Scots Poetry', *Scotland and the Lowland Tongue: Studies ... in honour of David D. Murrison*, ed. J. Derrick McClure (Aberdeen), 18–49.

—— (ed. Caroline Mcafee) 2002. *The Older Scots Vowels: A History of the Stressed Vowels of Older Scots,* STS 5th ser. 1 (Edinburgh).

Alexander, Flora M. 1983. 'Richard Holland's *Buke of the Howlat*', *Literature of the North*, ed. David Hewitt and Michael Spiller (Aberdeen), 14–25.

Allen, Valerie 2007. *On Farting: Language and Laughter in the Middle Ages* (Basingstoke).

Amours, F. J., ed. 1892–97. *Scottish Alliterative Poems in Riming Stanzas,* 2 vols, STS 1st ser. 27, 38 (Edinburgh and London).

——, ed. 1903–14. *The Original Chronicle of Andrew of Wyntoun*, 6 vols, STS 1st ser. 50, 53–54, 56–57, 63 (Edinburgh and London).

Batho, Edith C. and H. Winifred Husbands, eds, 1938–41. John Bellenden, *The Chronicle of Scotland Compiled by Hector Boece*, 2 vols, STS 3rd ser. 10, 13 (Edinburgh).

Bawcutt, Priscilla 2000. '"My bright buke": Women and their Books in Medieval and Renaissance Scotland', *Medieval Women: Texts and Contexts in Late Medieval Britain: Essays for Felicity Riddy*, ed. Jocelyn Wogan-Browne et al. (Turnhout), 17–34.

—— 2008. 'The Contents of the Bannatyne Manuscript: New Sources and Analogues', *Journal of the Edinburgh Bibliographical Society* 3, 95–133.

—— and Felicity Riddy, eds 1987. *Longer Scottish Poems Volume One 1375–1650* (Edinburgh).

Beattie, William 1938–45. 'An Early Printed Fragment of the "Buke of the Howlat"', *Transactions of the Edinburgh Bibliographical Society* 2, 393–97.

Borroff, Marie 1962. *Sir Gawain and the Green Knight: A Stylistic and Metrical Survey* (New Haven).

Bradley, Ritamary 1954. 'Backgrounds of the Title *Speculum* in Medieval Literature', *Speculum* 29, 100–15.

Brown, Michael 1997. '"Rejoice to Hear of Douglas": The House of Douglas and the Presentation of Magnate Power in Late Medieval Scotland', *Scottish Historical Review* 76, 161–84.

—— 1998. *The Black Douglases: War and Lordship in Late Medieval Scotland 1300–1455* (East Linton).

—— 2004. *The Wars of Scotland, 1214–1371*, The New Edinburgh History of Scotland 4 (Edinburgh).

Cameron, Sonja 2000. 'Sir James Douglas, Spain, and the Holy Land', *Freedom and Authority, Scotland c. 1050–c. 1650: Historical and Historiographical Essays presented to Grant G. Simpson*, ed. Terry Brotherstone and David Ditchburn (East Linton), 108–17.

Campbell, Colin 1995. *The Scots Roll: A Study of a Fifteenth Century Roll of Arms* (Kinross).

Carmody, Francis J., ed. 1939. *Physiologus Latinus: Éditions préliminaires Versio B* (Paris).

Coldwell, David F. C., ed. 1957–64. *Virgil's Aeneid Translated ... by Gavin Douglas*, 4 vols, STS 3rd ser. 25, 27–28, 30 (Edinburgh).

Cowan, Ian B. 1960. 'The Organisation of Scottish Secular Cathedral Chapters', *Records of the Scottish Church History Society* 14, 19–47.

Craigie, James, ed. 1951–58. *The Poems of James VI. of Scotland*, 2 vols, STS 3rd ser. 22, 26 (Edinburgh).

Craigie, William A., ed. 1923–25. *The Asloan Manuscript: A Miscellany in Verse and Prose*, 2 vols, STS ns 14, 16 (Edinburgh and London).

—— 1942. 'The Scottish Alliterative Poems', *Proceedings of the British Academy* 28, 217–36.

Cunningham, I. C. 1994. 'The Asloan Manuscript', *The Renaissance in Scotland: Studies ... Offered to John Durkan*, ed. A. A. MacDonald et al. (Leiden), 107–35.

Diebler, Arthur, ed. 1893. *Holland's Buke of the Houlate, publ. from the Bannatyne MS* ... (Chemnitz and Leipzig).

Donaldson, Robert 1980–83. 'An Early Printed Fragment of the "Buke of the Howlat" – Addendum', *Transactions of the Edinburgh Bibliographical Society* 5, iii, 25–28.

Duggan, Hoyt N. 1986. 'Alliterative Patterning as a Basis for Emendation in Middle English Alliterative Poetry', *Studies in the Age of Chaucer* 8, 73–105.

—— 2000. 'Extended A-Verses in Middle English Alliterative Poetry', *Parergon* 18, i, 53–76.

Durkan, John, ed. 1985. *The Protocol Book of John Foular 1528–34*, Scottish Record Society ns 10 (Edinburgh).

Economou, George 1972. *The Goddess Natura in Medieval Literature* (Cambridge MA).

Fletcher, Alan. J. 2000. *Drama, performance and polity in pre-Cromwellian Ireland* (Toronto).

Fox, Denton, and William A. Ringler, eds 1980. *The Bannatyne Manuscript: National Library of Scotland Advocates' MS 1.1.6* (London).

Fraser, William 1885. *The Douglas Book*, 4 vols (Edinburgh).

Froissart, Jean, tr. John Bourchier, lord Berners; introd. William P. Ker 1901–3. *The Chronicle of Froissart ...*, 6 vols (London).

Galbreath, Donald L., rev. Geoffrey Briggs 1972. *Papal Heraldry* (London).

Grant, Alexander 1988. 'Scotland's "Celtic Fringe" in the Late Middle Ages: The MacDonald Lords of the Isles and the Kingdom of Scotland', *The*

British Isles, 1100–1500: Comparisons, Contrasts, and Connections, ed. R. R. Davies (Edinburgh), 118–41.

Hanna, Ralph 1995. 'Robert the Ruyflare and His Companions', *Literature and Religion in the Later Middle Ages: Philological Essays in Honor of Siegfried Wenzel*, ed. Richard G. Newhauser and John A. Alford, Medieval and Renaissance Texts and Studies 118 (Binghamton NY), 81–96.

——, ed. 2008. *The Knightly Tale of Golagros and Gawane*, STS 5th ser. 7 (Woodbridge).

—— 2008a. 'Lambeth Palace Library, MS 260 and the Problem of English Vernacularity', *Studies in Medieval and Renaissance History* 3rd ser. 5, 131–99.

—— 2011. 'Literacy, Schooling, Universities', *The Cambridge Companion to Medieval English Culture*, ed. Andrew Galloway (Cambridge), 172–94.

Häring, Nikolaus M., ed. 1978. 'Alan of Lille, "De Planctu Naturae"', *Studi Medievali* 3rd ser. 19, 797–879.

Hervieux, Léopold, ed. 1893–99. *Les Fabulistes latins depuis le siècle d'Auguste jusqu'à la fin du moyen âge*, 2nd edn, 5 vols (Paris).

Higgins, Iain M. 2008. 'Shades of the East: Orientalism, Religion, and Nation in Late Medieval Scottish Literature', *Journal of Medieval and Early Modern Studies* 38, 197–228.

Holford, Matthew 2008. 'Family, Lineage, and Society: Medieval Pedigrees of the Percy Family', *Nottingham Medieval Studies* 52, 165–90.

Houwen, L. A. J. R., ed. 1990. *The Sex Werkdays and Agis: An Edition of a Late Medieval Scots Universal History* ... (Groningen).

Jordan, Richard, rev. H. Ch. Matthes 1934. *Handbuch der mittelenglischen Grammatik: I. Teil: Lautlehre* 2nd edn (Heidelberg).

Kingston, Simon 2004. *Ulster and the Isles in the Fifteenth Century: The Lordship of the Clann Domhnaill of Antrim* (Dublin).

Laing, David, ed. 1823. *The Buke of the Howlat*, Bannatyne Club (Edinburgh).

—— 1867. *Adversaria: Notices Illustrative of Some of the Earlier Works Printed for the Bannatyne Club*, Bannatyne Club 115 (Edinburgh).

Macdougall, Norman 2000. 'Achilles' Heel: The Earldom of Ross, the Lordship of the Isles, and the Stewart Kings, 1449–1507', *Alba: Celtic Scotland in the Middle Ages*, ed. Edward J. Cowan and R. Andrew McDonald (East Linton), 248–75.

Mackay, Margaret A. 1975. 'The Alliterative Tradition in Middle Scots Verse', unpublished PhD thesis, University of Edinburgh.

—— 1981. 'Structure and Style in Richard Holland's *The Buke of the Howlat*', *Proceedings of the Third International Conference on Scottish Language and Literature (Medieval and Renaissance)*, ed. Roderick J. Lyall and Felicity Riddy (Stirling and Glasgow), 191–205.

Mann, Jill 2009. *From Aesop to Reynard: Beast Literature in Medieval Britain* (Oxford).

Mapstone, Sally 1996. 'Scots and Their Books in the Middle Ages and the

Renaissance: An exhibition in the Bodleian Library, Oxford 10 June-24 August 1996' (Oxford).

—— 1999a. 'Invective as Poetic: The Cultural Contexts of Polwarth and Montgomerie's Flyting', *Scottish Literary Journal* 26, ii, 18–40.

—— 1999b. Review of *The Works of Geoffrey Chaucer and 'The Kingis Quair'*, *Review of English Studies* 50, 504–5.

—— 1999c. 'The *Scotichronicon*'s First Readers', *Church, Chronicle and Learning in Medieval and Early Renaissance Scotland: Essays Presented to Donald Watt* ..., ed. Barbara E. Crawford (Edinburgh), 31–55.

—— 2001. 'Introduction: William Dunbar and the Book Culture of Sixteenth-Century Scotland', *William Dunbar, 'The Nobill Poyet': Essays in Honour of Priscilla Bawcutt* (East Linton), 1- 23.

—— forthcoming 1. '*The Buke of the Howlat*', unpublished draft essay of March, 2010.

—— forthcoming 2. 'The Douglases and their Books', conference paper, presented at the symposium Border Families and their Books in Northern England and in Scotland, c.1400–1620, Merton College, Oxford, April 2010.

McAndrew, Bruce A. 2006. *Scotland's Historic Heraldry* (Woodbridge).

McDiarmid, Matthew P. 1969. 'Richard Holland's *Buke of the Howlat*: An Interpretation', *Medium Ævum* 38, 277–90.

McGladdery, Christine A. 2005. 'The Black Douglases, 1369–1455', *Lordship and Architecture in Medieval and Renaissance Scotland*, ed. Richard Oram and Geoffrey Stell (Edinburgh), 160–87.

McIntosh, Angus, M. L. Samuels, and Michael Benskin 1986. *A Linguistic Atlas of Late Mediaeval English*, 4 vols (Aberdeen).

McKim, Anne 2007. 'The Rossdhu Book of Hours: Tracing Connections', *Migrations: Medieval Manuscripts in New Zealand*, ed. Stephanie Harris and Alexandra Barratt (Newcastle), 202–15.

Millett, Bella 1999. 'Ancrene Wisse and the Conditions of Confession', *English Studies* 80, 193- 215.

Morrin, Margaret J. 1975. *John Waldeby OSA, c.1315–c.1372: English Augustinian Preacher and Writer* ... , Studia Augustiniana historica 2 (Rome).

Munro, Jean and R. W., eds 1986. *Acts of the Lords of the Isles 1336–1493*. Scottish History Society 4th ser. 22 (Edinburgh).

Murison, David D. 1974. 'Linguistic Relationships in Medieval Scotland', *The Scottish Tradition: Essays in Honour of Ronald Gordon Cant*, ed. G. W. S. Barrow (Edinburgh), 71–83.

Murray, Kylie 2012. 'Passing the Book: the Scottish Shaping of Chaucer's Dream States in Bodleian Library, MS Arch. Selden. B.24', *The Anglo-Scottish Border and the Shaping of Identity, 1300–1600*, ed. Mark P. Bruce and Katherine H. Terrell (Basingstoke), 121–39.

Panton, George, and James B. Murdoch, eds 1896. *The Bannatyne Manuscript, compiled by George Bannatyne 1568*, 4 vols, ([Glasgow]), *Howlat* at 4:867–97.

Parkinson, David 1986. 'Mobbing Scenes in Middle Scots Verse: Holland, Douglas, Dunbar', *Journal of English and Germanic Philology* 85, 494–509.

Pickering, O. S. 1981. 'Notes on the Sentence of Cursing in Middle English; or A Case for an Index of Middle English Prose', *Leeds Studies in English* n.s. 12, 229–44.

Pinkerton, John, ed. 1792. *Scotish Poems, reprinted from scarce editions*, 3 vols (London).

Riddy, Felicity J. 1986. 'Dating *The Buke of the Howlat*', *Review of English Studies* 37, 1–10.

—— 1988. 'The Alliterative Revival', *The History of Scottish Literature I: Origins to 1660 (Mediaeval and Renaissance)*, ed. R. D. S. Jack (Aberdeen), 39–54.

Royan, Nicola 2006. '"Mark your Meroure be Me": Richard Holland's *Buke of the Howlat*', *A Companion to Medieval Scots Poetry*, ed. Priscilla Bawcutt and Janet H. Williams (Cambridge), 49–62.

—— 2010. 'The Alliterative *Awntyrs* Stanza in Older Scots Verse', *Medieval Alliterative Poetry: Essays in Honour of Thorlac Turville-Petre*, ed. John A. Burrow and Hoyt N. Duggan (Dublin), 185–94.

Russell, Paul, ed. trans. 2005. *Vita Griffini Filii Conani: The Medieval Latin Life of Gruffudd ap Cynan* (Cardiff).

Sanderson, Margaret H. B. 2002. *A Kindly Place? Living in Sixteenth-Century Scotland* (East Linton).

Scheibe, Regina 1997. 'The Major Professional Skills of the Dove in *The Buke of the Howlat*', *Animals and the Symbolic in Medieval Art and Literature*, ed. J. A. J. R. Houwen (Groningen), 107–37.

Simms, Katharine 1989. 'Bards and Barons: The Anglo-Irish Aristocracy and the Native Culture', *Medieval Frontier Societies*, ed. Robert Bartlett and Angus MacKay (Oxford), 177–97.

Skene, F. J. H., ed. 1877–80. *Liber Pluscardensis*, 2 vols, The Historians of Scotland 7, 10 (Edinburgh).

Spearing, A. C. 1982. 'Central and Displaced Sovereignty in Three Medieval Poems', *Review of English Studies* 33, 247–61.

Stevenson, J. H. 1914. *Heraldry in Scotland*, 2 vols (Glasgow).

—— and Marguerite Wood 1940. *Scottish Heraldic Seals ...*, 3 vols (Glasgow).

Stewart, Marion M. 1972. 'Holland of *The Howlat*', *Innes Review* 23, 3–15.

—— 1975. 'Holland's "Howlat" and the Fall of the Livingstones', *Innes Review* 26, 67–79.

Thompson, A. Hamilton 1943. 'Diocesan Organisation in the Middle Ages: Archdeacons and Rural Deans', *Proceedings of the British Academy* 29, 153–94.

Thomson, Derick S. 1960–63. 'The Mac Mhuirich Bardic Family', *Transactions of the Gaelic Society of Inverness* 43, 276–304.

—— 1968. 'Gaelic Learned Orders and Literati in Mediaeval Scotland', *Scottish Studies* 12, 57–78.

—— 1969–70. 'The Poetry of Niall Mac Mhuirich', *Transactions of the Gaelic Society of Inverness* 46, 281–307.

—— 1974–76. 'Niall Mor Mac Mhuirich', *Transactions of the Gaelic Society of Inverness* 49, 9–25.

——, ed. 1983, 1987. *The Companion to Gaelic Scotland* (Oxford).

Thomson, Thomas, ed. (rev. T. G. S.) 1819 [1877]. *The Auchinkleck Chronicle: An Schort Memoriale* ... (Edinburgh).

Turville-Petre, Thorlac 1974. '"Summer Sunday", "*De tribus regibus mortuis*", and "The Awntyrs off Arthure": Three Poems in the Thirteen-Line Stanza', *Review of English Studies* 25, 1–14.

——, ed. 1989. *Alliterative Poetry of the Later Middle Ages: An Anthology* (London).

van Buuren, Catherine 1966. 'John Asloan, an Edinburgh Scribe', *English Studies* 47, 365–72.

——, ed. 1982. *The Buke of the Sevyne Sagis: A Middle Scots Version of the Seven Sages of Rome* ..., Germanic and Anglistic Studies of the University of Leiden (Leiden).

—— 1996. 'John Asloan and his Manuscript: An Edinburgh Notary and Scribe in the Days of James III, IV, and V (c. 1470-c. 1530)', *Stewart Style 1513–1542: Essays on the Court of James V*, ed. Janet H. Williams (East Linton), 15–51.

Wenzel, Siegfried 1984. *Summa Virtutum de Remediis Anime*, The Chaucer Library (Athens GA).

Woolf, Rosemary 1968. *The English Religious Lyric in the Middle Ages* (Oxford).

Wright, Aaron E., ed. 1997. 'Walter of England', *The Fables,* Toronto Medieval Latin Texts 25 (Toronto).